# RACING
# AGAINST
# HISTORY

# RACING
# AGAINST
# HISTORY

---

## THE 1940 CAMPAIGN
## FOR A JEWISH ARMY
## TO FIGHT HITLER

---

### RICK RICHMAN

Encounter Books
New York  London

© 2018 by Rick Richman

First American edition published in 2018 by Encounter Books,
an activity of Encounter for Culture and Education, Inc.,
a nonprofit, tax exempt corporation.
Encounter Books website address: www.encounterbooks.com

A portion of Chapter IV appeared, in different form, in the December 2013
issue of *The Tower Magazine*.

Manufactured in the United States and printed on
acid-free paper. The paper used in this publication meets
the minimum requirements of ANSI/NISO Z39.48–1992
(R 1997) (*Permanence of Paper*).

FIRST AMERICAN EDITION
LIBRARY OF CONGRESS CATALOGING-IN-PUBLICATION DATA
Names: Richman, Rick, 1945- author.
Title: Racing against history : the 1940 campaign for a Jewish army to fight
    Hitler / Rick Richman.
Description: New York ; London : Encounter Books, [2017] | Includes
    bibliographical references and index.
Identifiers: LCCN 2017031503 (print) | LCCN 2017032868 (ebook) | ISBN
    9781594039751 (Ebook) | ISBN 9781594039744 (hardback : alk. paper)
Subjects: LCSH: Weizmann, Chaim, 1874–1952—Travel—United States. |
    Jabotinsky, Vladimir, 1880–1940—Travel—United States. | Ben-Gurion,
    David, 1886–1973—Travel—United States. | Zionists—Travel—United
    States—History—20th century. | Jews—History, Military.
Classification: LCC DS125.3.W45 (ebook) | LCC DS125.3.W45 R53 2017 (print) |
    DDC 940.54/12089924—dc23
LC record available at https://lccn.loc.gov/2017031503

*To the memory of my parents,*
*Ruth Elaine Richman and Matthew M. Richman,*
*who instilled in me a love of books*
*and gave me the lasting gift*
*of a Jewish education.*
*And to my brother,*
*James D. Richman,*
*a blessing to them and to me.*

*We have been assailed . . . by a persecution against which the medieval persecutions are dwarfed into insignificance . . . Community after community has gone under . . . First Germany, then Czechoslovakia, and last of all, Poland. Poland! With the greatest Jewish community in Europe.*

Chaim Weizmann, January 16, 1940, addressing 4,000 people at the Shriners' Temple, New York City


*[T]here are still immense probabilities for quite decisive changes. One need not name them: enough to say that God's box of tricks is by far not emptied yet.*

Vladimir Jabotinsky, June 19, 1940, addressing 5,000 people at the Manhattan Center in New York City, after the fall of France


*There is no time to lose. History will never forgive us if we fail to do in time whatever is humanly possible to give the Jewish community the chance of defending itself.*

David Ben-Gurion, July 2, 1940, in a cable to the Zionist Organization of America, New York City

# CONTENTS

# ACKNOWLEDGMENTS

The popular conception is that writing a book is a solitary endeavor. I have found instead that to research, write, edit, design, and publish a book, it takes a *shtetl*. It is a pleasure to record my thanks to those who have helped me through this extraordinary process.

My most profound gratitude is to Anne Mandelbaum, my incomparable editor, who also acted as the agent for *Racing Against History*. No book—or author—could have a better friend. She immediately understood the significance of the project and gave me the immense benefit of her intelligence, insight, and inspiration; she not only edited the book but also assisted me in the research; gave the book its title; personally presented it to Roger Kimball, President and Publisher of Encounter Books; and co-designed the cover, with its suggestion of both a gathering storm and a light beyond the clouds. This is her book as well as mine.

I am deeply indebted to Roger and Susan Hertog for supporting the publication of this book.

I am enormously grateful to Norman Podhoretz, from whose encouragement I have benefited for more than a decade. I have used a technique he has frequently used in his books, providing frequent block quotations from primary sources, which permit a reader to evaluate an author's account more knowledgeably.

I have been blessed to have had an extraordinary group of people read the manuscript in whole or in part and offer their comments, including Gary Bialis, Professor Angie Cloke, Professor Phyllis K. Herman, Roger Hertog, Neal Kozodoy, Anne Lieberman, Seth Lipsky, Doris Wise Montrose, Norman Podhoretz, Magda Rados, David Richman, Judy Richman, Robert Richman, Dr. Robert Wexler, Professor Ruth R. Wisse, and Rabbi David J. Wolpe. Of course, any errors in this book are solely my responsibility.

I am grateful to Dr. David Hazony for publishing an early version of a part of Chapter 3 in The Israel Project's *Tower Magazine*; to Anne Lieberman and Seth Lipsky for impressing upon me Vladimir Jabotinsky's historical importance, and to Louis Gordon for sharing his lifelong knowledge of him; to Irving White for a very helpful conversation about Chaim Weizmann; and to Dr. Robert Wexler for his close reading of the manuscript and his significant insight about David Ben-Gurion. Norman Podhoretz, Neal Kozodoy, and Ruth R. Wisse were especially generous, on multiple occasions, with their time and suggestions.

I have been fortunate to have had access to many exceptional libraries, and have been the beneficiary of the efforts of their dedicated librarians, including the Ostrow Library at American Jewish University in Los Angeles (Patricia Fenton, Jackie Ben-Efraim, and Stephen Singler); the Dorot Jewish Division of the New York City Public Library (Eleanor Yadin and Stephen Corrsin); the Center for Jewish History and the YIVO Institute for Jewish Research in New York City (Gunnar Berg, Michelle McCarthy, and Vital Zajka); the Library of the University of Southern California Cinematic Arts Division (Edward Sykes Comstock); the Los Angeles Public Library; and the Jabotinsky Institute in Tel Aviv (Amira Stern).

I thank O'Melveny & Myers LLP, which provided me the office in which I wrote most of this book. I am grateful to my colleagues there for their assistance: Christopher C. Murray, who gave me the benefit of his expertise and experience on intellectual property law, and Eron Ben-Yehuda, who referred me to Einat Meisel, the head of O'Melveny's Israel practice, who in turn introduced me to Ella Tevet and Roee Laor of Gross, Kleinhendler, Hodak, Halevy, Greenberg & Co. (GKH), one of Israel's major law firms. They skillfully represented me in securing consents and releases for the letters, diaries, and speeches that form the heart of this book from the Archives at Yad Chaim Weizmann, Rehovot, Israel; the Jabotinsky Institute in Israel; and the Ben-Gurion Archives and Library, Ben-Gurion University of the Negev. Avi Shilon, PhD, searched the Ben-Gurion Archives for the diary entries and letters for the period covered by Ben-Gurion's 1940 trip. I am grateful to Aliza Perl Klainman and Ophir Klainman for their skillful translation of the Ben-Gurion documents from Hebrew into English for this book.

O'Melveny's Office Services team graciously accommodated my seemingly endless requests for copies, PDFs, supplies, mailings, and assistance with my temperamental computer: thank you to Jim Eshelman, José Torres, LaVonda Davis, Enrique Hilado, Ebony Mariano, and Douglas Orellana. I am grateful to O'Melveny's two stellar librarians, Patricia Smith and Deborah Fisher, for their help on many occasions.

For their generous assistance, advice, or encouragement, I thank Michal Gorlin Becker at the Shapell Manuscript Foundation; Rabbi Nosson Blumes of the Educational Institute Oholei Torah in Brooklyn, New York; Professors Michael Mandelbaum, Marc Saperstein, and Dan Schueftan; Adele Silver; my brother-in-law (and fellow author) Dr. Bill Cloke; and my friends Greyson Bryan, Michael Cohen, Mark Haloossim, Cary Lerman, Samuel W. Schaul, and Michael Silverstein.

It has been a pleasure to work with Encounter Books—especially Roger Kimball, Katherine Wong, Lauren Miklos, and Sam Schneider—and a great honor to be included in the roster of its authors. I thank each of them for the extraordinary attention they gave to this book.

I thank God for the sustaining love of my wife, Judy, and our extraordinary sons, Robert and David: blessings beyond compare.

November 2017
Los Angeles, California

# PREFACE

In 1940, in the opening months of World War II—more than a year before the attack on Pearl Harbor propelled the United States into the war—the three most prominent Zionist leaders in the world undertook missions to America.

They traveled across an ocean patrolled by German submarines to alert American Jews to a European crisis even more dire than they realized; to rally support for a Jewish homeland in Palestine; and to form a Jewish army to join the fight against Hitler. The three leaders were:

> (1) Chaim Weizmann, 65, the president of the Zionist Organization, founded by Theodor Herzl in 1897. In 1940, he was the leading Zionist figure in the world;[1]

> (2) Vladimir Jabotinsky, 59, the president of the New Zionist Organization, formed in 1935 when he withdrew his "Revisionist" Zionist party from the ranks of the Zionist Organization in opposition to what he considered Weizmann's too-moderate Zionism;[2] and

> (3) David Ben-Gurion, 53, the longtime leader of the Labor Zionist movement in Palestine and the head of the Jewish Agency, formed in 1922 to work with Britain to establish the Jewish national home under the League of Nations Mandate.[3]

*Chaim Weizmann*      *Vladimir Jabotinsky*      *David Ben-Gurion*

All three had been born in the nineteenth century in the Pale of Settlement, the area to which the czars confined the Jews and strictly regulated their lives. Weizmann and Ben-Gurion had grown up in small shtetls, while Jabotinsky grew up in the city of Odessa. Each had embraced Zionism at an early age and worked for decades in pursuit of a Jewish homeland in Palestine—sometimes together, often apart. They represented, roughly speaking, Zionism's left (Ben-Gurion), right (Jabotinsky), and center (Weizmann).

At the end of 1939, after Nazi Germany and the Soviet Union invaded Poland—with its three million Jews—the United States was the only country where a significant Jewish community lived in freedom. America, however, was frozen in isolationism, still smarting from the Great War it had entered two decades earlier on President Wilson's assurance it would make the world safe for democracy.[4] That war had produced hundreds of thousands of American casualties, without achieving its goal.[5] Very few Americans were in favor of participating in another European war.

Weizmann's trip to America lasted two months; Jabotinsky's five; and Ben-Gurion's four. There was thus a leading Zionist in America for virtually all of 1940, but they were never in the United States at the same time. Their relationships with one another, moreover, were frayed. Weizmann and Jabotinsky, close colleagues at the time of the 1917 Balfour Declaration, now favored different versions of Zionism. Ben-Gurion championed yet a third, and by the time of his trip to the United States, he was no longer on speaking terms with either Weizmann or Jabotinsky. The American Jewish community was divided as well, deeply apprehensive about its own precarious status in its relatively new home.

The story of these trips is a portrait, as the most consequential decade in modern Jewish history began, of three of the leading Zionists of the time, and of the American community they sought to engage. It is told using accounts from published sources, as well as from unpublished letters, speeches, and diaries, chronicling all three missions for the first time in a single volume.[6]

They were part of a heroic struggle at a critical time. The importance of the story, however, transcends that moment in history. Many of the issues the Zionist leaders confronted then about the identity of Jews and their role in the world endure more than seventy-five years later, with the Jewish state under continuing existential threat, as its enemies seek to acquire weapons of mass destruction.

# INTRODUCTION:
# THE WORLD IN 1940

On September 1, 1939—two decades after World War I—a new European war began, triggered by a pact between the two totalitarian powers that dominated the continent by then.

On August 23, 1939, Nazi Germany and the Soviet Union signed a ten-year "non-aggression pact," consisting of 280 words.[1] Its key provision was hidden in an undisclosed protocol, which by its terms was to be kept "strictly secret" by the signatories, specifying a "territorial and political rearrangement of the areas belonging to the Polish state." The secret protocol included a map with a line drawn through the middle of Poland, marking the contemplated division of Poland in the imminent "territorial and political rearrangement."[2]

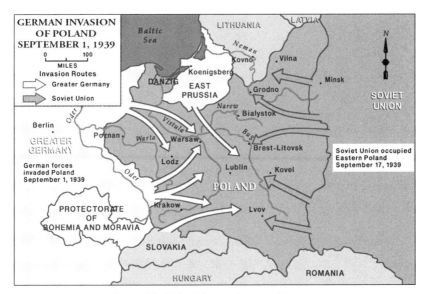

*Source: The U.S. Holocaust Memorial Museum*

The pact paved the way for what happened next. A week after signing it, Hitler invaded Poland from the West; two weeks later, Stalin invaded from the East.

By the end of September, Poland no longer existed as a country: it had been invaded, defeated, partitioned, and annexed by Germany and the Soviet Union.

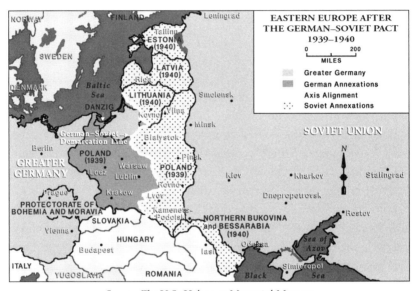

*Source: The U.S. Holocaust Memorial Museum*

The estimated Polish losses from the month-long Nazi invasion included 70,000 killed, 133,000 wounded, and 700,000 captured. An additional 50,000 Poles were killed in the Soviet invasion.[3] The elite of Poland's civil society and its ruling class were decimated, and Polish Jews of all classes were specifically targeted.[4] The Nazi and Soviet occupiers began cleansing Poland in their respective areas, with the Nazis employing racial standards and the Soviets using class criteria. Poland became a vast region of ideological reorganization, the entire population sorted, expropriated, expelled, confined, or murdered, with the land divided between the two invaders.[5]

What remained of the Polish military reorganized itself in Paris under General Wladyslaw Sikorski, who formed a government in exile that later made its headquarters in London.[6] From the scattered remnants of the defeated Polish army, Sikorski built a force that fought first in France in 1940; then elsewhere in Europe; and finally at Normandy in 1944, on behalf of a defeated Polish nation, trying to recover the land taken from it five years earlier.[7]

For the Jews of Poland—who comprised the largest Jewish community in Europe—matters were about to become extremely dire. The Jews had no army; they had no government in exile; they had no generals; they had no country to protect or shelter them; and the land they once possessed had been taken from them not five years before, but two millennia earlier.

NAZI GERMANY AND THE SOVIET UNION now controlled millions more Jews, who were unable to emigrate to Palestine or America. With the issuance of a new "White Paper" in May 1939, the British had prohibited any further significant Jewish immigration to Palestine— which Britain had already severely curtailed since the mid-1930s.[8] Virtually all Jews in Central and Eastern Europe were now held captive, trapped by two armed national ideological movements, one of which intended to annihilate them, while the other aimed to ban all religions. By mid-1940, all of Western Europe had fallen under the control of the genocidal Nazi empire as well, and Britain—the last remaining holdout—had come under ferocious attack.

In 1940, only one country in the world had a politically significant number of free Jews: the United States.[9] In America, however, the immigration-friendly laws of the early twentieth century had vanished after the Immigration Act of 1924, and American public opinion in 1939 was overwhelmingly against any new wave of immigration from Europe. The fate of the Jews in Europe—like that of the English and the French people themselves—would ultimately depend on the American response to European events. But American Jews, like almost all other Americans, wanted nothing to do with the European conflict.[10] In any event, America lacked a military force that would have enabled it to join the war effort. As of September 1939, the German Army had 200 divisions, consisting of almost three million men, with 400,000 horses and 200,000 military vehicles.[11] The United States Army had a total of five divisions.[12] In size and combat power, the American army ranked seventeenth in the world— behind Romania's.[13]

## THE NAZIS AND SOVIETS ADVANCE

On September 3, 1939, two days after the German invasion of Poland began, President Franklin D. Roosevelt addressed the American people by radio, assuring them the country would not participate in the new war: "Let no man or woman thoughtlessly or falsely talk of America sending its armies to European fields. At this moment, there is being prepared a proclamation of American neutrality."[14] He issued the proclamation two days later. The United States and the other Western Hemisphere countries declared an American Security Zone extending up to 600 miles from their coasts.[15] The Atlantic and Pacific Oceans would be their Maginot Line (the state-of-the-art defense line built by France in the 1930s on its border with Germany that ultimately proved useless).[16]

On the day that America declared its neutrality, Britain and France declared war on Germany. They had no choice: five months earlier, they had publicly committed themselves to the defense of Poland, after Hitler had violated the 1938 Munich "peace-for-our-time" agreement by taking over Czechoslovakia.[17] France and Britain had hoped that a public commitment to Poland would deter Germany from further aggression.[18] British Prime Minister Neville Chamberlain warned Hitler that "no greater mistake could be made" than believing the British would not come to Poland's defense, with "all the forces at [British] command."[19] Later in 1939, Britain proclaimed a formal treaty with Poland, confirming those security guarantees.[20]

In reality, however, Britain lacked the armed forces to meet its commitments. For years, despite Winston Churchill's warnings, there had been no significant military preparation in Britain; its army was not only small, but it also lacked sufficient officers even for its reduced size.[21] France maintained a large military, but having lost a million men in World War I, it was neither psychologically prepared to defend Poland, nor even to protect itself.[22] After the Nazi *blitzkrieg* on September 1, the French could not have mounted a counterattack until the end of the month, by which time Poland had already been defeated and divided.[23]

As soon as Hitler invaded Poland, both France and Britain sought to avoid their obligations to defend it. They declared war, but proceeded to fight it only half-heartedly.[24] On September 4, as an immediate response, Britain sent the British Expeditionary Force (BEF) to France—four divisions to be stationed in defensive positions along the Franco-Belgian border. But it was only a symbolic step.[25] Britain was simply not a significant military power at that time.[26] Hitler had a hundred divisions available for use against the West, saving the remainder of his forces for other purposes; the forces of the demoralized French and the under-armed British had only seventy-six divisions *combined*.[27] In the wake of the Polish invasion, Britain resolved to create a fifty-five-division army and a modern air force and navy—which it estimated would take two to three years.[28]

Through early 1940, British efforts on the continent consisted primarily of dropping leaflets over Germany urging the public to remove Hitler from power.[29] While battles continued to rage in Scandinavia, with the Soviet Union moving against Finland and occupying the Baltic States, the public in both Britain and France believed the new war posed no real threat to them. Daily life there continued more or less as usual.[30] After sending the BEF to France and deciding to build a serious military force in the coming years, Britain waited to see what would happen next.[31] The battle in Europe settled into a deceptively low-level conflict that became known as the "phony war."[32]

## WINSTON CHURCHILL

In January 1940, at the age of 64, Winston Churchill was the head of the British Admiralty. Had his story ended there, he well might have been remembered as a political failure. Over the previous forty years, he had been involved in almost every major issue in the political life of Great Britain—invariably on the losing side. He had switched parties twice; and had taken unpopular positions on issues such as the women's vote, the Gallipoli disaster, the gold standard, and Indian self-government, among others.[33] But in the words of British historian Andrew Roberts, he had a "preternatural eloquence and world-historical sense."[34] In an essay he wrote when he was only 23, entitled "The Scaffolding of Rhetoric," Churchill had observed that:

> Of all the talents bestowed upon men, none is so precious as the gift of oratory. He who enjoys it wields a power more durable than that of a great king. He is an independent force on the world. Abandoned by his party, betrayed by his friends, stripped of his offices, whoever can command this power is still formidable.[35]

On January 20, 1940, although he would not become prime minister for another five months, Churchill addressed the nation as First Lord of the Admiralty, since, as he said, "[e]veryone wonders what is happening about the war."[36] He reported that "[a]ll Scandinavia dwells brooding under Nazi and Bolshevik threats." The "small but ancient and historic States which lie in the North" and the "anxious peoples in the Balkans or in the Danube basin" all were "wondering which will be the next victim"—each hoping "if he feeds the crocodile enough, the crocodile will eat him last." Churchill presciently assured the public that the size of the German army would not be the determining factor in the war, because "very few wars have been won by mere numbers alone":

> Quality, will power, geographical advantages, natural and financial resources, the command of the sea, *and above all, a cause which rouses the spontaneous surging of the human spirit in millions of hearts*—these have proved to be the decisive factors in the human story. [Emphasis added.][37]

The "phony war" ended abruptly on May 10, 1940, when Germany launched another predawn *blitzkrieg* on Holland, Belgium, Denmark, and later, on France—all of which was as stunning as the attack against Poland eight months earlier. Chamberlain resigned immediately, and Churchill assumed office that day. He cabled President Roosevelt that the Low Countries had been "simply smashed up, one by one, like matchwood."

Three days later, in his first speech to the House of Commons as prime minister, Churchill said Britain was about to face "an ordeal of the most grievous kind," with "many, many long months of struggle and of suffering." But, he said, "without victory, there is no survival."[38] A week later, he made his first broadcast to the nation as prime minister, later known as his "Be Ye Men of Valor" speech. The Nazis had broken through French defenses and were proceeding toward Paris, virtually unopposed. Churchill said Britain would have to rescue "not only Europe but mankind from the foulest and most soul-destroying tyranny which has ever darkened and stained the pages of history." He noted that he was broadcasting on Trinity Sunday—the day on which Christians honor the Father, the Son, and the Holy Ghost—but he closed his address by citing a passage not from the New Testament, but from the Jewish Apocrypha:

Centuries ago words were written to be a call and a spur to the faithful servants of Truth and Justice: *"Arm yourselves, and be ye men of valor,* and be in readiness for the conflict; for it is better for us to perish in battle than to look upon the outrage of our nation and our altar. As the Will of God is in Heaven, even so let it be."[39] [Emphasis added.]

The quotation is from the Book of Maccabees (I Maccabees 3:58–60), the story of the Jewish heroes who miraculously prevailed over a vastly more powerful Greek force.[40]

### THE JEWISH SITUATION IN AMERICA IN 1940

As of 1939, there were some 15.8 million Jews in the world, with two-thirds—9.7 million—in Europe and 80 percent of that number in just four countries: Poland (3.2 million), the Soviet Union (3.0 million), Romania (850,000), and Hungary (625,000). Those 7.7 million Jews comprised half the Jews in the world. Germany had comparatively few (345,000), as did France (320,000) and Britain (380,000).[41]

There were about 450,000 Jews in Palestine, of whom 130,000 lived in Tel Aviv (a Jewish city founded in 1909 on the coast of the Mediterranean Sea) and about 80,000 in Jerusalem (comprising 60 percent of its total population). Another 800,000 Jews lived in Arab countries. The American Jewish Yearbook for 1940 listed 432,000 stateless Jews throughout the world.[42]

One-third of all the Jews in the world lived in the United States: 4.8 million, nearly four percent of the American population.[43] The 1940 Annual Report of the American Jewish Committee (AJC), prepared in the opening months of 1940, expressed both the scope of the disaster facing the European Jews and the opposition of Jewish leaders in the United States to American participation in the new war.[44] The AJC, founded in 1906 to combat discrimination against American Jews, was anxious lest the new war in Europe be perceived in America as a "Jewish" war. The first paragraph of the Report acknowledged that the war would affect "half our brethren who live in the countries directly or indirectly involved," but emphasized that the war was part of a larger, non-Jewish concern: "The [Jewish situation] in Central and Eastern Europe, intensely tragic as it is, is part of a calamity almost world-wide in its scope." The AJC was "convinced . . . of the futility of war," and was thus pleased not to be involved in the new one: "Happily," the AJC concluded, "our country is not a party in this conflict."

### ANNUAL REPORT OF THE EXECUTIVE COMMITTEE

*To the Members of the American Jewish Committee:*

For the second time in the history of the Committee, we meet but a few months after the outbreak of a major European conflict. Like its predecessor, the war is bound to affect the lives and to determine the destiny of millions of human beings, including half of our brethren who live in the countries directly or indirectly involved. The disastrous effects of the war on the Jews of Central and Eastern Europe, intensely tragic as it is, is a part of a calamity almost world-wide in its scope. Happily, our country is not a party in this conflict. Convinced as we are of the futility of war, knowing as we do its incalculable material and moral costs, we hope and pray it may be possible for our country to remain at peace.

Turning first to Germany, the Report informed its readers that the Nazis now had 1.5 million more Jews under their control and that:

The well-known Nazi techniques . . . are being applied with indescribable ferocity and ruthlessness in German occupied Poland. Its 1,500,000 Jewish inhabitants are being robbed of all their belongings; stripped of their professions and businesses; condemned to forced labor amidst the debris of cities devastated by the military attack; segregated in Warsaw in districts wholly inadequate to house their number. . . .

The Report further noted that the Nazis planned to round up all Jews and send them to a small area near Lublin, a Polish town with a population of 100,000:

If this fantastic plan is carried out, it would mean that the 2,000,000 Jews now in Germany or in territories under German domination would be confined in what would be a large concentration camp, where they would be doomed to degradation, misery and death.

Concerning the Soviet-occupied portion of Poland—which added about 1.5 million Jews to Soviet control—the AJC reported that the situation was the same as in the Nazi-controlled sector:

> Such meager reports as have reached the United States indicate that, just as in territories newly-acquired by Germany, the Nazi system is quickly applied, so in areas on the Russian side of the line of partition the Bolshevik system is but a short step behind the military forces.
>
> These reports tell of such measures as the banning of religious teaching in Jewish schools, of the complete closing of Hebrew schools, of the launching of an anti-religious campaign by the Moscow League of the Godless, of the over-crowding of prisons with Jewish leaders, of the conversion of synagogues and communal buildings into communist clubs, and of the deportation of rabbis to interior cities. These are all part of the established Soviet pattern. . . .

The change that had occurred in the position of the European Jews within their societies in fewer than two decades was dramatic.[45] In the 1920s, European Jews had been the best-educated group in Europe, accomplished in science, literature, theater, and music. But in the following decade, they were increasingly marked as scapegoats for every social, economic, or political problem, damned in inherently contradictory terms: as both revolutionary communists and capitalist exploiters; practitioners of an outmoded religion and atheistic proponents of a non-religious culture; cliquish people and people inappropriately trying to assimilate into the larger society; people insufficiently cultured and people too educated and supercilious about their knowledge.[46]

This was true not only in Nazi Germany, but also in most of Europe.[47] The horrific situation that the Jews of Eastern Europe faced had long been known in America, at least to readers of *The New York Times*. On February 7, 1937, an extensive article written by Otto D. Tolischus, one of the *Times'* most experienced correspondents (and later the recipient of a Pulitzer Prize in 1940 for his reporting from Berlin), described the wave of anti-Semitism sweeping Eastern Europe. His article began with a prescient sentence:

> Anti-Semitism, raised by Adolf Hitler in Germany to the status of a political religion, is rapidly spreading throughout Eastern

Europe and is thereby *turning the recurrent Jewish tragedy in that biggest Jewish center in the world into a final disaster of truly historic magnitude.*[48] [Emphasis added.]

# JEWS FACE CRISIS IN EASTERN EUROPE

## Anti-Semitism, Sweeping Five Countries, Is Threatening 5,000,000 With Disaster

## WAVE AT PEAK IN POLAND

## Government Fights Violence, but Its Economic Measures Are Pauperizing Jewry.

### By OTTO D. TOLISCHUS
Wireless to THE NEW YORK TIMES.

WARSAW, Poland, Feb. 6.—Anti-Semitism, raised by Adolf Hitler in Germany to the status of a political religion, is rapidly spreading throughout Eastern Europe and is thereby turning the recurrent Jewish tragedy in that biggest Jewish center in the world into a final dis-

days of the Crusades, the Black Death and other periods of anti-Jewish persecution.

### Pilsudski Curbed Movement

This brand of anti-Semitism, which is nothing new in Poland, but which had been suppressed for a time by the late Marshal Josef Pilsudski's iron hand, began to raise its head anew after his death and that was also the signal for the revival of Nationalist opposition to his political heirs.

last three months in university rioting, twenty of them for life.

Efforts to obtain official figures on these excesses have proved unavailing, but the unofficial figures were confirmed in part by no less an authority than Premier Felicien Slawoj-Skladkowski. He revealed to the Sejm that in the Province of Bialystok alone there had occurred during the last year 348 assaults on Jews, including twenty-one mass riots or pograms; ninety-nine cases of Jew-baiting, and 161 cases of window-smashing, although he gave the total casualties at only three Jews killed and seven severely injured.

### Differs from Nazi Wave

Despite their outward similarity, this new Polish anti-Semitic wave differs from previous outbreaks in Czarist Russia and National Socialist Germany.

In both these States anti-Semitism found no support in either a social or economic upheaval but was the direct result of the anti-Semitic policies of their respective governments, based on either a need for the diversion of popular attention from other issues or a racial creed that designates the Jew as the only racial enemy.

*The New York Times, February 7, 1937*

Tolischus' article—which covered five columns in the first section of the Sunday *Times*—reported that the "disaster is now taking place in Latvia, Lithuania, Hungary and Rumania and is approaching a high-water mark in Poland, the country with the biggest Jewish population outside the United States." Tolischus described the tragedy in very stark terms:

> In all these countries the majority of the Jews, totaling 5,000,000 souls, or 30 percent of the whole Jewish population in the world, are now facing the prospect of either repeating the Exodus on a bigger scale than that chronicled in the bible, and somehow making it through the immigration barriers erected against them everywhere, or spending the rest of their lives in an atmosphere of creeping hostility and dying a slow death from economic strangulation.

Two years later—a month after the outbreak of World War II—the October 1939 issue of the *Brooklyn Jewish Center Review,* the monthly publication of one of the leading American Conservative synagogues, featured an article by Rabbi Elias N. Rabinowitz entitled "How Will the Conquest of Poland Affect Its Jews?" It described the situation in Poland as follows:

> The tragedy of Poland has, probably, never been equaled in the
> recorded annals of history. . . . [T]he present dismemberment has
> come so rapidly and in a way so unexpectedly that one, at times,
> finds difficulties in visualizing it. . . . The plight of the Polish
> Jew beggars description. He has been uprooted, he has been
> destroyed. . . . The Polish Republic contained the second larg-
> est Jewish community in the present Diaspora, approximately
> 4,000,000 souls. . . . As reports reach us from various sources,
> starvation is rampant. The number of suicides is reported to be
> overwhelming.[49]

By the end of 1939, Poland, Austria, and Czechoslovakia had all been
conquered by Hitler. A sizable percentage of the European Jewish population had fallen under the control of totalitarian anti-Semitic states.
Their disaster had been reported in *The New York Times* since at least the
beginning of 1937.[50] But for many American Jews, it all seemed very far
away—and not merely geographically.

## THE JEWISH HISTORICAL EXPERIENCE IN AMERICA

Most American Jews in 1940 viewed the United States as the new Zion. It
was the country that had welcomed them from the very beginning, from
the days of George Washington, and indeed even earlier.[51] Beginning in
the late nineteenth century, after unprecedentedly brutal pogroms in Russia, America had facilitated a massive movement of millions of Jews from
Europe to the United States.[52] The Jews had found unparalleled opportunities in the American economy and in its political process. They became
both an American success story and a Jewish one.

But Jewish success in the United States—combined with the continuing Jewish catastrophes in Europe—produced an identity crisis of its own
for American Jews.

Between 1820 and 1880, the Jewish population in America had increased a hundred times over, from 3,000 in 1820 to 300,000 in 1880.[53]
These immigrants were mainly German-speaking Jews from Central Europe, who assimilated into cities across the country—New York, Philadelphia, Cincinnati, Cleveland, St. Louis, New Orleans, and Atlanta,
among others. They had little desire to carry forward the religious identity
they associated with so much sorrow in the Old World: history was not

something they wished to remember, but rather to forget. Some suggested sardonically that the biggest graveyard of *tallitot* (the traditional Jewish prayer shawls) was the New York harbor.

For those who chose to retain their religious identity in America, many were drawn to Reform Judaism, which sought to adapt Judaism to the modern era. Rabbi Isaac Mayer Wise, the principal leader of the movement in America, urged that "[t]he Jew must become an American in order to gain the proud self-consciousness of the free-born man." He argued that Jews "must be not only American citizens," but "Americans through and through."[54] He wrote that he himself had begun "to Americanize with all my might."[55]

In Reform congregations across the country, the traditional Jewish head coverings and prayer shawls were abandoned; services were shortened; English replaced Hebrew in the prayer book; rituals of Protestant prayer such as organ music were adopted; men and women sat together; services were moved to Sunday—and the traditional prayer for the return to Zion was omitted entirely from the liturgy.[56]

*Rabbi Isaac Mayer Wise, circa 1876*

The movement of Reform Judaism away from the orthodoxy and traditions of the Old World was epitomized on July 11, 1883, in a seminal event in the history of American Judaism. On that date, the Hebrew Union College, established by Rabbi Wise in 1875, graduated its first class of rabbis and held a lavish banquet in their honor at the luxurious Highland House resort and restaurant in Cincinnati. There were 215 invited guests, including local Christian clergy and other dignitaries. The occasion became notorious because its menu, printed in French, contained only "*tref*" (Yiddish for non-kosher food).[57] The dinner consisted of clams, crab, shrimp, lobster, frogs' legs, and meat mixed with milk.[58] What became known as "The *Trefa* Banquet" was an audacious declaration of independence from Jewish law. Partly in response, leading Orthodox Jews founded the Jewish Theological Seminary of America in 1886, and the Conservative Jewish movement in America was strengthened by it.[59] Henceforth religious American Jews would be split among three different groups.

## ZIONISM AND ANTI-ZIONISM IN AMERICA

In 1885, Rabbi Wise invited Reform rabbis to a conference in Pittsburgh, which adopted a set of principles that would constitute the basic tenets of Reform Judaism for the next half century. The "Pittsburgh Platform" stated that the kosher laws had been adopted "under the influence of ideas entirely foreign to our present mental and spiritual state"; they failed to impress "modern Jews"; and they tended "rather to obstruct than to further modern spiritual elevation."[60] The Platform also asserted that the Bible itself reflected "the primitive ideas of its own age," often clothed "in miraculous narratives" rather than reason, and that henceforth only the "moral laws" of the Bible were binding. All rituals other than those "adapted to the views and habits of modern civilization" were rejected. In a critical part of the Platform, the rabbis also rejected Zionism:

> We consider ourselves no longer a nation, but a religious community, and therefore expect neither a return to Palestine, nor a sacrificial worship under the sons of Aaron, nor the restoration of any of the laws concerning the Jewish state. . . . We recognize in Judaism a progressive religion, ever striving to be in accord with the postulates of reason.

What this meant in practice was illustrated by the example of Rabbi David Marx, a young Reform rabbi who in 1895 had assumed the pulpit of the Hebrew Benevolent Congregation, a thirty-year-old synagogue in Atlanta. Within his first five years, Rabbi Marx adopted the dress of Christian clergy, banned the traditional wearing of hats in the synagogue, abolished the bar mitzvah ceremony, held services on Sunday rather than Friday evening and Saturday, and repudiated Zionism. He became a local celebrity, a guest columnist for the *Atlanta Journal*, and a frequent speaker in the city's churches. His congregants said he made them proud to be Jews, although some observed that their pride seemed to be not in Judaism, but rather in their acceptance by the Gentile community.[61]

In 1897, the year after Theodor Herzl, the Austrian Jewish journalist who had witnessed the anti-Semitic trial of Alfred Dreyfus in France in 1894, published *The Jewish State*—the founding document of the modern Zionist movement in Europe—Rabbi Wise publicly announced his opposition to the idea. He argued it would "turn the mission of Israel from the province of religion and humanity to the narrow political and national field, where Judaism loses its universal and sanctified ground and its historical signification." He thought the idea of a Jewish state was "utopian" and "foreign." In an address to the Central Conference of American Rabbis (CCAR), the leading group of Reform rabbis, on July 6, 1897, he said "all this agitation on the other side of the ocean concerns us very little":

> We are perfectly satisfied with our political and social position. It can make no difference to us . . . in what particular spot of the earth's surface we occupy. . . . That new Messianic movement over the ocean does not concern us at all . . . [nor the fact that] so-and-so many rabbis advocated those political schemes. . . . [They are] the fantastic dupes of a thoughtless Utopia, which to us is . . . a momentary inebriation of morbid minds, and a prostitution of Israel's holy cause to a madman's dance of unsound politicians.[62]

A year later, the Jewish Congregational Union of America—representing Orthodox rabbis—announced its support of Zionism. Its platform rejected "the idea that we are merely a religious sect, and maintain that we are a nation, though temporarily without a national home." The "restoration to Zion," the Orthodox asserted, was the "legitimate aspiration of scattered Israel, in no way conflicting with our loyalty to the land in which we dwell or may dwell at any time." But this was a minority view among the Orthodox Jews, who generally rejected Zionism on the basis that the messiah had not yet arrived. For many Orthodox rabbis, Zionism was a movement that weakened traditional Judaism and was in significant part a rebellion against the Jewish past.[63]

In 1917, when Britain issued the Balfour Declaration, committing itself to foster the establishment of a Jewish national home in Palestine, the reaction among many Jews in America differed dramatically from those in Palestine. Several months after the Declaration, *The New York Times* reported that the Zionist enthusiasm among the Jews of Palestine was "striking," and that "[v]irtually all the able-bodied Jews of Palestine have applied . . . for service" in the Jewish battalions supporting the British in World War I.[64] At the same time, in the United States, the CCAR closed its seven-day session in Chicago by adopting resolutions that expressed appreciation for the goodwill underlying the Declaration—but nonetheless opposed a Jewish home in Palestine.[65]

As conditions for the Jews in Russia (and in the Soviet Union after 1917) and Eastern and Central Europe progressively worsened, the Reform movement eventually came to re-examine its official attitude opposing Zionism—but only slightly. At its 1935 annual meeting in Chicago, the movement adopted a new position of neutrality: "We are persuaded that acceptance or rejection of the Zionist program should be left to the determination of the individual members of the Conference themselves." The CCAR took "no official stand on the subject of Zionism." In May 1937, as the conditions for European Jews continued to deteriorate, the CCAR moved closer to acceptance of Zionism, adopting principles that "affirm the obligation of all Jewry to aid in [the] up-building [of Palestine] as a Jewish homeland by endeavoring to make it not only a haven of refuge for the oppressed but also a center of Jewish culture and spiritual life." But the Reform movement did not endorse a Jewish state—only a "haven" and a "center." They were wary of anything that might suggest loyalty by American Jews to a different nation.

In June 1937, the Rabbinical Assembly of the Conservative Movement issued its own "Pronouncement on Zionism," which emphasized the central importance of Palestine:

> We reaffirm our historic claim to Palestine, as the land where for more than a thousand years our fathers lived a national life and built a religious civilization. . . . This land, further sanctified by

the vision and message of the prophets, by more than eighteen centuries of unfaltering hope and tear-drenched prayer, and by the blood and sweat of the modern Jewish pioneer and martyr, has become inextricably intertwined with our religious faith and has assumed a central and all-important position. . . .

As the disastrous decade of the 1930s continued its march toward the annihilation of European Jewry, the three major Jewish movements in America lacked a unified position on Zionism.[66]

### "JEWS IN AMERICA" VERSUS "AMERICANS WHO ARE JEWS"

In its June 20, 1938, issue, *Time Magazine* devoted an article to the split between Zionists and non-Zionists. In a report entitled *"Jews v. Jews,"* the magazine informed its readers that:

> There are two kinds of U.S. Jews. One kind (in its own words) is composed of "Americans who are Jews"—Americans who, as individuals, practice the Jewish faith, or, if they are not religious, admit their Jewish ancestry.
>
> The other kind is a smaller but more articulate group of "Jews in America"—Jews who have not only a common religion but a common culture; who believe they are members of a scattered nation; who tend to approve Zionist aims toward a Jewish homeland. Between these two groups there is deep-rooted animosity.

*Time* designated Dr. Cyrus Adler—head of the American Jewish Committee (AJC)—as the Number One "American who is a Jew." The AJC had been formed in 1906 in response to the brutal pogroms in Russia in 1903 and 1905; its goal was to "prevent infringement of the civil and religious rights of Jews and to alleviate the consequences of persecution." As of 1940, the members of the AJC included such prominent American Jews as Irving Lehman, Joseph M. Proskauer, and Sol M. Stroock, leading members of the Bar; and the investment banker, Frederick M. Warburg. It was a non-Zionist—indeed an anti-Zionist—group, concerned with protecting Jewish rights in America and other places Jews lived, seeking to end prejudice against Jews, but not to support a separate Jewish state.[67]

As for the Number One "Jew in America," *Time* identified Rabbi Stephen S. Wise—a charismatic Reform rabbi (unrelated to Rabbi Isaac

*Cyrus Adler*                                    *Rabbi Stephen S. Wise*

Mayer Wise) who had been born in Budapest in 1874, the grandson of a chief rabbi of a nearby town, and who came to New York as a child. Unlike most Reform rabbis and their congregants, he became a Zionist, after meeting Theodor Herzl at the second Zionist Congress in 1898. In 1920, he founded the American Jewish Congress as a Zionist organization to compete with the AJC. He became president of the Zionist Organization of America in 1936 and was president of the American Jewish Congress in 1939.[68]

*Time* called Rabbi Wise "ardently Zionist"—as someone favoring a boycott of Nazi Germany and supporting mass protests against Hitler—and the magazine, describing him as speaking with "his Mosaic profile bobbing," quoted him as criticizing German Jews for their naiveté:

> The [German Jews] said they were Germans first. Germans who happened to be Jews. I am a Jew who is an American. I was a Jew before I was an American. I have been an American all my life, 64 years, but I've been a Jew for 4,000 years.

According to *Time*, Cyrus Adler's AJC represented "U.S. Jewry at its richest and most conservative, ardently non-Zionist, lukewarm toward boycotts and protests."[69] *Time* reported that "between President Adler and President Wise there is intense personal dislike," and that Wise's group was out of step with the rest of the Jewish community. *Time* asserted that

*(Photo from his 1941 Autobiography)*

organizations with membership of more than one million had rejected Wise's concept of "Jews in America."

The rejection of Zionism by most "Americans who are Jews" was reflected in the writings of Rabbi David Philipson—one of the first four graduates of the Hebrew Union College, in whose honor the *Trefa* Banquet had been held a half century earlier. In 1940, he had retired after a distinguished fifty-year career as rabbi of Cincinnati's Rockdale Avenue Temple, the oldest congregation west of the Allegheny Mountains. He was the author or editor of eleven books and the dean of the American Reform Rabbinate, and his vehement opposition to Zionism had marked his entire career. What was happening to the Jews in Europe as of 1940 had not affected his opposition in the slightest.[70]

In retirement, Rabbi Philipson prepared a 526-page autobiography, published in 1941 as *My Life as an American Jew*. It included this paragraph, written in the first month of World War II, summarizing his feelings about the predicament of the Jews of Eastern Europe:

As of this writing (September 1939) the situation is even worse [than in Germany], if such a thing were possible. The rape of Austria and Czechoslovakia and the conquest of Poland subject the millions of Jews in those three lands to the same horrible fate that has been the portion of their co-religionists in Greater Germany since the gang of criminals, headed by Adolf Hitler, came to power. *Have all these horrors caused me to change my attitude on the Palestine question? Fundamentally, no. A Jewish state in Palestine will not solve the Jewish problem.*[71] [Emphasis added.]

Rabbi Philipson rejected the idea of a Jewish homeland because, in his view, the "Jews constitute a universal people" whose mission was "hope"—which is "our religious heritage" and the message to be delivered by Jews throughout the world. For "us American Jews of universalistic tendencies," he wrote, Palestine represents "an outgrown phase of Jewish historical experience":

We are Americans, not Palestinians. Our interest in Palestine is philanthropic, not political. The so-called Jewish problem will never be solved by the acquisition of a so-called Jewish homeland in Palestine. Every land is the homeland for its Jews—the United States for me, as England for my English Jewish brother, France for my French Jewish brother, and so in every country. . . . For us there is no Jewish nation—only a Jewish religious community.[72]

Rabbi Philipson was not simply unconvinced by Zionism; he went further and claimed that it had performed a "great disservice to Judaism and the Jews the world over." In his view, it was "a complete misreading and misinterpretation of Judaism's past and future."[73]

## A SONG, A BOOK, AND A MOVIE

The conflicting influences on American Jews at the beginning of World War II were reflected in a popular song, a widely read book, and an award-winning movie.

## THE SONG: *GOD BLESS AMERICA*

On Armistice Day, November 10, 1938, at a time when radio was the principal means of mass communication, Kate Smith—one of the most

*Irving Berlin, circa 1940*

popular American singers of the century—introduced her millions of lis-teners to a song written by Irving Berlin: *God Bless America*.[74] In its orig-inal form, the lyrics included an introductory verse, preceding its soon-to-be-famous chorus—a prayer of gratitude for living in America and not in Europe:[75]

> While the storm clouds gather far across the sea,
> Let us swear allegiance to a land that's free.
> Let us all be grateful that we're far from there,
> As we raise our voices in a solemn prayer.
> God Bless America, land that I love . . .

The song mirrored Berlin's own story: born to a religious Jewish family in Ukraine in 1888 as "Israel Beilin," he came to America as a four-year-old, when his family fled the pogroms. In New York, he became "Izzy" Beilin; then he was "Irving" Beilin; and finally, "Irving Berlin." America was his "home sweet home," and he told *The New York Times* his song was "not a patriotic song, but rather an expression of gratitude for what this country has done for its citizens."[76]

Smith sang *God Bless America* on her program a total of fifty-eight times. It remained on the *Billboard* charts for fifteen weeks and sold more than 500,000 copies in sheet music. It became an unofficial anthem, sung at churches and schools, adopted by both the Republicans and Democrats at their respective 1940 conventions as their theme song.[77] The National

Committee for Music Appreciation gave the song its award as the out-standing composition of the year.[78]

But in February 1939, as the song exploded in popularity, Berlin changed its third line. Berlin replaced "Let us all be grateful *that we're far from there*" with a new line: "Let us all be grateful *for a land so fair.*" He amended the line because the song's premiere on Kate Smith's show had coincided with the wave of Nazi pogroms in Germany and Austria only the night before, known later as *Kristallnacht.*[79] As the full scope and significance of the horrific assault on central European Jewry emerged, Berlin understood that a quasi-religious musical paean to being "far from there" was unseemly, particularly for an American Jew living in the safety of the United States.

In fact, some negative reactions to the song suggested that the Jews of America might, in fact, not be quite as "far from there" as they thought. In a July 1940 sermon, Rev. Edgar Romig, a progressive Protestant minister at the West End Collegiate Church in Manhattan, founded in 1628, whose sermon topics were listed each week in *The New York Times*, criticized the song as "doggerel," unlike the "great national anthem that . . . came out of the hearts of men who knew what it was to sacrifice for America."[80] Peter Marshall, minister of the New York Avenue Presbyterian Church in Washington, D.C.—and later the Chaplain of the Senate—went even further. In a September 15, 1940, sermon, he called the song "pseudo-patriotism" and warned, pointedly, against Jewish control of Hollywood, whose morals "infect our national life."[81]

The September 30, 1940, issue of *Time Magazine,* in an article entitled "Badgered Ballad," reported that *God Bless America* had brought on "a wave of snide anti-Semitism directed at Composer Berlin," and that Kate Smith's business manager frequently received letters "berating him . . . for swelling Jewish coffers" with royalties—a charge all the more appall-ing because both Berlin and Smith had donated their royalties and rights from writing and performing the song to a trust for the Boy Scouts, Girl Scouts, and other youth organizations.[82]

## THE BOOK: *IT CAN'T HAPPEN HERE*

Sinclair Lewis' 1935 novel, *It Can't Happen Here*, was a widely read satirical novel and cautionary tale about fascism coming to America. It was pro-duced as a play in many cities, including a Yiddish version in New York.[83] MGM hoped to turn it into a movie—first in 1936, and then in 1939.

The novel opens with an argument between a liberal newspaper editor and his industrialist friend, who tells the editor that with twenty-eight million people on relief, things were "beginning to get ugly." The industrialist goes on to assert that "Jew Communists and Jew financiers [are] plotting together to control the country" and that a "strong man" might be a good thing, but that unfortunately this "could not happen in America." The editor replies, "The hell it can't":

> Look how Huey Long became absolute monarch over Louisiana, and how the Right Honorable Mr. Senator Berzelius Windrip owns his State. Listen to Bishop Prang and Father Coughlin on the radio—divine oracles to millions. Remember how casually most Americans have accepted Tammany grafting and Chicago gangs and the crookedness of so many of President Harding's appointees? Could Hitler's bunch, or Windrip's, be worse? Remember the Ku Klux Klan? Remember our war hysteria [during World War I] . . . [and] wartime censorship of honest papers? . . . Remember our Red scares and our Catholic scares . . . and the Republicans campaigning against Al Smith, [telling] the Carolina mountaineers that if Al won, the Pope would illegitimatize their children? . . . Remember how trainloads of people have gone to enjoy lynchings?
>
> Not happen here? Prohibition—shooting down people just because they might be transporting liquor—no, that couldn't happen in America! Why, where in all history has there ever been a people so ripe for a dictatorship as ours! We're ready to start on a Children's Crusade—only of adults—right now."

MGM bought the movie rights, but the industry association pressured it to forgo making the film, because it would be "inflammatory" and adversely affect the market for American films in Germany.[84] In 1939, when MGM again considered producing the film, the association pressured it yet a second time. Joseph Breen, the association's anti-Semitic head of standards, enforced a policy barring any film that did not "fairly" discuss Nazi Germany.[85]

In the face of such opposition, MGM dropped the film project entirely. What is particularly noteworthy, however, is that among those who lobbied against making the movie were two prominent Jewish organizations: the Anti-Defamation League and the American Jewish Committee. They argued that Jews must be wary of placing themselves in the public spotlight with such a film.[86]

## THE MOVIE: *CONFESSIONS OF A NAZI SPY*

Many Jewish directors—such as Fritz Lang, Max Ophuls, and Billy Wilder—had fled Germany and Austria in the 1930s for Hollywood, where they translated their harrowing European experience into *film noir,* which did not directly address the situation in Europe but conveyed a pervasive sense of evil and impending doom. The Jewish-run studios, however, were publicly silent about Nazism throughout the 1930s.[87] To the extent that studio executives expressed their opposition at all, they did so largely in private.[88]

The first overtly anti-Nazi film from a major Hollywood studio was Warner Bros.' *Confessions of a Nazi Spy* (1939), starring Edward G. Robinson (born Emanuel Goldenberg in Romania) as an FBI agent investigating a Nazi spy ring in New York.[89] The movie was based on a true story: the ring had been tried and convicted in 1938.[90] The National Board of Review of Motion Pictures named it the best film of the year, citing its "artistic merit and importance," ranking it ahead of *Wuthering Heights, Goodbye, Mr. Chips*, and *Mr. Smith Goes to Washington*.[91]

Warner Bros.' Harry Warner—a religious Jew, the son of a cobbler who had fled Russian pogroms to come to America in 1883—was the only industry leader who spoke out publicly against Nazism.[92] But he did so not as part of a personal campaign to stop events in Europe, but rather to warn that what was happening there could happen in America. On June 5, 1940, he convened the first company-wide gathering in Warner Bros. history, summoning nearly 6,000 employees to hear a long and emotional speech, in which he told them:

> We must unite and quit listening to anybody discussing whether you or I am a Jew or a Catholic or a Protestant or of any other faith—and not allow anyone to say anything about anybody's faith—or we will fall just the same as they did over there. . . . [M]y father and mother lived under such a system [as the Nazis], and that's why we were brought here . . . and that's why I'm so carried away.[93]

Harry Warner continued with a statement of policy: "We don't want anyone in our employ who . . . [are] Communists, Fascists, Nazis, or other un-American believers."[94] He emphasized that he was not advocating U.S. participation in the European war—only domestic action against those who would encourage the growth and spread in America of the European disease:

> I don't want you to leave here thinking that I am telling you or anybody in this world that I want war. . . . God knows I want peace. I long and pray for it, but the only certain way of insuring our peace is to be so strong in arms and defense that we can command peace. And we will never be strong enough to see this ideal realized until we have ejected from our midst, those enemies who are boring from within. . . .

Warner urged his company's employees to report any suspicious individuals to the Federal Bureau of Investigation (FBI). He had even arranged to include the local FBI director on stage with him. The July 1940 issue of *Warner Club News* included extensive coverage of the speech, and copies were sent to the White House and to members of Congress.[95]

A little more than a year later, Warner was called before a subcommittee of the Senate Committee on Interstate Commerce, chaired by Senator D. Worth Clark (D-Idaho), to testify on the ominously titled subject of "war propaganda disseminated by the motion picture industry."[96] The lead witness, Senator Gerald P. Nye (R-N.D.), told the committee that "were I determined to name those primarily responsible for propaganda in the moving-picture field, I would . . . confine myself to four names, each that of one of the Jewish faith. . . ." He said he opposed anti-Semitism ("I have splendid Jewish friends") and "there are people of the Jewish faith as ardent in support of the nonintervention cause as I count myself to be." But he claimed that:

> [T]he fact remains that the voices of those who occupy places of leadership [in the Jewish community] . . . entertain solicitation about causes abroad that blind them to American causes and that bring burdens of terrible weight upon all Americans.[97]

In his testimony, Warner defended *Confessions of a Nazi Spy* and sought to rebut the subcommittee's "industry expert," who had characterized the film as "definitely propaganda."[98] Warner acknowledged that "in September 1939 . . . I said publicly . . . and I say today, that the freedom which this country fought England to obtain, we may have to fight with England to retain." But he assured the committee he had meant providing Britain with spare supplies, and did "not think that it is necessary for America to send men, to go to war."

The chairman of the committee said he knew Warner was "almost fanatical in his Americanism," but that even the *premise* of his testimony was dangerous:

> [I]f you start out with the premise that England's fight is our fight . . . you cannot end up anywhere, in my judgment, but in a wish to go to war now. . . . [T]here is a great body of people in this country—and polls show 70 or 80 percent . . . who just simply differ with you on that score; who believe that England is not fighting our fight; that she is fighting the same battle she has fought throughout the centuries, for trade, gold, and commerce.[99]

The hearing transcript reports that, at this point, the spectators burst into "loud applause."

Senator Clark ended by warning Harry Warner that he "should be careful in using this great and powerful moving-picture industry, as [you and others] seem to have done over a period of years . . . for the purpose of influencing public opinion on this phase of a very controversial question."[100] The other witnesses included the presidents and officers of other studios, but they testified only briefly.[101] The subcommittee's extended confrontation with Warner, in a contentious hearing covered by *The New York Times*, was sufficient to send a message that it was dangerous—even for an established Jewish film executive, well known for his "fanatical Americanism"—to speak out publicly against Nazism and the German assault on Europe.[102]

## ANTI-SEMITISM MOUNTS IN AMERICA IN 1940

A 1940 article in the American Jewish Congress *Bulletin* reported that there was mounting fear among American Jews.[103] The public anti-Semitism of such well-known figures as the industrialist Henry Ford, the clergymen Father Charles Coughlin and Rev. Gerald L. K. Smith, radio personality Fulton Lewis, syndicated columnist Westbrook Pegler, national hero

Charles Lindbergh, among others, increased the anxiety of Jews about the security of their position within American society.

Henry Ford's newspaper, the *Dearborn Independent*, whose circulation had reached 900,000 at its height in 1925, had blamed American participation in World War I on "the clustering of Jewry about the war machinery of the United States."[104] In a November 20, 1938, broadcast, Father Coughlin—a vitriolic anti-Semite with up to thirty million radio listeners—asserted that Nazism was "a political defense mechanism" against communism, which he attributed to "a group of Jews who dominated the destinies of Russia." Public opinion polls in 1939 showed that 80 percent of the American public was opposed to increasing immigration quotas for German Jewish refugees.[105] A 1940 survey asked, "Have you heard any criticism or talk against Jews in the last six months?" and 46 percent responded "yes," with about 60 percent saying they had negative impressions of Jews.[106] Distribution of anti-Semitic pamphlets and articles was a common occurrence.[107] Restrictive covenants preventing the sale of real estate to Jews were legal.[108]

A half century later, a scholarly survey of anti-Semitism in the United States concluded that, as of 1939:

> American Jews, seeing what Hitler had done in Germany and
> now personally experiencing the impact of discrimination and
> racial rhetoric in the United States, seemed more fearful about
> the future than ever before. . . . A sense of foreboding continued
> to spread among Jews in the United States. . . .[109]

American Jews were eager to be considered patriotic citizens, and they were exceedingly wary of taking positions at variance with the isolationist consensus of their fellow citizens.[110] Zionism was a minority view among the Jews in America and, for many, it was a threat to their identity as progressive Americans, or simply an imprudent position to take in American society. Few of them endorsed Zionism publicly or espoused it wholeheartedly even privately.

The three most prominent Zionist leaders in the world—messengers from the old world, traveling to the prosperous new one, seeking to mobilize American Jews to help fight a European war and to champion a Jewish homeland in Palestine—faced a deeply daunting task.

# CHAIM WEIZMANN

## *January–March 1940*

*At the beginning of 1939, Chaim Weizmann did not intend to travel to America to promote Zionism. In his diary, David Ben-Gurion noted that Weizmann "told [me] he is exhausted. . . . He won't go to America. He is sixty-five already. Sixty is retirement age."[1] Weizmann wrote to his assistant, Doris May, "I have been tired beyond human bounds."[2] He began working on his memoirs.[3]*

*Once the new European war began, rumors reached Weizmann of German plans "so hideous as to be quite incredible," and he received a letter from a friend with good sources in Germany, who told him that if Hitler overran Europe, "Zionism would lose all its meaning, because no Jews would be left alive."[4] In October, Weizmann decided that he would go to America.*

Had chaim weizmann retired in early 1939, he could have looked back on one of the most distinguished careers in modern Jewish history. By then, he had more than enough material to write an autobiography of considerable historical importance.

Born in 1874, Weizmann had played a major role in the formative years of the Zionist movement. At the landmark 1903 Zionist Conference, he had led the Russian students opposing Herzl's plan for a Jewish state in Uganda rather than Palestine. In 1917, he was a driving force behind the adoption of the Balfour Declaration, which committed Britain, if it prevailed against the Ottoman Empire in Palestine in World War I, to "facilitate" a Jewish national home there.[5] The following year, the British government appointed him to lead a commission to Palestine to plan the Jewish home, and in 1919 he met with Emir Feisal, a key leader of the Arabs, and entered into an agreement (later repudiated by Feisal's followers) to support Arab nationalist aspirations in exchange for Arab support of the Balfour Declaration. After World War I, he led the Zionist delegation at the Peace Conference at Versailles, and in 1920 became president of the Zionist Organization, which he led well beyond the usual retirement age of 60. He had gone from a small *shtetl* with a one-room school to study in Germany; then on to a prestigious university in Switzerland where he earned his doctorate in chemistry; finally to England as a researcher and lecturer, where his chemical work produced synthetic materials that significantly aided the British war effort in World War I. He became a British subject and enjoyed friendships with many at the highest levels of the government and in the aristocracy.

Weizmann's 482-page autobiography, *Trial and Error,* was ultimately published in 1949. It consisted of a single volume divided into two "books": "Book One," written largely in 1941, and "Book Two," written in 1948–49 at the end of the tumultuous decade following the disastrous events of

1939. Given his age—65 years old—and his long career, Weizmann was understandably weary in 1939, both physically and psychologically. But his eventful life in Zionism, which had begun in the nineteenth century, was about to enter its most challenging decade of all.

## THE BRITISH RETREAT FROM THE MANDATE FOR PALESTINE

In 1937, the British Peel Commission—established after Arab riots and pogroms in Palestine had reached new levels of violence in 1936— recommended the partition of Palestine into an Arab and a Jewish state, with a small area assigned to the Jews.[6] The Zionist Organization accepted partition in principle, but the Arabs adamantly rejected the existence of even a minuscule Jewish state.

*Peel Commission Partition Plan*
*Source: Jewish Virtual Library*

Given Arab intractability, Britain began to consider a different plan: a single state, with an Arab majority and a one-third Jewish minority, with stringent limits on future Jewish immigration, which would be restricted to 10,000 a year for five years, with discretionary increases to a maximum of 25,000 during that period, but no immigration thereafter. The plan barred Jews from buying any additional land in Palestine, with minor exceptions. The new plan would effectively negate the League of Nations Mandate for Palestine, and make a Jewish national homeland impossible to achieve.

In February 1939, the plan circulated within the British government in the form of a draft new White Paper on Palestine to replace the one of 1922, which had affirmed that the Jewish people were in Palestine "as of right and not on sufferance" of others, based on their "ancient historic connection" to the Jewish homeland.[7] Weizmann learned of the draft almost immediately, when a British official mistakenly sent a copy to him that had been intended for review by the Arabs. Although he may have been ready to retire a month earlier, he was now suddenly faced with the effective destruction of the central accomplishments of his life: the Balfour Declaration and the British commitment to a Jewish homeland, as well as decades of efforts to strengthen the Jewish economy and to foster the institutions in Palestine necessary for an eventual state.

On March 24, 1939, as he left London on a personal mission to Palestine, Weizmann wrote directly to Prime Minister Neville Chamberlain, with a plea to reject the proposed new plan:

> Through all the ups and downs of more than twenty years, I have found support in the thought that, to quote Lord Balfour's words, we were "partners in the great enterprise" which means life or death to my people. . . . Please consider the events of the past twelve months . . . [1] Hitler's entry into Vienna; [2] the expulsion of Jews from Italy and from Danzig; [3] the Nazi occupation of the Sudetenland; [4] the November pogrom in Germany [Kristallnacht]; [5] the anti-Semitic measure in Slovakia; [6] the Nazi invasion of Bohemia and Moravia; and [7] now Memel [part of Lithuania annexed by the Nazis on March 21, 1939]. In times so deeply disturbed, could we not avoid adding to the turmoil?

*Hitler touring Memel in March 1939. The banner reads:
"This country will always be German"*

Three weeks later, Weizmann cabled Chamberlain from Palestine, informing him that he had "found [the] Jewish community united [in] resolute determination [to] oppose with all its strength [the] contemplated new policy." He appealed to Chamberlain "out of deep anxiety for all concerned" and warned him that the new policy would lead to a "supreme tragedy":

> Proposed liquidation of Mandate and establishment of independent Palestine State coupled with reduction [of] Jewish population to one-third total and with restriction [on] area [of] Jewish settlement to small sector [of] country are viewed as destruction [of] Jewish hopes and surrender [of] Jewish community [in] Palestine to rule [of] Arab junta responsible for terrorist campaign. . . . Jews are determined [to] make supreme sacrifice rather than submit to such regime. Feel it my solemn duty [to] draw attention of His Majesty's Government to grave consequences involved before irrevocable step [of] adoption and announcement of policy is taken.

Weizmann also cabled Justice Louis D. Brandeis, who had resigned from the Supreme Court in February 1939 after twenty-three years. Brandeis was the most prominent Zionist in the United States, and enjoyed a close relationship with President Roosevelt, who admired his long career and considered him a prophet (indeed, in his private letters to Brandeis, Roosevelt addressed him as "Dear Isaiah"). On April 19, 1939, Weizmann sent Brandeis a telegram:

> Beg you make last minute effort [to] induce President [to] urge British Government [to] delay publication [of] their proposals and reconsider their policy. . . . [It] will drive Jews who have nothing to lose anyhow to adhere to counsels of despair. . . . If new policy imposed Jews will conduct immigration [and] disregard legal restrictions, will settle and without permission, even if exposed [to] British bayonets. . . . By violation [of] Mandate British Government loses moral and legal title [to] govern country and becomes mere coercive authority. . . . Please impress President [that] owing to advanced state matter no ordinary diplomatic representations but only extraordinary emphatic step can possibly produce effect.[8]

Brandeis appealed to the President more than once, but to no avail.[9]

On April 24, Weizmann sent a message to William Bullitt, the American ambassador to France, in the hope that he would convey it to the State Department, telling him the Jewish political leadership in Palestine had decided that "no sacrifice would be too heavy":

> I have conveyed all this in a telegram to the Prime Minister and warned him, in as restrained language as I could use in such circumstances, of what was here at stake. . . . I can only say this, that if the Government really adopts this policy outlined to us in London and endeavors to carry it into effect, it will bite granite. At a time when millions of Jews are undergoing a sadistic persecution such as the world has not known since the darkest ages, the Jews of Palestine will not put up with the land in which a National Home was solemnly promised to them by the civilized world being closed to their harassed brethren.[10]

On April 27, 1939, Weizmann wrote to the newly appointed British ambassador to the United States, Philip Henry Kerr (Lord Lothian), who had been Prime Minister Lloyd George's private secretary at the time of the Balfour Declaration, and who was strongly sympathetic to Zionism. Weizmann told him that the British bureaucracy suffered from "a kind of pharaonic blindness" in its treatment of the Jews, and that it would eventually affect the entire British Empire:

> The British Empire . . . cannot be run by the methods by which authoritarian states conduct their internal and external affairs. It lives essentially on the moral authority which it inspires, on its tradition of legality, on its attachment to its pledges. . . . I cannot emphasize enough the gravity of the situation and I have warned the Prime Minister of it. . . . I am conscious of having uttered it as much in the interest of the British as of the Jews.[11]

Weizmann continued his agitated correspondence into May, writing to as many influential friends as he could. On May 3, 1939, he wrote to Albert Cohen, the Zionist emissary to the League of Nations, to describe Britain's changed Palestine policy as "a sort of Munich [referring to Chamberlain's disastrous appeasement of Hitler] applied to us at a time when Jewry is drowning in its [own] blood":

> [P]eople come in daily [to Palestine] on leaky dangerous boats, after having undergone untold suffering for weeks on sea; pirate captains exploit this poor human cargo, starve them, rob them, strip them of their belongings, but they are ready to undergo everything, as long as there is a faint chance of getting on land. . . .
>
> [T]he British have no moral right to denounce a Treaty which has become part of International Law and of the fabric of history in the post-war troublesome period. They have no moral or legal right to jeopardize a great piece of constructive work, the lives of hundreds of thousands of people who have come to Palestine trusting to the promise of England, France and other civilized powers, sanctioned and ratified by the League of Nations.

A week later, Weizmann cabled Chamberlain to inform him he was flying back to London from Palestine and would be "grateful for the privilege of an interview" the following day. He met with Chamberlain the next evening, but the meeting produced no results.[12] On May 13, the British Colonial Secretary, Malcolm MacDonald, invited Weizmann to MacDonald's country house for tea; it turned into a bitter confrontation in which Weizmann called the new British policy a "betrayal" and Mac-Donald himself a "hypocrite."[13] Weizmann later said he "had never spoken so rudely and so straight to any man."[14]

Weizmann's increasing despair was reflected in a letter he wrote the following week to one of his oldest British acquaintances, Sir George King-Hall, in which he noted that for twenty years "we have cooperated, we have compromised, we have done our best to make the task of the [British] Administration [in Palestine] as easy as we could":

> And the result of all this—it is the policy to which I have given
> my life—has been the White Paper which, if it is carried into
> effect, will hand us over to our bitter enemies—a permanent
> minority within a virtually Arab State.[15]

On May 17, 1939, the day after the British issued the White Paper, Weizmann spoke to a Zionist conference. Departing from his usual understated rhetoric, he openly criticized the British:

> [The British government] has found it necessary to formulate and
> inaugurate this policy in the blackest hour of Jewish history—at
> a time when our enemies, cruel and relentless, seek to destroy the
> Jewish people body and soul. . . . This document forgets, or tries
> to forget, all those noble motives which brought British states-
> men in 1917 and 1918 to issue the Balfour Declaration. . . .
>
>    We have never relinquished our claim to Palestine; we have
> never ceased to maintain contact with that country throughout
> the thousands of years during which we have been forcibly sepa-
> rated from it. . . . [I]t seems almost—I will try not to use an un-
> parliamentary expression—almost ridiculous that a White Paper
> should stand across the road of our return to this country which,
> it is written in the stars, will be Jewish one day. . . .

Weizmann also addressed the larger issues relating to the British betrayal of the Jews:

> [I]t may be appropriate, in this tragic and solemn hour, to re-
> mind the Powers that they are in Palestine, that they were en-
> trusted with the Mandate for Palestine, because of us. . . . [T]he
> moral right to be in Palestine today was conferred upon Great
> Britain by the civilized nations of the world for the explicit and

direct purpose of helping to build up the Jewish National Home. Long before the Balfour Declaration, God had decreed that our destiny is bound up with Palestine, and against this decree, all decrees of humans, however mighty they may appear to themselves and at the time, are as naught; they will blow away like chaff before the wind.[16]

Parliamentary debates on the White Paper were held on May 22 and 23, 1939, during which Winston Churchill opposed the new policy in a stirring address.[17] Afterward, Weizmann sent Churchill a two-sentence note: "Your magnificent speech may yet destroy this policy. Words fail me [to] express my thanks."[18] Churchill's words had indeed been eloquent and moving.[19] But on May 23, Weizmann cabled David Ben-Gurion, the leader of the *Yishuv*, the pre-State community of Jews in Palestine, with a one-sentence report about the rest of the debate: "Many friends readied for battle [but] failed to speak."[20] The House of Commons adopted the new policy by a vote of 268–179.

On May 30, 1939, Weizmann wrote to Solomon Goldman, the president of the Zionist Organization of America, reporting that relations with the British government "are very strained, non-cooperation has already set in."[21] Several weeks later, the British announced the suspension of all Jewish immigration to Palestine until March 1940—a ten-month period in which Britain would seek to block Jews from entering the place mandated as their homeland, at a time when Hitler's existential threat was all too apparent.[22]

## THE NEW WORLD WAR BEGINS

On August 29, 1939—two days before the Nazi invasion of Poland, as the international situation grew increasingly ominous—Weizmann wrote to Chamberlain to assure him that, in the event of a new European war, the Jews would "stand by Great Britain and will fight on the side of the democracies," regardless of the ongoing dispute about Palestine:

> In this hour of supreme crisis, the consciousness that the Jews have a contribution to make to the defense of sacred values impels me to write this letter. . . . The Jewish Agency is ready to enter into immediate arrangements for utilizing Jewish manpower, technical ability, resources, etc. . . .[23]

Chamberlain disregarded Weizmann's offer. In his September 2 reply—sent the day after the Nazi invasion—he wrote that he was pleased "that in this time of supreme emergency when those things which we hold dear are at stake, Britain can rely upon the whole-hearted cooperation of the Jewish Agency." But, he said, "You will not expect me to say more at this stage than that your public-spirited assurances and welcome aid will be kept in mind."[24]

On September 5, Weizmann wrote to the British Secretary of State for War, Leslie Hore-Belisha, telling him that a "movement for the formation of Jewish volunteer units to serve on the side of the Allies has arisen in different countries," and that the Jews stood ready to "take definite action, without delay." Weizmann asked Hore-Belisha to spare him "a few minutes in the course of the next day or two" to discuss the subject, but no meeting was granted. The Secretary declined, citing the pressure of other problems.[25] Weizmann wrote again on September 11, yielding to the Secretary's assertion that the discussion was premature, but nevertheless enclosing a draft memorandum entitled "Arguments in Favor of Immediate Formation of a Jewish Military Unit."[26] That memo, too, met with no response.

On September 15, 1939, as Nazi forces swept through Poland, Weizmann formally requested that Britain admit 20,000 Jewish children from Poland into Palestine—a number within the 25,000-person quota established in the White Paper. Weizmann set forth his request to British Colonial Secretary Malcolm J. MacDonald in dramatic terms:

> Hundreds of thousands of Jews in Poland will have to face the Polish winter without a roof over their heads, dying of starvation. Whatever food can be removed from the Polish countryside will be taken for Germany; little will reach the towns, and still less the Jewish population. . . . [T]he [German] administration will be of the extremist anti-Semitic character. This is a catastrophe of a magnitude such as not even we have yet experienced.
>
> In these circumstances, we ask you for immediate permission to remove these children from Poland to Palestine, say of the ages between thirteen and seventeen years. The economic burden of supporting them naturally will fall upon the Jewish people inside and outside Palestine. We pledge ourselves to provide for them. It therefore depends on your decision alone whether the lives of Jewish children shall be saved or not.[27]

MacDonald replied five days later, saying that although he sympathized with the plight of the Jews of Poland, he was unable to admit large numbers of additional Jewish immigrants to Palestine, because it might "seriously embarrass Great Britain and her Allies in their endeavor to bring the war to a victorious issue."[28] These were code words, signaling British fear that bringing Jewish children into Palestine might cost Britain the support of the Arabs. Even though the number was within the strict limits set by their own White Paper, the British barred the children.

## WEIZMANN PLANS HIS TRIP TO AMERICA

In October, as the war entered its second month, Weizmann wrote to Lazar Braudo, one of the founders of the Zionist movement in South Africa, about his plans for his trip to the United States:

> My principal task in America will, naturally, be to do what I can to raise the funds so badly needed to meet the present critical economic situation in Palestine, but apart from this, my visit will, of course, have its political aspects. You know my view that this is a war in which we, as Jews, must bear a special and additional responsibility; it is with this conviction in mind that I shall approach my task in the United States.[29]

Weizmann disclosed that his efforts in London to gain approval for a Jewish military unit "have so far met with no success." He had accordingly lowered his sights: he wanted to establish a war industry in Palestine to assist the British, and to have the British consider training a few hundred Jewish officers in England for a possible future Jewish force.[30] At the same time, he knew—as he wrote in a letter sent the same day to Jan Christiaan Smuts in Pretoria, the Prime Minister of the Union of South Africa and a World War I hero of the South African theater—that the new war "is going to be a grimmer business than most people realize":

> I have felt strongly that, for people like myself, the war has a double significance—we fight in it as British citizens, but also as Jews. Perhaps few people have realized, when the Nazi challenge was first thrown down to the Jews, that it was not a challenge to the Jews alone, but to the whole Christian world. But today, there can be few who fail to realize that what is at stake in this

war is the whole of Western civilization . . . I expect to leave early in November for the United States, and shall there do my best to bring home to my people this aspect of the situation, and the special responsibility which devolves upon them as Jews in the present conflict.[31]

Weizmann continued to send memoranda to his contacts within the British government, reiterating the desire of the Jewish Agency to provide a Jewish division for military service.[32] He wanted to put "on record" both the "readiness and ability of our people to make some tangible contribution to the British Cause in this war."[33] He emphasized that Jewish support for Britain would continue notwithstanding the White Paper, but that the issue would not disappear:

> I fully agree that Jewish cooperation with the Allied War-effort is, and will continue to be, unconditional. . . . [W]e all realize only too well the decisive role which England is playing in this gigantic struggle for the preservation of moral values forming the very foundation of our civilization. . . . [But] After victory has been won the Jewish problem will still be there in all its ghastly nakedness as a challenge to the new world which may arise, and I am deeply convinced that only in Palestine and through Palestine an equitable and lasting solution can be found.[34]

## WEIZMANN'S VOYAGE TO THE UNITED STATES

Weizmann's trip to America was repeatedly delayed, as he addressed problems the White Paper had already created for the Jews in Palestine. He continued his correspondence and conversations with members of the British government, seeking at least preliminary approval of a Jewish military unit in the belief that it could help him make a favorable impression on American Jews on his trip. But no such British approval was in the offing. Eventually, on December 21, 1939, he left London, accompanied by his wife, Vera, heading first to Paris and then to Lisbon, where he planned to fly to New York on the Pan-American Clipper.

Lisbon was, in Weizmann's words, "the fire escape to the West," a neutral city where people could still arrange transportation out of the continent.[35] When he arrived, he found transatlantic flights canceled because of weather and wartime danger, and he spent ten days awaiting new travel arrangements. Lisbon was "an extremely ugly little world," he later recalled, marked by "rampant spying, rumors everywhere, and an air of secrecy."[36] There was "no one to speak to, and if there had been, one did not dare to speak."[37] He had discovered—months into the war—that it was hazardous to talk about it in public, in a foreign country, to strangers.

Pan-American eventually arranged transportation by ship, on the Italian luxury liner *Rex*, known as the "Riviera Afloat" because of its swimming pools surrounded by real sand. It was considered one of the most beautiful liners in the world.[38] Within months, it would be taken out of commission—its large size made it too easy a target for German submarines.[39] But this voyage was uneventful, and the ship arrived safely in New York harbor on January 12, 1940, with 879 passengers on board, including several well-known figures.[40]

*The New York Times* covered Weizmann's arrival as part of an article about those who arrived on the Rex. Weizmann is mentioned at the end after Anne Morgan—J. P. Morgan's sister—the film star Ingrid Bergman, and General Joseph Haller, commander of the Polish army in World War I, among others. Weizmann told the *Times* the main purpose of his trip was to enlist American Jews in developing Palestine "as a haven and homeland for tens of thousands of Jews" uprooted from Central Europe.[41] The Jewish Telegraphic Agency (JTA) reported the trip was intended to seek Jewish capital for Palestinian enterprises and to encourage non-Zionist Jews to assist the work of the Jewish Agency in Palestine.[42] Weizmann had downplayed his goals in his statements to the press.

## WEIZMANN SPEAKS TO 4,000 PEOPLE

On January 16, 1940—four days after his arrival in New York—Weizmann addressed an audience of 4,000 in Manhattan at the Mecca Temple of the "Ancient Arabic Order of the Nobles of the Mystic Shrine," popularly known as the "Shriners."[43] It was the major address of his trip.[44] He began by noting that he had not been to America for the past "six fateful years, which will rank even in our tragic history as our blackest years." He said there was a "fundamental difference" between what Polish Jews had undergone and what the Polish people in general had experienced:

> However great and deep the tragedy of the Poles may be, the
> Polish peasant is still on his land. He is rooted, he can still grow

*The photograph of Chaim Weizmann that
appeared in* The New York Times,
*January 13, 1940*

perhaps a miserable harvest of which a great part will be taken
away—but he will go on staying on his land. The Jew in the
small town or in the big city when driven out is . . . radically
uprooted. He becomes a wanderer. . . .

In Poland, Weizmann continued, the entire Jewish society had gone
under, and it was a Jewish community *ten times* the size of the Jewish
community of Germany. He said he could describe in a single sentence
the Nazi and Soviet control over Polish Jews: "In one [place] the Jews are
being destroyed; in the other Judaism is being destroyed." Nonetheless,
Weizmann made a statement that he felt required "a certain amount of
daring" to say:

[Even these world-shaking events] are merely a passage in our
long history of martyrdom. It is merely another link in the great
chain of tragedy which constitutes Jewish history: Egypt, Baby-

lon, Rome, the Middle Ages, the Inquisition, the exile from Spain, Czarism, Revolution and aftermath of the Revolution, and the events of the Great War, followed by the Petluras [pogroms in Ukraine] and all the others. . . . [W]e believe that a better future is coming . . . a time when the peoples of the world will remember what small nations have meant to the civilization of the world. And in remembering this, they might possibly remember that Greece and Judea have given the world all those values which have been fundamental to our civilization.

Weizmann next described the work in Palestine—which he emphasized had "never been merely a place of refuge" but was also a "home"—since the Balfour Declaration had granted the Jewish people an internationally recognized right to their homeland:

Twenty-five years have passed. A short span indeed in the life of an ancient people like ourselves. A very short span in the life of a country! In these 25 years it has passed from tribulation to tribulation. World Jewry has been shaken to its very foundation. The great Russian Jewish community . . . has disappeared.

We began our work . . . surrounded by widespread indifference, by the skepticism of many, but also by enthusiasm, chiefly of the poor. We encountered difficulties inside the country as well as outside in the Jewish and non-Jewish world; we were without experience in country building; and we were forced to rely on a population which was primarily and fundamentally European, and which had to be transformed and adapted to the hard life of the conquest of an ungrateful soil. . . .

In these last seven years, almost a quarter of a million persons entered [Palestine]. In the last four years, 80,000 fresh *olim* [immigrants] came in. . . . They are still coming; they are travelling now as I address you; travelling through submarine-and mine-infested seas.

Weizmann was convinced that the Jewish national home was "a solid fact woven into the fabric of Jewish history and of world history." He was "very sorry about the White Paper, which I fought to the best of my ability and which we have not and will not accept." But it "is not, I am convinced, the last word of British statesmanship."

Weizmann also addressed the question of the Arabs in Palestine, and described what he said might be "a new set of circumstances" in which "the Arab mind is also evolving":

> These three and a half years of trouble [since the Arab pogroms began in 1936] have taught us a lesson which I think thoughtful Arabs are also beginning to understand. I am not speaking of the small group of Arabs who may be guided by the same hand which has destroyed us in Poland and in Germany. I am now speaking of the vast majority of the Arabs who love their country and who love their Zion as we love ours. . . .
>
> I think these people are beginning to learn the futility of destruction. . . . It is a long and tedious road. It is an educational process. . . . But the beginnings of it are there.

As he neared the end of his address, Weizmann compared the building of the Jewish national home in Palestine with the creation of the United States. Both countries depended, he said, on more than purely physical factors:

> Countries like your own commonwealth were built up out of two great moral factors; people tried to escape persecution and people hoped to build up a better life with a new start. . . . And this—not the fertility of its land—is the secret of Palestine.

Finally, Weizmann noted that he and his wife had traveled at an advanced age, under hazardous conditions, because of a single powerful imperative—"maintaining the structure in Palestine":

> We [in Europe] are doing our best, but our best is very small. You are still, and I pray that you may stay so, a powerful and in a certain degree prosperous community, sheltered under the wing of a great government. From those to whom much is given, much is expected. We in Europe, and particularly those who are responsible for guarding the movement, look about for help to maintain the structure of Palestine.

*The New York Times* coverage of Weizmann's address focused on neither the Jewish crisis in Europe nor the Jewish homeland in Palestine, but on the dispute with the Arabs. The *Times* reported that Weizmann had said he "detected in thoughtful Arabs a realization of the futility of strife, and even the possibility that the internal difficulty in Palestine might be resolved to a 'family quarrel' which could be worked out by the 'cousins' themselves."[45]

Over the next month, Weizmann spoke to Zionist meetings in New York, Baltimore, Chicago, Detroit, and Cleveland. On January 28, he addressed several thousand people from 144 communities attending the General Assembly of the Council of Jewish Federations and Welfare Funds. The JTA reported that Weizmann praised the Council for channeling American Jewry's "impulses of devotion" toward aiding European Jewry and building the Jewish national home:

> "In the world I have but recently left," he said, "there are today literally millions of Jews who find in the American Jewish community a great reservoir of material and spiritual strength. . . . [T]he Jewish communities of central and eastern Europe have been forced in large measure to relinquish their leadership in Jewish life throughout the world, and have watched with tortured hope the assumption by American Jewry of pre-eminence in the communal existence of Jewries everywhere."

## WEIZMANN VISITS JUSTICE BRANDEIS

On February 6, 1940, Weizmann visited the 83-year-old retired Supreme Court Justice Louis D. Brandeis at home in Washington. He had been one of the most prominent Justices in American judicial history, the author of landmark opinions on free speech, privacy, and other significant issues. In 1914, when he had a national reputation as "the people's lawyer," he had assumed the leadership of the American Zionist movement.

Brandeis' association with Zionism had given it a standing in America that no one else could have provided. At the time, there were about 12,000 members in the Federation of American Zionists, out of a total of three million American Jews.[46] In the first few years after he became its leader, its membership more than quintupled. His greatest intellectual contribution to Zionism was to equate it with Americanism.[47] He had become convinced that "[t]he Jewish spirit, the product of our religion and experiences, is essentially modern and essentially American."[48] "My approach to Zionism," he wrote, "was through Americanism":

> In time, practical experience and observation convinced me that Jews were, by reason of their traditions and their character, pe-

culiarly fitted for the attainment of American ideals. Gradually it became clear to me that to be good Americans, we must be better Jews.

Weizmann and Brandeis had worked closely in 1917 and were instrumental in the issuance of the Balfour Declaration. As Weizmann worked with members of the British War Cabinet on successive drafts of the Declaration, Brandeis discussed Britain's plans for Palestine with President Woodrow Wilson, and Wilson's backing played a key role in the British decision to issue the Balfour Declaration on November 2, 1917.[49]

In the years following 1917, however, Weizmann and Brandeis had a falling out, as their views on Palestine diverged. Weizmann saw Palestine as the pre-eminent Jewish "home," the place where Jewish culture and civilization would be preserved. For American Jews, by contrast, the United States was already "home," and they did not consider themselves in exile.[50] They envisioned Palestine as a haven for Jews not fortunate enough to live in America, but not as a potential home for themselves.[51]

Brandeis supported a Jewish state as a laboratory for democracy that would complement Americanism; he wanted it established as soon as possible, and emphasized the importance of such projects as mining the mineral deposits in the Dead Sea, applying the principles of land management and irrigation, draining the swamps, eliminating the scourge of malaria from the land, and of attracting investors to enterprises there. Weizmann favored the slow organic growth of Jewish cultural institutions, such as the Hebrew University, and wanted the homeland to be a place where Jewish culture could flourish among Jews dedicated to preserving it. The distinction between a "home" and a "haven" had important implications for the way the Zionist movement and its projects would evolve; and the relationship between Weizmann and Brandeis eventually became a casualty of their serious differences in policy, perspective, and personality.[52]

In its account of the Weizmann-Brandeis meeting in 1940, the JTA reported that it was the first time they had met in twenty years. JTA said that the two aging leaders had agreed that Palestine "held out the largest if not the only hope" for a solution of the Jewish problem. They told the press of their belief that "at the conclusion of the war," the civilized nations would arrange to make Palestine "a home and haven for the Jews."[53]

The reference to both "a home and a haven" reflected a renewed unity between Weizmann and Brandeis. Their longstanding differences had been overtaken by events.[54]

### WEIZMANN'S MEETING WITH PRESIDENT ROOSEVELT

Two days after his meeting with Brandeis, Weizmann visited President Roosevelt at the White House, in a half-hour meeting arranged by Britain's ambassador, Lord Lothian. It was their first encounter.

Weizmann wanted to discuss Britain's restrictions on Jewish immigration to Palestine, and he emerged from the meeting to tell the press that FDR was confident that when the war was over, a solution for the Jewish problem might be reached.[55]

In his autobiography, Weizmann was more candid about the meeting. He wrote that Roosevelt "showed himself friendly, but the discussion remained theoretical."[56] An even clearer picture is provided in Weizmann's contemporaneous memorandum, which summarized FDR's response to Weizmann's informing him that he had addressed large audiences across the country:

> The President remarked that there were a good many Jews here [in America] who were not exactly obstructionists so far as Palestine was concerned, but who were not too friendly [to the idea of Zionism]. Dr. Weizmann said, "Certainly that was so, but that on the whole sentiment for Palestine was very strong." The President said, "Yes, I agree."

The memorandum stated that the discussion with the President had turned to developments in Palestine, and the prospect of other places for Jews to emigrate:

> [Dr. Weizmann said he] was not going to attempt to harrow the President's feelings by a description of what was happening to the Jews of Central and Eastern Europe. No doubt he knew the situation well enough, but the fact was that today Palestine and the United States were the only countries which were taking substantial numbers of immigrants. The President asked whether Dr. Weizmann did not think that other countries too might absorb refugees, and referred to Colombia.

According to his memorandum, Weizmann replied that no place could substitute for Palestine. Weizmann did not record the President's reply, if any, to Weizmann's reference to the American immigration policy. Later in 1940, however, the United States moved to restrict Jewish immigration to America even more stringently.[57]

Weizmann told FDR that, not including the Jews who had been "swallowed up by the Russian system and [had] disappeared," and the number of Jews who would perish by the end of the war "if the present rate of destruction continued," there would be about 2.5 million Jews in need of help after the war. Many would be too old, he said, or be otherwise unsuitable for immigration to Palestine; they might move to another country or might just remain where they were. But after adjusting for those figures, Weizmann said, he estimated that one million "younger and more vigorous" Jews could be "drawn off into Palestine" over a period of years.

To support his statement that Palestine was economically viable to support one million additional Jewish refugees, without displacing any Arabs, Weizmann cited a 1939 Department of Agriculture report by Dr. Walter C. Lowdermilk, a soil conservationist who had proposed a "Jordan Valley Authority" comparable to the Tennessee Valley Authority. Lowdermilk had called for a "TVA on the Jordan" to irrigate large areas of Palestine.[58] FDR replied that he had read Lowdermilk's study, had found it a "wonderful" report, and that the Jews had "done very well." He told Weizmann that Brandeis thought there was room for at least *two million* additional people in Palestine, to which Weizmann replied that "it all depended on the extent of development."

The Lowdermilk report was in fact far more optimistic than either Weizmann or Brandeis. Lowdermilk believed a "JVA" in Palestine would enable many millions of people to live there. He had led a team of soil scientists and archaeologists for three months of field studies in Palestine. He had concluded that the Jewish land conservation efforts were "the most remarkable we have seen while studying land use in twenty-four countries." He and his team were "astonished" and "amazed" at the "methods and achievements" and the difficulties the Jews had overcome.[59] He proposed a project that would, he concluded, "provide room and work for millions of Jewish refugees now suffering persecutions in many lands of Europe."

Lowdermilk's 1944 book, *Palestine: Land of Promise*, based on his 1939 report, became a best-seller.[60] He lectured widely to spread the news about the opportunities for developing the region and later made extended television appearances as well. But in 1940, although the report was known at the highest levels of the American government, nothing resulted from Weizmann's discussion of it with FDR.[61]

Weizmann turned to the political status of Palestine and told the President that he believed the 1939 White Paper would not be the last word on British policy. According to Weizmann's memorandum of the meeting, his statement evoked this exchange:

> The President asked: "What about the Arabs? Can't that be settled with a little *baksheesh*? [Persian for "tip" or "bribe"] Dr. Weizmann said it wasn't as simple as all that. . . . One result of the disturbances had been, [Weizmann] thought, to bring much nearer the possibility of an arrangement with their Arab neighbors; despite a campaign of violence . . . the latter had completely failed in their efforts to dislodge the Jews. That was a fact which was likely to have a fundamental effect on future relations with the Arabs. Already there were signs—he was not going to exaggerate them, but they were unmistakable—that the Arabs were realizing this failure, and were casting around to see if they could not arrive at some modus vivendi.
>
> The President said: "When the war is over you will settle it. First, of course, the war must be won." Dr. Weizmann agreed.

Neither FDR nor Weizmann could know how long the war would last, nor how many Jewish lives would be extinguished "if the present rate of destruction continued." But history would eventually record that six million European Jews were no longer alive at the war's end.

## WEIZMANN'S THOUGHTS ON HIS AMERICAN TRIP

Weizmann returned to London on March 5, 1940. In his autobiography, he wrote that he had found America in a "strange prewar mood . . . violently neutral, and making an extraordinary effort to live in the ordinary way." He believed he had to be "extremely careful" expressing himself, finding it necessary to speak "always with the utmost caution . . . avoiding anything that might be interpreted as [pro-war] propaganda." He felt he "had to maintain silence," lest he be accused of promoting American involvement in the European war at the behest of the Jews. The mere mention of the Jewish tragedy unfolding in Europe, he wrote, could have been "associated with warmongering."

In one of his private lectures during his trip, Weizmann referred sardonically to the strictures under which he was operating in America: "I am not sure whether mentioning the Ten Commandments will not be considered [an impolitic] statement of policy, since one of them says: Thou shalt not kill."[62]

He maintained a studious public silence on anything that might be construed as suggesting that America, or American Jews, should actively respond to what was transpiring in Europe, other than by assisting in building Palestine through investments and contributions.

During Weizmann's trip, Britain issued draconian regulations to implement the White Paper, seeking to halt Jewish acquisition of land in Palestine.[63] Rabbi Solomon Goldman, president of the Zionist Organization of America (ZOA), organized a protest, but he received no support from Weizmann, who ignored Goldman's message to him.[64] Rabbi Stephen S. Wise and Louis Lipsky, vice president of the ZOA, organized a protest meeting at Carnegie Hall. But according to a report by a Ben-Gurion associate who attended it, the "hall was not full; the press gave no coverage to the meeting . . . and Stephen Wise, after he had finished his speech, sent me a note, 'We should shout in low tones.'"[65]

Weizmann remained in America for two months. Only his New York speech is included in the published collection of his papers, speeches, and correspondence that covers 1940. In his memoir, he described the atmosphere in America in 1940 as having been "artificial" and "uncomfortable," and "not a satisfactory one." "It was," he wrote, "a genuine relief to get back to the realities of England where, if the truth was harsh, it was at least being faced."[66]

From London, in July 1940, Weizmann wrote to a Chicago friend, Albert K. Epstein, of the "world of shadows" he had found in America. He thought the attitudes there bore "no relation to the grim realities which today face humanity at large and the Jews in particular."[67] American Jews, he told Epstein, appeared to be oblivious to "the hurricane which is breaking over our heads":

> [I]t seems that the Jews are just as incurably complacent as many
> of their neighbors, and equally heedless of the warnings and

signs of the times. Then, when catastrophe reaches their gates, they will start up perplexed and wondering, as though something totally unexpected had happened.

Weizmann wrote that he hoped "American Jewry will prove itself worthy of the terrible responsibility which rests upon it"—because "3,000 miles of water will not save American Jewry, or America itself, if they refuse to take the right decisions now." As for himself, Weizmann said, he had "no plans at present." He believed his place was in London, where "[w]e live here from hour to hour." His final words of advice to his American friend were these:

> Every conceivable effort of American Jewry should be devoted towards helping the Allies in this struggle—which is our struggle. If the battle here should be lost, there will be no hope for you, and very little for America as a whole.
> This should therefore be the guiding principle of your lives, and everything else must, for the time being, take second place.

Those words were much stronger, and far more urgent, than any Weizmann had uttered in public in America—where he mentioned nothing of fighting on the side of Britain, nor of joining a battle to save the civilization of which the Jews were a part, nor anything else that might be criticized as "warmongering."[68]

### THE RESULTS OF WEIZMANN'S TRIP

In terms of generating a strong response from the American Jewish community, Weizmann's 1940 trip was a failure. But perhaps that outcome was not solely the result of the pervasive fears Weizmann encountered within the American Jewish community.

Weizmann was earnest but uncontroversial in public, ever wary of "warmongering." He was not a gifted orator, preferring private diplomacy to public speeches.[69] He complimented American Jews on their accomplishments and sought their economic assistance for projects in Palestine, but he did not challenge them concerning the horrific situation in Europe. In his autobiography, Weizmann claimed that he had had "nothing too specific in mind" for his 1940 visit, and that he had viewed it as an "exploratory trip" to get his bearings and "lay the groundwork" for later trips.[70]

Faced with an existential crisis, however, one does not make an "exploratory" trip, nor does one go on a trip that is focused on preparations for "later trips." Weizmann's description of his 1940 trip in his 1949 book seems a retrospective rationalization of his failure, a downplaying of the importance of his trip in light of its meager results. Weizmann's later description, moreover, does not recount what he knew was at stake at the time, which he expressed in private letters both immediately before and after his trip.

There may have been a deeper reason for the failure of the trip—one that extended beyond Weizmann's innate caution and his public reticence. In 1916, in his introduction to a book of essays entitled *Zionism and the Jewish Future,* Weizmann wrote that the "natural progress of the emancipated Jews" in foreign lands was assimilation, making it impossible for them to lead Zionism.[71] In the post-World War I conferences to implement the League of Nations Mandate for Palestine, Weizmann had told the Americans, "We are different, absolutely different. There is no bridge between Washington and Pinsk."[72] He thought American Jews did not have a true Jewish national consciousness; that they had "built a Monroe Doctrine around Zionism," which had resulted in a "moral cleavage" between them and other Jews.[73] He thought Americans had reduced Zionism to a charity project.[74]

When he came to America in 1940, Weizmann held deeply conflicted views about American Jews and American Zionism. In a handwritten letter dated June 20, 1937, to Orde and Lorna Wingate, British friends who were ardent Zionists, he described a person he identified only as "S" as being a representative American Jewish figure:

> S. belongs to the type of an "assimilated" Jew. He thinks himself an American and his connection with Jewry is a loose religious bond. His religion is a poor imitation of Protestantism. It has nothing in it of the austerity, severity and the real tradition of Jewry sanctified by so much martyrdom. At best he is prepared to be charitable to his "poorer brethren" to show he is inclined to send some of his surplus but with whom he would not like to consort. Palestine is a challenge to these Jews. It stirs some memories in them that they have tried to bury under their American civilization.

Weizmann suggested to the Wingates that American Jews were seeking an escape from Zionism; and that this made them of only marginal use, if any, to the movement:

> They fasten on the Arab problem which offers them a sort of escape from their Jewish consciousness; they are mostly useless to us, if not harmful. Between these fully assimilated Jews and us stands a clan of Jews who at some time or another toyed with Zionism, but never could rise to giving up the fleshpots offered by the non-Jewish world . . . [T]hey always prefer an already established running concern to something which has to go through the pangs of creation. May I be forgiven if I'm doing them an injustice.[75]

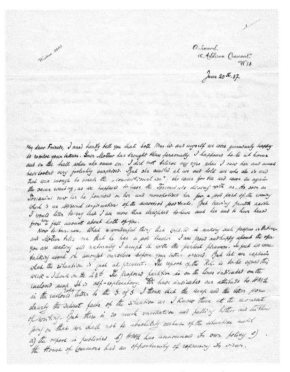

*First page of Chaim Weizmann's 1937 letter to the Wingates*

Weizmann came to America two and a half years after writing that letter, still believing the future of Zionism lay in diplomatic relations with the British, and he left America with that conviction unchanged, disappointed once again in American Jews.

But what if Weizmann had challenged the American Jewish community more directly, more publicly, with an eloquence matching the urgency he himself saw in the existential crisis? What if a Zionist leader had employed in America what the young Churchill called "the scaffolding of rhetoric"—an eloquence that "wields a power more durable than that of a great king" and that creates "an independent force on the world"? Under those circumstances, might American Jews have responded differently?

We can answer that question by considering the mission to America that year of the second great Zionist leader—one whose oratorical power approached that of Churchill.

# VLADIMIR JABOTINSKY

## March–August 1940

*On Monday, August 5, 1940, as New Yorkers leafed through The New York Times, there was nothing particularly surprising to see. The wars in Europe and Asia continued, as did speeches and demonstrations protesting any American involvement in them. The Times reported stories of a world on fire—and of Americans determined to avoid the flames.*

*Jewish readers of that day's newspaper suffered a profound shock, however, as they came to page 13. In the center, they found a picture and an article running the entire length of the page, reporting news from a small town in the Catskill Mountains, of special relevance to them. The news was so stunning that, by noon on the following day, 25,000 Jews lined the streets of New York.*

O N MARCH 6, 1940, the day after the Weizmanns left America, *The New York Times* carried a notice under the headline "Jabotinsky to Give Lecture":

> Vladimir Jabotinsky, president of the New Zionist Organization of the World, will lecture on "The Fate of Jewry" at Manhattan Center, 311 West Thirty-Fourth Street, on Tuesday, March 19, at 8:30 p.m., it was announced yesterday.

A week later, Jabotinsky arrived from England, traveling on the Cunard Line's 500-passenger *Samaria*, with 350 refugees from Nazi-controlled countries on board. He made the crossing without his wife, Joanna; to his great frustration, he had been unable to obtain a visa for her to accompany him.[1] The *Times* covered his arrival:

> Mr. Jabotinsky, who commanded the Jewish Legion in Palestine during the [First] World War, said that he had conferred in London with British leaders about Jewish participation in the present war. "As long as the war remains a military stalemate I don't see much scope for any additional troops," he said. "But if there is going to be a real military war, there is going to be a Jewish army, fighting under a Jewish flag on the side of the democracies."

Before undertaking his mission to America, Jabotinsky had written a 255-page book, entitled *The Jewish War Front*, in which he had argued that it was incumbent on the Jews of the world to form a Jewish army, take an active part in the struggle against Nazism, and persuade the Allies to make one of their war aims a Jewish state, because the Jewish problem in Eastern Europe was:

. . . of immense importance to the world's health and peace, clearly distinct from all other problems, *a problem which means literally life or death to five or six million people*, and affects the fate of sixteen million; that these men and women are just as anxious to help in solving their problem as any normal nation can be; and that they possess a total sum of moral and material power that can go a long way towards that solution, and ought to be given a chance to do so.[2] [Emphasis added.]

Jabotinsky envisioned an army assembled from the more than half a million stateless Jews in the world—432,000 Jewish refugees scattered among several European countries, more than 210,000 Jews in Palestine, and many Jews in neutral countries. He was confident he could build a Jewish military force, because he had already done so—twenty-five years earlier.

Shortly after the outbreak of World War I in 1914—when, at the age of 34, he was working as a foreign correspondent for a Russian newspaper—Jabotinsky was the moving force behind the creation of the Jewish Legion,

# LEADER SAYS JEWS WILL FIGHT AS UNIT

### Head of New Zionists, Here on Samaria, to Form Army Under Own Flag if 'Real War' Comes

### BABY BORN DURING VOYAGE

### Refugees' Son to Get U. S. Name, 'Sam'—350 Emigres Are Among 499 Passengers

The Samaria, one of the five Cunard White Star liners in regular transatlantic operation, arrived here yesterday morning on her fourth wartime voyage. She brought 499 passengers, among whom were Vladimir Jabotinsky,

The New York Times, *March 13, 1940*

a regiment of thousands of British, American, Canadian, and Palestinian Jews who fought alongside British forces in 1917–18, under the command of British Lieutenant Colonel John Patterson, to help liberate Palestine from the rule of the Ottoman Turks. It was the first organized Jewish military force in two millennia.[3]

## JABOTINSKY'S EARLY CAREERS

By 1914, Jabotinsky had already achieved remarkable success as a journalist, poet, writer, translator, playwright, activist, and public speaker. He was fluent in seven languages (Russian, Yiddish, Hebrew, Italian, English, French, and German). He was born in Odessa in 1880, at a time when it was a relatively young city, created on land seized by Russia from the Ottomans in an eighteenth-century war between the two empires. As of the nineteenth century, Odessa was part of "New Russia" bordering on the Black Sea. Jews there enjoyed a relative freedom of mind unknown in the Jewish towns and villages (*shtetls*) of Russia.

Odessa's population included Jews, Greeks, Italians, Armenians, Romanians, and Ukrainians—all of whom Russia had welcomed to the city as the labor necessary to build a major port. Jews constituted one-third of the city's 400,000 inhabitants; and the fact that there was no single ethnic group in the majority itself created for them a sense of freedom. Many of the "port Jews" of Odessa abandoned the traditional piety of the "*shtetl* Jews," and Odessa eventually became both famous and infamous, its reputation captured in the Yiddish expression that secular Jews used to describe it—*leben vi Got in Odess* ("to live like God in Odessa")—and the contrasting saying that Orthodox Jews used: *zibn mayl arum Odess brent dos gehenem* ("the fires of hell burn for seven miles around Odessa"). The city became a center of the new, emerging faith of Jewish nationalism, the city of Leo Pinsker, whose 1882 pamphlet, *Auto-Emancipation*, was the seminal Zionist response to the brutal pogroms that had swept through Russia in the year before.[4] The pamphlet was the *Common Sense* of its time.[5]

Jabotinsky had left Odessa at 17 to study law in Switzerland and then studied further in Italy, while serving as a foreign correspondent for a liberal Odessa newspaper, covering politics, literature, theater, and opera in a regular, widely read column he wrote under the pen name "Altalena" (the Italian word for "seesaw" or "swing"). Rome in those days was still filled with stories of Mazzini, Garibaldi, and Cavour, who together had been responsible for the rebirth of Italy as a modern state in the nineteenth century, the result of the Italian *Risorgimento* (the "Revival" or "Resurrection"). Jabotinsky would later write about the powerful effect that his time in Italy had on his Zionist thinking:

> My whole attitude toward the problems of nationality, state, and society took shape during those years under Italy's influence. I learned to appreciate the art of the architect, the sculptor, and the painter. . . . My professors . . . planted in my heart a belief in the justice of socialism that I preserved as something self-evident until it was utterly annihilated by the spectacle of the Red Experiment in Russia. The story of Garibaldi, the writings of Mazzini, the poetry of Leopardi and Giusti, enriched and deepened my superficial Zionism, and developed it into a tangible concept. . . .[6]

In his magisterial history of modern Italy, the late British historian Professor Christopher Duggan described the origins of the Italian Revival in a way that makes evident its relationship to the underlying spirit of Zionism. The *Risorgimento* had started with a small group of educated men and women who had questioned why the land that had produced the Roman civilization and had been part of the Renaissance should not become a nation again, as other European countries were:

> Much of the discussion focused on the problem of the Italian character, using concepts that had been made familiar by writers of the eighteenth century (and earlier) who had endeavored to account for the rise and fall of states and empires in essentially moral terms. The task . . . was not just to secure the independence of Italy from foreign rule . . . but more fundamentally to eradicate the vices that centuries of despotism and clerical rule had allegedly engendered—for example, subservience, indiscipline, excessive materialism and a lack of martial ardor.[7]

Mazzini, Garibaldi, and Cavour took their divided and dejected people and—through a combination of intellectual power (Mazzini), diplomacy (Cavour), and military efforts (Garibaldi)—built a new Italy, based on the concept of a new Italian man. The analogy to another people, not only divided and dejected but also dispersed, and whose ancient capital had been as glorious as Rome, was obvious. Indeed, the first great Zionist tract—*Rome and Jerusalem*, written by Moses Hess in 1862 at the time of the unification of Italy as a modern state—had made precisely that connection.[8]

Jabotinsky would eventually see Zionism not only as a movement of cultural preservation (as did Weizmann), nor as the opportunity to build a socialist utopia (as did Ben-Gurion), but also as a movement to create a new Jewish character.

### JABOTINSKY TURNS TO ZIONISM AS A YOUNG MAN

In June 1901, at the age of 20, Jabotinsky returned to Odessa for the summer and decided to remain there when the newspaper *Odesskaya Novosti* (*New Odessa)* offered him a position as a columnist at a substantial salary. His Odessan friend, Shlomo Saltzman, loaned him works by Theodor Herzl and Pinsker, and Jabotinsky began writing and speaking on behalf of Zionism in the city's debate clubs.[9]

Two years later, in 1903, a Russian boy was murdered near Kishinev, 90 miles from Odessa, and rumors immediately spread among the Russians that the Jews were responsible—purportedly for blood allegedly used to bake their Passover matzos, a despicable slander with roots extending to eleventh-century England, resuscitated in Damascus in the nineteenth century, and endemic throughout Europe, Russia, and the Middle East by the early twentieth century. Weeks later, on Easter Sunday, a particularly horrific pogrom erupted in Kishinev: scores of Jews were murdered, Jewish women were raped in front of their families, and more than 1,000 Jewish homes and stores were sacked and looted. *The New York Times* reported that the massacres were "worse than the censor will permit [us] to publish . . . the Jews were taken wholly unaware and were slaughtered like sheep . . . [and] scenes of horror attending this massacre are beyond description."

Joining a clandestine Jewish defense force, the 22-year-old Jabotinsky traveled to Kishinev to help distribute money and supplies to the survivors. Walking down a deserted street, he found in the debris a scrap of Torah, which he would retain for years. It read: "*I have been a stranger in a strange land*," the words of Moses in Exodus 2:22, and they crystallized for Jabotinsky the position of the Jews in Russia. He composed a poem describing the verse:

Just a few words from the Bible, but the sum
Of all one needs to understand
About a pogrom.

Jabotinsky included this poem in the introduction to his Russian translation of Chaim Nachman Bialik's *In the City of Slaughter*, an epic poem in
Hebrew that castigated the "concealed and cowering" reaction in Kishinev
of "the sons of the Maccabees." Jabotinsky's translation captivated Russian Jews, who circulated it widely in handwritten copies and read it aloud
at meetings.[10] The translation carried his name far beyond Odessa.

Jabotinsky translated other poems into Russian (including Edgar Allan Poe's "The Raven" and works of Dante), wrote plays for the Odessa
theater, and was one of the small number of Jews who could likely have
succeeded as a Russian writer, living outside the Pale of Settlement.[11] The
Russian author Alexander Kuprin later wrote that Jabotinsky had "a God-
given talent [and] could have been an eagle of Russian literature had you
[Jews] not stolen him from us." Instead, at the age of 23, Jabotinsky became a delegate from Odessa to the Sixth Zionist Congress in Basel in
1903 (the same Congress at which Chaim Weizmann would lead a student
revolt against Herzl's Uganda plan). From that point forward, Zionism
became the central mission of Jabotinsky's life.[12]

## TURKEY'S ENTRY INTO WORLD WAR I
## AND ITS EFFECTS ON PALESTINE

In 1914, Jabotinsky accepted an assignment to cover the new European war
for *Russkiya Vyedomosti* (*Russian Monitor*), reporting on the wartime atmosphere in several countries: Egypt, Sweden, England, and then France.[13]
In December 1914, in the fifth month of the war, he saw a news poster in
Bordeaux, announcing that Turkey had joined the war as an ally of Germany. "Until that morning," he later recalled, "I had been a mere observer
. . . [wanting] peace as soon as possible," but:

Turkey's move made this war "my war." In 1909 I had been
chief editor in Constantinople of four Zionist newspapers . . .
and [while there] I reached the steadfast conclusion that where
the Turk rules neither sun may shine nor grass may grow, and
that the only hope for the restoration of Palestine lay in the dis-

memberment of the Ottoman Empire. . . . I never doubted that once Turkey entered the war, she would be defeated and sliced to pieces . . . [and] the right thing for the Jews would be to form a regiment of their own and participate in the conquest of Palestine.[14]

Jabotinsky's insight was not only that the war would end the Ottoman Empire (long known as the "sick man of Europe"), but even more importantly that the Jews could not expect to participate in the postwar division of territory unless they participated in the war. In his view, neutrality was inimical to Zionist goals. To propose a Jewish military force, however, to a people with no modern military experience, and an ingrained moral resistance to it, was a radical idea.[15] Lt. Col. Patterson later described the opposition that Jabotinsky faced:

> When Jabotinsky embarked on the Jewish Legion venture, every-thing was against him. . . . First of all, it was a precedent-breaking idea. Since the fall of Judea and the Jewish dispersion all over the globe, there never was a Jewish military unit anywhere in the world. For two thousand years, the Jews had had neither a state organization . . . nor any military formation of their own.
>
> Furthermore, by the very fact of the Jewish dispersion, the Jewish people had a stake in every land, and this was later to be one of the chief arguments of the opponents of the Jewish Legion. "How can we dare," they would say, "to join either of the warring alliances, thus endangering the Jewish populations of the other alliance?" . . . [T]hey claimed that if a Jewish Legion was formed within the framework of the British Army, the Jews of Germany, Austria, Bulgaria and Turkey would pay the price, for surely vengeance would engulf them. . . .
>
> It is against this background of thorough passivism conse-crated by hundreds of years of tradition that Jabotinsky's idea of a Jewish Legion has to be seen. . . . [The] idea was not simply precedent-breaking; it was contrary to all precedents.[16]

Jabotinsky consulted Zionist leaders, virtually all of whom advised against any participation by Jews in the war as Jews. The sole exception was Weizmann, six years Jabotinsky's senior. They worked together on Jabotinsky's proposal. Jabotinsky later recalled:

In London we came still closer together. We even lived together
for three months in a small house . . . a stone's throw from the
Thames. . . . In those months we became great friends . . . [and]
Dr. Weizmann was in favor of my plans.[17]

Weizmann understood that a plan for a Jewish Legion would help in
his discussions with the British on a declaration concerning post-Ottoman
Palestine. Most of his colleagues, however, thought a Jewish Legion would
endanger the Jewish community in Palestine, then living under Ottoman
rule, or would associate the Zionist movement with "militarism."[18] When
Patterson discovered that "in certain quarters of influential English Jewry
there was a violent hostility to Zionist aspirations, and to the very idea of
a Jewish Regiment," he summoned twenty prominent Jews, on both sides
of the issue, to an August 8, 1917, meeting at the British War Office. The
attendees included Lord Rothschild, Major Lionel de Rothschild, Captain William David Ormsby-Gore, Cecil Sebag-Montefiore, Weizmann,
Jabotinsky, and two Secretaries to the British War Cabinet—Colonel Sir
Mark Sykes and Lt. Col. Leopold S. Amery. Patterson later described his
astonishment at the divisions in the meeting:

I was, of course, aware that there was somewhat of a cleavage
amongst the Jews on this question, but the bitterness and hostility shown was quite a revelation to me.

I could not understand how any Jew could fail to grasp this
Heaven-sent opportunity and do all in his power to further the
efforts of the British Government on behalf of the Jewish people. Imagine my surprise, therefore, when certain of the Jews
in opposition vigorously denounced the formation of a Jewish
Regiment, and equally vigorously damned the aspirations of the
Zionists!

Dr. Weizmann gave a slashing reply to the [opponents] from
the Zionist point of view . . . and Jabotinsky, in his address for
the cause he had at heart, lifted the debate to a level immeasur-
ably above the point of view of his opponents.[19]

The formation of a "Jewish Regiment" was finally announced in the
*London Gazette* on August 23, 1917, and Patterson was appointed its commander. Later, in his book *The Story of the Jewish Legion* (1928), Jabotinsky
described how the first battalion, consisting of Jews previously denigrated

*38th Battalion, Royal Fusiliers marching in London before leaving for Middle East*
*First on horseback: Lt. Col. Patterson. First on foot, behind the second horse:*
*Lt. Jabotinsky.*

by others as mere "tailors," marched through the streets of London before their deployment to Palestine:

> There were tens of thousands of Jews in the streets, at the windows and on the roofs. Blue-white flags were over every shop door; women crying with joy, old Jews with fluttering beards murmuring, "shehecheyanu"; Patterson on his horse, laughing and bowing, and wearing a rose which a girl had thrown him from a balcony; and the boys, those "tailors," shoulder to shoulder, their bayonets dead level, each step like a single clap of thunder, clean, proud . . . with the sense of a holy mission, unexampled since the day of Bar-Kochba. . . .[20]

Jabotinsky himself, at the age of 37, enlisted in the Jewish Legion as a private; he was promoted to lieutenant, and departed for Palestine to fight in 1917–18. In his book, *With the Judeans in the Palestine Campaign* (1922), Patterson effusively praised both the Legion and Jabotinsky's leadership.

In his own history of the Legion, however, Jabotinsky argued that its greatest significance was not military but rather political: it had demonstrated that Zionism's adherents were serious and prepared for sacrifice. He believed that it had a compelling effect on the British War Cabinet as they debated whether to issue the Balfour Declaration in 1917. Jabotinsky wrote that:

> [T]he efforts made in the years of the war were only a small part of the earlier strivings of the Jewish people for Palestine. For the Balfour Declaration we have to thank Herzl and Rothschild and Pinsker and Moses Hess; still more, the Bilu [the Jewish pioneers in Palestine] and those who followed them. . . . Not to mention that which, more than anything else, helped to establish our claim: the Book which is holy to them as to us. . . . [But] I say with the deep and cold conviction of an observer: half the Balfour Declaration belongs to the Legion. . . .[21]
>
> And to each one of the five thousand [members of my brigade] I say what I once said to my "tailors" [in Palestine] . . . "Far away, in your home, you will one day read glorious news, of a free Jewish life in a free Jewish country—of factories and universities, of farms and theaters, perhaps of MPs and Ministers. . . . Then you shall stand up, walk to the mirror, and look yourself proudly in the face . . . and salute yourself—for 'tis you who have made it."[22]

Two decades later, at the outbreak of the Second World War—a war waged not only against Britain and France but against the Jewish People itself—the idea of forming a Jewish military force was not a theoretical or fanciful one. It had been done in the First World War, a war in which the Jews were not specifically threatened. And the leader of that force was ready to form it again, now that they were.

On September 3, 1939, two days after the Nazi invasion of Poland, and the same day Britain declared war on Germany, Jabotinsky called Lt. Col. Patterson to ask that they meet as soon as possible. They met that afternoon and agreed to work together to form not a legion but a Jewish army.[23] Jabotinsky knew that the heart of the effort would have to be to engage the American Jews through a trip to the United States. As he wrote to Rabbi Louis I. Newman the following month, "it surely cannot be enough . . . for an American Jewry left almost alone and lost in a ruined Jewish

*Jabotinsky with soldiers of the Jewish Legion in Jaffa, 1918*

הגדוד ה־38 הגדוד הראשון ליהודה

*38th Battalion, Royal Fusiliers, First Judeans, January 1918*

diaspora, to cater for repatriating refugees, no matter how many." The curse under which the Jewish people were operating, Jabotinsky observed, was "being 'not on the map,' having no place at all among anybody's war-aims except Hitler's." He told Rabbi Newman that the "mission now is to stir American Jews into some such effort of an unprecedented magnitude and daring."[24]

## JABOTINSKY ADDRESSES 5,000 PEOPLE IN NEW YORK

In March 1940, Jabotinsky assembled a small group of senior aides in New York, including his executive assistant, Benzion Netanyahu, 30, the editor of a Palestine daily (the son of the renowned Zionist orator Rabbi Nathan Mileikowsky, and the father of Israeli Prime Minister Benjamin Netanyahu, born in 1949). The others included Eliahu Ben-Horin, 38, a Zionist journalist and editor from Palestine, and Benjamin Akzin, a 36-year-old Russian-born professor with doctorates in law and political science from European universities, seeking yet a third doctorate at Harvard.[25]

On March 19, 1940, an eager crowd—exceeding the 4,600-person seating capacity—converged on the Manhattan Center for Jabotinsky's lecture.[26] He began by calling Eastern Europe the "Zone of Jewish Distress," a place where the danger was of historic magnitude, and he invoked a vivid metaphor to describe it: "Anti-Semitism elsewhere may be comparable to a headache, but in that Zone it is a cancer." He didn't know whether the "quasi-war" in Europe was destined to become "a real war and spread," or whether it would "fizzle out in a precarious peace." But either way, he predicted, the result would be "a thorough shakeup, a worldwide revision of all international and national conditions":

> Should the democracies lose the war, their eclipse—especially that of France, which is Europe's main window to fresh air—will enthrone medievalism right up to the Atlantic shore. But even an allied victory, if the present policy with regard to Jews is to continue, threatens to leave those Jews in the lurch. That policy now consists in keeping the Jews off the war-map. When the war broke out we hoped to be recognized and treated as one of the allied peoples, offered Jewish troops and other important forms of collaboration. All that was rejected: the Jewish ally is not wanted. His problems are rigorously excluded from the list of war aims.

Jabotinsky believed that history was repeating itself in the Jewish reliance on universalist ideals to ameliorate their situation:

> The old fallacy, the curse of our past, has been revived: that
> there is no Jewish problem; that all our troubles can be cured en
> passant by general measures of progress, and there is no need to
> worry about any special remedies. The allied victory will ensure
> democracy and equality . . . and that will be enough for the Jews.

Formal political and civil rights alone were no solution: such rights had existed for Jews for decades in Eastern Europe, yet had failed to prevent the harrowing situation in which they now found themselves. In the 1930s, for the first time in their history, Jews had been citizens of every country in which they lived, but anti-Semitism had nevertheless grown. Indeed, Jabotinsky argued, it had grown *because* of their new status:

> [T]hose countries [in Eastern Europe] had all been given dem-
> ocratic constitutions since 1918, yet the plight of the Jews grew
> worse day by day. . . . For the last seven years, every Jew in the
> Zone, no matter how well-off himself, no matter how attached to
> the land of his birth, had only one wish for his children: "a visa"—
> a chance to go and live elsewhere. But today it is really a frozen
> "stampede" of millions, frozen because all gates are closed.

For Jabotinsky, the idea that the fortunes of European Jews could be improved simply by restoring their civil and political rights was thus demonstrably false:

> Such a situation cannot be solved just by proclaiming equal
> rights. Democracy there can only be effective if at the same time
> the Jews are given a real choice to stay or to leave; and that real
> choice can only mean a Jewish State adapted for a mass repatri-
> ation of unprecedented multitudes within the shortest period
> possible.

Jabotinsky described a situation that he said was intolerable irrespective of whether the Allies prevailed. If they lost the war, it "would be a catastrophe." But even if they won, it would only return the Jews to their *status quo ante*—which would be, in Jabotinsky's phrase, "an 'as you were' of agony." Accordingly, the Jews required both a Jewish army *and* a Jewish state, and only Jews themselves could take the necessary steps to form them:

The allies will have to make room, on their various fronts, for a
Jewish army, just as they have in the case of the Polish army. In
their governing Councils they will have to make room for some
kind of Jewish Embassy. In the list of their war aims they will
have to insert not only the Covenant of Equality—not only an
international convention outlawing anti-Semitism, just as slavery
is outlawed—but above all the Jewish State and the Max Nordau
Plan [for immigration to Palestine] . . . whose true absorptive capacity is what I said . . . in 1937: "room enough for the million
Arabs who live there, for another million of their progeny, for
three or four or five million Jews, and for peace."[27]

Jabotinsky closed his speech with a call for two "practical lines of action": a union of the two worldwide Zionist organizations (Weizmann's
Zionist Organization and Jabotinsky's New Zionist Organization) together with the formation of a new "World-Jewish Headquarters"; and free
immigration into Palestine, since "the agony of the refugees is so great."
    The next day, *The New York Times* reported Jabotinsky's speech:

More than 5,000 persons jammed the Manhattan Center to hear
the man who headed the Jewish Legion in Palestine in the World
War, in a two-hour statement of his party's case. . . . None of the
leaders of the Zionist Organization of America, which differs
with the Jabotinsky point of view in many ways, was observed in
the audience . . .

### NEW ZIONIST LEADER HEARD BY 5,000 HERE

#### Jabotinsky Reiterates Demands for Restored Jewish State

Vladimir Jabotinsky, world leader of the New Zionist Organization, addressed last night the largest gathering ever assembled under its auspices in this city.
    More than 5,000 persons jammed the Manhattan Center to hear the man who headed the Jewish legion in Palestine in the World War, in a two-hour statement of his party's

differs with the Jabotinsky point of view in many ways, was observed in the audience although at times Mr. Jabotinsky and other speakers seemed to be addressing themselves to the Z. O. A.
    "In the list of their war aims," Mr. Jabotinsky said, "the Allies will have to insert not only a covenant of Jewish equality, not only an international convention outlawing anti-Semitism. Among the war aims for which they fight there must be restoration of the Jewish state."
    He reiterated the assertion he made when he arrived last Wednesday that a Jewish army could be raised to assist the democracies.
    Other speakers were Rabbi Morris M. Rose, Rabbi Louis I. Newman, Aaron Propes, and Professor Benjamin Azkin, who presided.

The most remarkable fact reported by the *Times* was not the size of the audience—although 5,000 attendees, in isolationist America, in the dead of a New York winter, was remarkable enough. It was that the leadership of the American Zionist movement had been conspicuously absent.

What caused them to spurn Jabotinsky's speech? What were the "many ways" in which they differed with "the Jabotinsky point of view"? What was it about his public call for a Jewish army and a Jewish state, for unrestricted Jewish immigration into Palestine, and for a unified world Jewish organization, that made the American Jewish leaders unwilling to join thousands of other Jews at the Manhattan Center, to hear Jabotinsky speak on "The Fate of Jewry"?

The short answer is that these American Jewish leaders considered Jabotinsky "right wing," ideologically different from their own position as staunch, pro-Roosevelt liberals. They considered Jabotinsky a "militarist," using means they deemed inconsistent with Jewish values. They regarded him as an "extremist" in matters they thought required moderation and quiet diplomacy, not impassioned public discussion.[28] They further perceived Jabotinsky as a challenge to their own leadership. Professor Melvin I. Urofsky, in his admiring biography of Rabbi Stephen S. Wise—who, in 1940, aligned himself not with Jabotinsky, but rather with Weizmann and the "General Zionists"—writes that "[i]n the winter and spring of 1940, the Jewish community in general and the Zionists in particular seemed completely confused over what to do regarding European Jewry, the war, and the [British] Mandatory power [in Palestine]."[29] American Jewish leadership became alarmed at the institutional challenge to their own positions, as foreign Zionists came to the U.S. seeking funds for their projects, often ignoring the American leadership.[30]

The issue extended, however, beyond the Jewish community's fears, passivity, and internecine rivalries. The American Jewish leadership opposed Jabotinsky's public call for a Jewish army for reasons involving the uneasiness of American Jews about their position within American society. Urofsky elucidated that there was a difference between the leaders and many within the Jewish community who wanted to act:

> Jabotinsky, much to Wise's anger, campaigned for a Jewish army [to fight the Nazis], thus violating [FDR's] call for neutrality and American Jewry's reluctance to be labeled as a separate ethnic group. . . . [But] the idea appealed to many persons frustrated

by the inability of either western Jews or the free democracies to help those trapped in Hitler's grip.[31]

After the overwhelming turnout at Jabotinsky's rally, Louis Lipsky of the Zionist Organization of America (ZOA) wrote to his colleagues that he feared Jabotinsky was "making an impression on American Jews." He argued it was necessary to "destroy the influence that Mr. Jabotinsky is exerting on the American public."[32] The major American Zionist organizations all joined in printing a lengthy pamphlet warning against the "seductiveness" of Jabotinsky's rhetoric, "particularly when supported by [his] powerful personality." They castigated his "notorious Evacuation Scheme," accusing him of "abetting the anti-Semitic desire to treat Jews as aliens and drive them out of their lands of residence."[33]

### JABOTINSKY'S "EVACUATION SCHEME"

The "Evacuation Scheme" was Jabotinsky's plan, published in 1936, for mass emigration to Palestine—an expanded version of the proposal of Herzl's principal associate Max Nordau in 1920, following the Balfour Declaration.[34] Jabotinsky's plan envisioned 1.5 million Jews moving to Palestine from Poland, Hungary, and Romania over a ten-year period, to establish in Palestine both a place of refuge and an eventual majority to form a Jewish state. Jabotinsky met with the rulers of those three countries and secured preliminary support from them for his plan.[35] Weizmann, however, opposed it, and mainstream Zionists criticized Jabotinsky for negotiating with anti-Semitic governments in the first place, accusing him of exposing Jews there to charges of dual loyalty. Jabotinsky was savaged for what his opponents called his "evacuationism."

In February 1937—the same month in which *The New York Times* reported that five million Eastern European Jews were facing "the prospect of a new Exodus of bigger than Biblical proportions or a slow death from economic strangulation"—Jabotinsky testified in London before the Peel Commission as it considered the future of Palestine.[36] He quoted from the *Times* article and said that the magnitude of the problems facing the Jews went far beyond the attitudes of particular governments:

> [I]t would be very naïve—and although many Jews make this
> mistake I disapprove of it—it would be very naïve to ascribe
> that state of disaster . . . only to the guilt of men, whether it be
> crowds and multitudes, or whether it be governments. The thing

goes much deeper than that. I am very much afraid that what
I am going to say will not be popular with many among my co-
religionists, and I regret that, but the truth is the truth. We are
facing an elemental calamity, a kind of social earthquake. . . . We
have got to save millions, many millions. I do not know whether
it is a question of re-housing one-third of the Jewish race, half of
the Jewish race, or a quarter of the Jewish race; I do not know;
but it is a question of millions. . . . [And] with 1,000,000 more
Jews in Palestine today you could already have a Jewish majority.
But there are certainly 3,000,000 or 4,000,000 in the East who
are virtually knocking at the door asking for admission, i.e., for
salvation.

Jabotinsky told the Commission that he appreciated the desires of Arab
nationalism; he realized the Arabs of Palestine would want Palestine "to
be the Arab State No. 4, No. 5, or No. 6":

[T]hat I quite understand. But when the Arab claim is confronted with our Jewish demand to be saved, it is like the claims
of appetite versus the claims of starvation.[37]

*Jabotinsky testifying before the Peel Commission*

In August 1938, Jabotinsky traveled to Warsaw—a year before it would
be decimated by the Nazis—to address the largest Jewish community
in Europe. He spoke on Tisha b'Av (the Ninth of Av), the Jewish day of
mourning that memorializes the destruction of the ancient Temples in
Jerusalem and other Jewish tragedies. To the Jews of Poland, he set forth
both a warning and a vision. This was the warning:

It is for three years that I have been calling on you, Jews of Poland, the glory of world Jewry, with an appeal. I have been cease-
lessly warning you that the catastrophe is coming closer. My
hair has turned white and I have aged in these years, because
my heart is bleeding, for you, dear brothers and sisters, do not
see the volcano which will soon begin to spurt out the fire of destruction. I see a terrifying sight. The time is short in which one
can still be saved.

I know: you do not see, because you are bothered and rush-
ing about with everyday worries. . . . Listen to my remarks at the
twelfth hour. For God's sake: may each one save his life while
there is still time. And time is short.

And this was the vision:

I want to say one more thing to you on this day of the Ninth of
Av: Those who will succeed to escape from the catastrophe will
merit a moment of great Jewish joy—the rebirth and rise of a
Jewish State. I do not know if I will earn that. My son, yes! I believe in this just as I am sure that tomorrow morning the sun will
shine once again. I believe in this with total faith.[38]

In 1939, the month after the British White Paper was released, Jabotinsky published a long analysis in *The Jewish Herald*, entitled "A White Paper Against Diaspora Jewry." He urged Jews in the Diaspora not to treat
the Paper as one that affected only Palestine. The British abandonment of
its commitment to facilitate a Jewish national home would, he predicted,
have adverse consequences for *all* Jews, lowering their status and robbing
them of alternatives, with changes to their status that might be impercep-
tible as they occurred, but serious at the end:

I warn you, dear readers, against the natural but dangerous tendency to comfort yourselves with the fact that all these consequences have not yet been introduced; that perhaps they will
not be introduced at all; that my conclusions are based only on
theoretical logic and "life is not always logical." I warn you that
at least where it is a matter of our Jewish troubles, life is always
logical, and every stone breaks a pan and every spark becomes a
flame. . . .

Today—today and not the day after tomorrow, not even tomorrow morning—is the time to remind the world, and first of all the Governments of all the European areas of distress, that the problem of Jewish migration hunger is and remains one of the urgent, first-line problems of the immediate future. . . .[39]

On September 4, 1939—the week World War II began—Jabotinsky wrote to Prime Minister Chamberlain "[o]n behalf of a movement whose origin is that Jewish Regiment which, under Allenby, crossed the Jordan in 1918." He pledged that there would be "neither stint nor limit to the sacrifices which the Jewish people will eagerly consent" to support Britain in her "resolve to cut out the cancer choking God's earth." Jabotinsky offered to form a national army to stand "on all fronts as well as on our Palestine guard" and thereby "produce untapped resources of manpower" for the fight.[40]

Chamberlain ignored the offer, just as he had ignored one the week before from Weizmann. Once in America, Jabotinsky wrote to Lt. Col. Patterson that the "Jewish Army issue . . . is not on the map nor even on the horizon just now, with this fake war slipping off to the back pages of the newspapers and everybody in America really feeling proud to be out of it." But Jabotinsky believed that it was likely that the war would expand, not contract, and that there was still the possibility of "striking the imagination of our masses at a moment like this."[41]

In March 1940, however, the American Jewish leaders attempted to render Jabotinsky's views beyond the pale of public discussion, certainly not worthy of a trip to the Manhattan Center to hear him speak.[42] They thought the proper approach was the one Weizmann had adopted, studiously avoiding any public proposals to mobilize American Jews, much less asserting that England's cause was America's too. They considered it better to work privately with the British, to try to form a Jewish military unit after the British government might decide to allow it.

## JABOTINSKY ADDRESSES JEWISH GROUPS AND BETAR, HIS YOUTH ORGANIZATION

In the weeks following the Manhattan Center rally, Jabotinsky addressed a series of groups in New York, including a gathering of the Jewish War Veterans, a Brooklyn meeting of several hundred rabbis and Orthodox Jews, and the National Council of Young Israel.[43] He spoke to 1,500 American supporters of the youth organization he had founded, known by its Hebrew acronym, Betar.[44] As of 1938, Betar had 78,000 members worldwide (half of them in Poland).[45] He recalled the group's origins—an incident at an East European university two decades earlier, when a female Jewish student had been bullied as other Jewish students stood idly by:

> That was a sample of the ghetto mentality which made us wish for the creation of a new Jewish mentality. . . . This was the origin of the Betar and you here [in America] are an outpost of what was a very great movement in Eastern Europe until the recent catastrophe destroyed its central fortress, the Polish Betar. . . .[46]

Jabotinsky gave the Betar assembly a summary of the goals of his "Revisionist" Zionism and its one-word slogan, *Hadar*, a Hebrew word that combined honor, civility, and self-esteem.[47] *Hadar* was the essence of the Betar hymn, which Jabotinsky had composed, as he told the group that evening:

> The Jew wants to take his place among the foremost of all civilized peoples; wants to possess every bit of splendor and glory and greatness they possess. He wants to have an independent state. . . .
>
> The main principle of the Betar is . . . *Hadar*, a word that includes the meaning of grandeur, magnificence and royalty. The second stanza of your [Betar] hymn says: "Whether you be a beggar or a hobo / You were born a son of kings / Crowned with the crown of David / In daylight or in darkness / Never forget your crown."

Jabotinsky urged his fellow Jews to remember that they were the descendants of kings, entitled to their state in the place it had stood before, encompassing the entire area that the League of Nations had mandated as the Jewish homeland in 1922. He argued that a Jewish state should be the immediate and overriding objective of Zionism, not subjugated to other "isms" such as the socialism of Ben-Gurion's Labor Zionist movement or the slow "organic" approach favored by Weizmann.[48] He did not believe it would be possible to attain a state by diplomacy or by organic growth alone, but that the "mightiest force on earth is a *justa causa*—if you have the courage to fight for it." He advised Jews to "learn to shoot."[49]

At the conclusion of his speech, Jabotinsky spoke about America, and about the siren song for Jewish youth of one of the competing ideologies of the day:

> My last word to you Betarim [Hebrew plural for "members of Betar"] will be about America. This is the country destined to lead the world civilization in the near future. Those of you born in America should always be conscious of this privilege. Those of you who are newcomers must remember that a country which gives the Jew hospitality and treats him decently must be treated by Jews as a partner. . . .
>
> But I also want to say something to your parents. Jewish youth in recent years has been morally estranged from Jewry because the spiritual contents of Jewry seemed to them so poor and gray in comparison to the splendor of the slogans animating the great world movements outside. The Betar ideology is an attempt to clothe the Jewish ideals in a royal splendor of their own. This is one reason that you should help us to recruit your children in the Betar. The other reason is that the only real rival . . . [that] the Betar actually has in Jewish life is Communism.[50]

### ABRAHAM CAHAN ATTACKS JABOTINSKY
### IN THE *JEWISH DAILY FORWARD*

On March 31, 1940, Abraham Cahan, the prominent editor of the *Jewish Daily Forward*—the most influential Jewish publication in America, founded in 1897 as the organ of the Jewish socialist movement, with a nationwide circulation of more than 250,000—published a full-page, harshly negative article, entitled "Vladimir Jabotinsky, What Sort of Person is He?"[51]

Cahan had not attended Jabotinsky's March 19 lecture, but several of his close friends had, and had given him what he called "a very accurate point-by-point report." Cahan proceeded to ridicule the idea of a Jewish army: "Believe me, the whole idea about a Jewish army, which is one of the main points in Jabotinsky's plan, sounds like a story out of *A Thousand and One Nights*." According to Cahan, Jabotinsky was "a man with exceptional abilities," including "oratorical power" and "the talent to write beautifully." But even Jewish nationalists, Cahan asserted, thought his advocacy of a Jewish state as soon as possible was a program built on "wish and wind." Jabotinsky had told his audience at the Manhattan Center that "waiting is a crime"—to which Cahan responded that the "best" he could say about Jabotinsky was that he was "very competent but basically a very naïve person and a great fantasizer."

Cahan focused on the part of Jabotinsky's speech in which he had noted that Weizmann had said a million Jews could be settled in Palestine but that when asked what would become of the other five million at risk, Weizmann had answered: "I don't know."[52] Jabotinsky told his audience he had been astonished by Weizmann's answer and that it was unworthy of a Jewish leader.[53] Cahan defended Weizmann's response, writing that the issue of six million homeless Jews was a question "loaded with incredible difficulties," which he said Jabotinsky refused to consider:

> Such questions depend upon thousands, and perhaps millions, of different circumstances that can change daily. One would have to be a prophet to be able to foretell the character of tomorrow's problems. God Himself wouldn't be able to guess, but with [Jabotinsky] everything is predicted beforehand and as clear as day. Weizmann understands the difficulties that are in the path of settling even one million Jews in Palestine. He understands that this cannot happen at once. You must take into consideration all kinds of problems, and one is forced to be satisfied with plans on accomplishing this little by little. Jabotinsky, however, does not want to know of any difficulties.

Cahan also denigrated Jabotinsky's notion of becoming an "ally" of England and France: to be an "ally," Cahan wrote, "you must first have an independent, well-organized and militarily-equipped state, [but] that doesn't occur to Jabotinsky." Cahan believed "the fate of the Jews is mainly dependent on the outcome of the war," because "[i]f the Allies win, and Hitlerism is destroyed, democracy will develop, and wherever true democracy exists, there is no place for anti-Semitism."

Jabotinsky made no public reply to Cahan. Instead, eleven days later, he sent Cahan a private letter, marked "not for publication."[54] He wrote that Cahan's personal accusations against him were "not for me to discuss," and that he wanted instead to address an "infinitely more essential" subject. He wanted to call Cahan's "special attention" to the economic situation facing the millions of Polish Jews. There were plans to herd them into a single city (Lublin), and their jobs were already being re-assigned to non-Jewish Poles. The crux of their economic position, Jabotinsky wrote, was this:

> The ousted Jew may be sent to Lublin or to the next ditch around the corner—the place does not matter; what matters is the statistical fact that two million mouths will soon be "removed" from Poland's economy and those three to four hundred thousand jobs that kept them alive transferred to Poles.
>
> Should the war last a year or two, these two million mouths may of course die out, in which case there would be no problem left. But if they survive, and then the Allied victory comes and Poland becomes a democracy and equal rights are established— then the situation will be this: two million mouths will return from "Lublin" (or the ditches) and they will be compelled, economically speaking, to claim the 300 to 400 thousand jobs which, in the meantime, for a year or two have already been occupied by Poles. Poland is a poor country, and after a war of this kind it will emerge even poorer.
>
> Please try and calculate what it would mean, in proportion, for America: ten to twelve million newcomers admitted to the USA within one year, or rather all at once, claiming (as of right!) about 2.5 million urban jobs to feed all those mouths. . . .

Jabotinsky wrote that it would be strange if a man of Cahan's intellect failed to understand that a democratic constitution and equal rights could not possibly solve the Jewish problem in Poland:

> It is bad for the Jews not to realize that when Poland is restored and democratized much more than that will be needed to ensure a livelihood for all those ousted Jews. And if you add those who are being ousted from the other countries under Gestapo rule, there will be not two but nearly three million; and if the war spreads to Romania and Hungary—there may be five. . . .
>
> Some people believe, of course, that Socialism—if introduced after the Allied victory—would solve this problem too. Maybe. I doubt it, but maybe. But in this case Jews should be told that an Allied victory without Socialism is no remedy to their plight; and we all know that the Allies have not the slightest intention to allow East-Central Europe to become Socialist if they will win the

war and be the masters of this situation. As things stand and as
they loom on the horizons of realism—even to optimists like you
and I who hope the Allies will win—the only practical remedy
remains the exodus.

Jabotinsky concluded his letter by seeking to elevate the issue above
the personal:

> The question of whether [Cahan] or [Jabotinsky] does or does
> not believe in the possibility of a mass exodus is one which it
> would be useless to argue. I have written this [letter] only to
> point out to you the negative aspect: Allied victory and de-
> mocracy are no help to the most important of Europe's Jewish
> communities.
>
> And, speaking as an old Jewish journalist to another, I still ex-
> pect you to warn America's Jewry of this situation, for it will be
> theirs to deal with its unprecedented burdens, and it is you who
> are the doyen of the Jewish press.[55]

Jabotinsky and Cahan were alike in many ways. Both had been born
in the Pale of Settlement in the nineteenth century and had grown up in
the era of horrific pogroms; both had achieved distinguished careers in
journalism; both had written novels of lasting literary merit.[56] But Cahan
came to America in 1882 at the age of 21, and his lifelong passion was socialism, not Zionism.[57] He established a Yiddish daily that became a national newspaper, influencing the politics of the Jews and the entire labor
movement. In 1917, he disparaged the Balfour Declaration in an editorial
entitled "The 'Victory' of Zionism and the Socialist Enlightenment of the
Masses," asserting that the idea of a Jewish homeland arose from a "messianic hysteria" that "socialist enlightenment" had thankfully cured.[58] He
later traveled to Europe, met Weizmann and others, and became more
sympathetic to Zionism. But even then he remained concerned that the
Zionist movement would endanger equal rights for Jews "in their true
homes"—in Europe.[59] Eventually he grew increasingly supportive of Jewish efforts in Palestine, but his feelings would always remain mixed.

Cahan concluded the 1940 exchange with Jabotinsky by saying that
they looked at things "from two different points of view," and he gave
Jabotinsky a supremely backhanded compliment, saying he was familiar
with Jabotinsky's literary talent and regretted "that you have not devoted

your great gifts to journalism and literature . . . [s]o much so that the part
you play in the Zionist movement is of secondary importance from my
point of view."[60]

History would not look kindly on Cahan's condescension: the Jews of
Poland ultimately suffered a fate far worse than simply losing their jobs
and being sent to Lublin.[61]

*Abraham Cahan, 1937 (Library of Congress,*
*Prints & Photographs Division)*

## THE NAZIS OVERWHELM WESTERN EUROPE,
## AND JABOTINSKY TAKES MORE STEPS
## TO MOBILIZE THE JEWS

On May 10, 1940, after the second German *blitzkrieg* overwhelmed Western Europe, Chamberlain resigned as Britain's prime minister. Churchill
succeeded him and was informed that British forces faced complete annihilation on the continent. He decided to withdraw the entire British Expeditionary Force from France on an emergency basis. Two weeks later,
the evacuation from Dunkirk began. The sole objective was the safe removal of the British and Allied troops, without regard for the arms they
left behind. More than 300,000 soldiers managed to escape, but they had
to abandon 475 tanks, 38,000 vehicles, 12,000 motorcycles, 90,000 rifles,
and 7,000 tons of ammunition.

On June 3, the German Air Force bombed Paris, and German forces prepared to enter the French capital. The next day, Churchill addressed the House of Commons to defend the frantic withdrawal from France: he explained that eight or nine German divisions had nearly surrounded the Belgian, British, and French armies. He had feared "the greatest military disaster in our long history"—the loss of the "whole root and core and brain of the British Army." He acknowledged that "our losses in materiel are enormous" and that the "best of all we had to give had gone to the British Expeditionary Force . . . and that is gone." It was "a colossal military disaster," he said, but Britain would "go on to the end." Then he uttered words remembered to this day:

> We shall defend our Island . . . we shall fight on the beaches, we
> shall fight on the landing grounds, we shall fight in the fields and
> in the streets, we shall fight in the hills; we shall never surrender.

In New York, Jabotinsky responded to the German blitzkrieg and Churchill's assumption of power by sending Churchill a cable on May 12, renewing his offer to organize a Jewish army of 130,000 soldiers, to be "available on all fronts."[62] He sent a letter dated May 17 to the new Secretary of State for Air in Churchill's government, Archibald Sinclair, repeating his offer of a Jewish army that he had discussed with Sinclair months earlier.[63] The same day, Jabotinsky wrote to the Executive Committee of the New Zionist Organization in London, summarizing his efforts, telling members that he could accomplish much "within a few months" if he could awaken America and the American Jewish community.[64]

Jabotinsky sent a cable on May 20 to Weizmann and Ben-Gurion (both of whom were in London), which read:

> Propose to you joining efforts to establish united Jewish front
> for policy and relief. Urge immediate consultations between our-
> selves or deputies.[65]

Jabotinsky also sent identical letters to every major American Jewish leader: Justice Louis D. Brandeis, Rabbi Solomon Goldman, Rabbi Stephen S. Wise, Rabbi David de Sola Pool, Abraham Cahan, Paul Baerwald, Henry Monsky, and Louis Finkelstein. Each letter read:

> In view of a situation so grave, it seems to me that steps should
> be taken here to establish without delay some kind of "Vaad

Olami"—a World Jewish Committee to concentrate the care and defense of the interests of our people in the Eastern hemisphere.

In the face of dangers never yet paralleled in our history, a common platform could now perhaps prove easier to find than ever before.

I am writing in the same sense also to [Brandeis, Goldman, etc.] and I take the liberty to propose, with all the earnestness warranted by the moment, that from among this group of leaders the initiative should come to convene a preliminary consultation for devising ways and means.[66]

On Jabotinsky's file copy of his letter, in the archives of The Jabotinsky Institute in Israel, there is his handwritten note, dated May 21, which reads: "Finkelstein has already politely declined. No different answers expected [from any of the others]."[67] And in fact the other answers—from those who replied—were the same.[68]

JABOTINSKY PLANS A SECOND RALLY
AT THE MANHATTAN CENTER

Most of Jabotinsky's own associates thought the size and enthusiasm of his first rally could not be duplicated, but his assistant, Benzion Netanyahu, urged him to schedule a second one, and Netanyahu proceeded to book the Manhattan Center again for June 19.[69] Jabotinsky decided to make the second rally a broader expression of support for a Jewish army, with an immediate goal of aiding the British. He dispatched Benjamin Akzin to Washington to meet with diplomats, government officials, journalists, and others to inform them of the rally. On May 26, he sent a telegram to Lord Lothian, whom he had long known personally. The telegram consisted of two sentences, saying Akzin was "carrying information of essential importance" and asking the British ambassador to receive him "urgently." The telegram was signed simply "Jabotinsky."[70]

In Washington, Akzin reported that the people most resistant to the idea of a Jewish army were those he sardonically called the "Society for Trembling Jews," who feared that public support would ignite the dreaded accusation of "dual loyalty."[71] Rabbi Stephen S. Wise publicly criticized Jabotinsky's idea of a "mass evacuation" of European Jewry, saying he was afraid it might result in the forcible ejection of Jews from Europe.[72]

On May 28—at the beginning of the calamitous Dunkirk evacuation—
Akzin met with Lord Lothian and presented to him Jabotinsky's plan
to form a Jewish army to fight on the side of the British.[73] On June
5, the Polish ambassador told Akzin he had learned that Lord Lothian
supported the plan and was cabling London for instructions about the
June 19 rally.[74] Three days later, Lord Lothian met with Col. Patterson,
who came away believing Lord Lothian was on their side.[75] On June 12,
Jabotinsky and Lord Lothian themselves met for lunch in New York, and
two days later—a week before the rally—the British embassy sent a letter to Jabotinsky informing him that the British consul-general in New
York would attend.[76]

The American Zionist organizations learned of the British decision and
mobilized to reverse it. On June 17—two days before the rally—they sent
their own delegation to Washington, comprising Rabbi Stephen S. Wise,
Louis Lipsky, and two others, to meet with the British ambassador. After
the meeting, the delegation issued a curt statement to the press: "American
Zionist organizations are not associated with Mr. V. Jabotinsky's activities
in any way."[77] Given the opposition from American Jewish leaders, Lord
Lothian withdrew his consul-general from the rally.

## TWO DAYS IN JUNE, THREE HISTORIC SPEECHES

On June 18 and 19, 1940, three great leaders delivered three historic
speeches: (1) the British prime minister, in an address still admired in Britain, America, and beyond; (2) a French general, in a speech now celebrated
annually by his countrymen; and (3) a Jewish leader, speaking in New York
to a crowd of 5,000 people, in an address largely unknown. The leaders
were Winston Churchill, Charles de Gaulle, and Vladimir Jabotinsky.

Churchill spoke to the House of Commons on June 18, delivering a
thirty-six-minute speech describing what Hitler would soon visit upon
Britain.[78] The mood in the House was subdued.[79] Churchill urged members to forgo recriminations over the humiliating Dunkirk evacuation and
to direct their attention instead to the future. The speech would ultimately
be most remembered for a single sentence—its last:

> Let us therefore brace ourselves to our duties, and so bear our-
> selves that, if the British Empire and its Commonwealth last for
> a thousand years, men will still say, "This was their finest hour."

Churchill's speech was a turning point, rallying the spirit of a people who, at that moment of national disgrace, lacked the military resources to achieve the goals Churchill set forth, but who possessed a national character to which he successfully appealed with his stirring words.[80] Six months earlier, he had told the nation that the decisive factor in war and human history was not material, but spiritual: "above all, a cause which rouses the spontaneous surging of the human spirit in millions of hearts." The June 18 speech expressed that cause for his fellow Britons.

On the same day, Charles de Gaulle, who had escaped from France and flown to London in a small plane, spoke to the citizens of France from a BBC radio studio. He sought to build a resistance against Marshall Pétain's collaborationist government, which was arranging an armistice with Hitler. De Gaulle—a general without an army—argued for fighting on:

> Must we abandon all hope? Is our defeat final and irremediable? To those questions I answer—No! Speaking in full knowledge of the facts, I ask you to believe me when I say that the cause of France is not lost. . . . The destiny of the world is at stake.
>
> I, General de Gaulle, now in London, call on all French officers and men who are at present on British soil, or may be in the future, with or without their arms; I call on all engineers and skilled workmen from the armaments factories who are at present on British soil, or may be in the future, to get in touch with me.

The following day, de Gaulle broadcast a second speech from the BBC studio, calling on the soldiers of France, "wherever you may be," to arise:

> Faced by the bewilderment of my countrymen, by the disintegration of a government in thrall to the enemy, by the fact that the institutions of my country are incapable, at the moment, of functioning, I, General de Gaulle, a French soldier and military leader, realize that I now speak for France.

Posters quoting de Gaulle's words appeared all over London, and on June 22, he gave a third radio address.[81] His first address would eventually be remembered in France on a par with Churchill's "finest hour" speech. June 18 is now a commemorative day in France, celebrated each year.[82] De Gaulle's address, delivered at France's darkest hour, was the beginning of a resistance that would—ultimately and improbably—succeed.

## JABOTINSKY'S JUNE 19, 1940, ADDRESS

The evening after Churchill gave his "finest hour" speech and de Gaulle the first of his "I speak for France" addresses, Jabotinsky took to the stage a second time at the Manhattan Center.

That morning's *New York Times* had reported on the "complete military and political collapse" of France. The German High Command's war communiqué, published in the *Times*, reported that "[y]esterday alone far more than 100,000 prisoners were taken," with "booty" comprising "the complete equipment of numerous French divisions." The *Times* published photographs of Hitler and Mussolini standing together before a cheering crowd in Germany, the *Times* headline reading: "Munich is Gay as Dictators Meet." The dispatch reported that "all Munich [is] riding on the crest of an exhilarating wave," bathed in the "bright sunlight of the thought that this war may now be almost ended." On its front page, the *Times* described the enthusiastic crowd Wendell Willkie had drawn in Brooklyn, where he said America "could best serve the cause of democracy by keeping out of the European war."

France was the sixth nation to fall to Germany in fewer than nine months.[83] An estimated 600,000 French lives had already been lost.[84] Within weeks, Hitler would order the beginning of the Battle of Britain, at a time when Germany commanded at least two million more men-at-arms than Britain's under-equipped and under-trained forces.[85] The British were an embattled people, whose leaders for years had left them unprepared for the German assault. The French were now living under a Nazi-controlled regime. But the British had a leader of extraordinary eloquence—whose words often drew inspiration from the Bible—and the French had an eloquent general addressing his countrymen, seeking to build a military force for his defeated nation. The Poles were reconstituting their own vanquished military to recover their land.

As for the European Jews, an almost unimaginable fate awaited them—for which they had neither a prime minister nor a general, much less a military to reconstitute. But they too had a leader of extraordinary eloquence, who had already organized a significant Jewish military force during World War I, and who now wanted them to join the fight again.

Jabotinsky called his June 19 presentation "The Second World War and a Jewish Army."[86] To generate maximum interest, he held a press conference at the Commodore Hotel, telling reporters that, just as he had felt in 1916 that Jews must participate in World War I on Britain's side, he felt even more strongly now that the Jews must join the war, since they were the explicit targets of the Nazi barbarism: "It is up to us to offer sacrifice and help at least as much, if not more, than any other people." He told the press he hoped "to get soon the Allied recognition of a co-belligerent Jewish Army, available on all fronts"—a force he thought could quickly exceed 100,000 men, recruited from the hundreds of thousands of refugees and other stateless Jews, and from the Jews of Palestine, where men were "ready to defend their own homeland and the Allied cause in the Middle East," as well as from volunteers in neutral countries. And he thought a Jewish army would be of "tremendous moral significance":

> The example of Jews, long known as a most peaceful of peoples, volunteering in large numbers to fight for truth and sacrifice their lives, will inspire humanity to ever greater sacrifices at the present critical hour. It will easily upset the ridiculous whispering campaign still going on to the effect that the Jews want all others to fight in their interest, but they themselves remain at home.
>
> . . . In the first World War, where the very idea of Jewish military units was unfamiliar and strange, where both the Allied governments and Jewish opinion did still oppose it, 15,000 fighting Jews were easily got together from Palestine, England, the United States, Canada, and Argentine. This time, where the stakes are greater and the responsibility heavier, I am hopeful that progress will be both speedier and greater."[87]

More than 4,000 people arrived at the Manhattan Center that evening, filling the huge hall again beyond its stated capacity, with a standing-room-only crowd pressed against the walls. The closest thing the Jews had to a military leader in 1940 warned his audience not to "forecast historical events on the basis of last week's headlines," because while the impending attack on Britain would be fierce:

> [T]he Channel, after all, is much more of a barrier than the river Somme, and if there will be an invasion it will not be millions of men nor thousands of heavy tanks. The figures are bound to be on a much smaller scale. And that means that foreign help, to be effective, need not wait till millions of soldiers can be sent over.

This meant, Jabotinsky continued, that "every division may now prove decisive," and that a Jewish army could play an important role:

> [T]here are strong chances that the hostilities are to continue—and if so, there is still time ahead of us for changes to come in; there are still immense probabilities for quite decisive changes. One need not name them: enough to say that God's box of tricks is by far not emptied yet. This is why my belief in the ultimate defeat of the rattlesnake is not shattered—provided we all remember the principle by which all great nations live and without which they die, the principle which is the secret of our own Jewish people's survival through all these centuries of torture: No Surrender.

This time, Jabotinsky said, what was required was not merely a Jewish Legion but an entire Jewish army, with a status like the Polish army-in-exile, to "signify that the Jewish people choose a cloudy day to renew its demand for recognition as a belligerent on the side of a good cause." He wanted not only to see the "giant rattlesnake destroyed," but to see it destroyed "with our help." Then he told of things he said had not been reported in the European press:

> American readers . . . would be astonished at the almost complete silence of some among the most important London and Paris organs with regard to the fate of Polish Jewry during the earlier months of the war. Those were the months when that section of our people was made to pay, in actual human suffering, in tears and hunger and massacre, much more even than the Poles themselves: yet it was distinctly felt that, in certain influential Western circles, there was a tendency to avoid acknowledging the Jews even as fellow-sufferers.

Jabotinsky informed his audience that there was in England and France a "moral underworld" that called the conflict a "Jewish war" and that saw no harm in the Nazi murder of the Jews:

> It is most regrettable that the enlightened sections of Allied society, instead of openly combating this kind of idiocy, should have tried pandering to it by hushing up the Jewish groan. The result is that the Jewish fellow-sufferer is denied even the last and

most elementary privilege of a sufferer: the privilege of having his losses registered in fair and proper perspective, so that he may at least hope, when the day comes for a general redress, for restoration and retribution, to present his claims on equal terms with other claimants.

But what was even more troubling to Jabotinsky was the silence of the Allied leaders. He did not castigate them by name, but rather challenged the thinking behind their silence:

> [I do] not wish to pillory these leaders as callous, for many . . . would probably repudiate, with sincere indignation, any attempt to construe their silence as unfriendly; they would insist that the demand for solution of the Jewish problem was omitted in their statements of war aims simply because such things obviously go without saying, etc. They ought to be told what Talleyrand once replied to a diplomat who used the same argument . . . "Si çela va sans le dire, çela ira mieux en le disant"—"if it goes without saying, it will go still better by being said."

Jabotinsky then returned to his major theme—that Jews could not simply stand by and watch, because "we want to be listed as a people among those that crushed the rattlesnake":

> There is stuff for well over 100,000 Jewish soldiers even without counting American Jews. . . . [H]ad our request for a Jewish Army had been granted early in the war when we first submitted it to the Allies, that source alone would have yielded three to four divisions. Even now it can yield two at least.

Noting that it had taken many months during World War I to form the Jewish Legion, Jabotinsky said that this time it would be much faster, and "everything [will] be righted again if only people will stick to that principle: *No surrender whatever the odds*." Jabotinsky ended by acknowledging the presence on the stage behind him of the Czech representative—and the absence of the French and British ones.[88] He promised that "the gallant spokesman of the Czechoslovak nation, trapped because she trusted, will see Masaryk's republic free again"; that "those Frenchmen who felt too shy to join us here will also live to see a different day"; and that England—the other "bashful absentee on this platform"—should take hope, because there was within the American public a sentiment not reported by the press:

> There were periods—there still are, there still will be in the months before us—when the impression is that England's plight leaves America only superficially rippled, while the basic attitude of this mighty nation is expressed in the words, "The Yanks are not coming." As an observer and a reporter, I contest this impression . . . [I would say:] "Mr. Churchill, they are coming!" But "they" will be delayed. It takes long to equip a battleship; smaller craft can be delivered quicker. I want the Jews "coming" at once.

In its report the next day, *The New York Times* quoted further from Jabotinsky's speech:

> This is the time for blunt speaking. I challenge the Jews, wherever they are still free, to demand the right of fighting the giant rattlesnake . . . as a Jewish Army. Some shout that we only want others to fight, some whisper that a Jew only makes a good soldier when squeezed in between Gentile comrades. I challenge the Jewish youth to give them the lie.

### JABOTINSKY ASKS JEWS FOR ARMY OF 100,000

#### Zionist Leader Calls for Men to Fight as Unit—4,000 Hear Plea

More than 4,000 persons assembled in the Manhattan Center, Thirty-fourth Street and Eighth Avenue, last night and heard Vladimir Jabotinsky, world president of the New Zionist Organization, outline his plan for a Jewish army of at least 100,000 men, recruited from all over the world, to assist the Allies in the task of defeating Germany.

He predicted that there would be no real peace between France and Germany and that France, with her navy and air force, would continue to fight side by side with England. He said that the Jewish army now being organized would fight wherever necessary under British command and would have the same status as the Polish Army.

Colonel John Henry Patterson,

The *Times* also quoted Col. Patterson's words at the Manhattan Center program:

> If I were a Jew, nothing would give me greater pleasure than to show the German criminals that the Jews of today are capable of fighting just as their forefathers were when in seven years of bitter warfare they shook the mighty Roman Empire to its very foundations.

Jabotinsky's second Manhattan Center address struck a nerve.[89] It received widespread coverage well beyond New York. Offers to serve in a Jewish army poured in to the American offices of the New Zionist Organization; the Canadian foreign ministry offered training camps; Benjamin Akzin enlisted the head of the Polish army-in-exile to press the British to permit a Jewish army; British Labor leader Clement Attlee said he would recommend it to the British cabinet. The NZO launched an organization to raise funds and conduct efforts in communities across the country.[90]

Jabotinsky had set forth a goal with a fervor and an eloquence that touched the hearts and minds of American Jews. Two days after the rally, he wrote to Lord Lothian, seeking to clarify his proposal for a Jewish army. First, he wrote, it would *not* be conditioned on the repeal of the British White Paper: "The reasonable course during the [current] crisis," Jabotinsky wrote, "is to leave controversial matters in suspense." Second, the

*Jabotinsky speaking at the Manhattan Center, in New York City, June 19, 1940*

Jewish army would *not* be raised from America: "In all our publications and negotiations we emphasize that the recruits are to be Palestinians, refugees and other volunteers, most of them probably non-naturalized emigrants; that recruiting offices and training camps would be in Canada and other allied lands."

Jabotinsky closed his letter by emphasizing that the Manhattan Center event had demonstrated that the Jewish army proposal had "caught on with the imagination of Jews and non-Jews, which after all is the main element of final success." He acknowledged nevertheless the difficulties of forming a Jewish army—including one he had run into before:

> I understand from the press that some of the difficulties arise
> from a faint-heartedness of a routine-bound Jewish leadership
> rather than from the British Government. Just as in 1916.[91]

On July 12, Jabotinsky published an article in *The Jewish Standard* entitled "The A.B.C. of the Jewish Army," in which he addressed "some of the questions facing the New Zionist delegation in the United States in their campaign for the creation of a Jewish Army."[92] He described the World War I Jewish Legion and summarized his proposal for an army of between 100,000 and 200,000, which he thought could be achieved "without counting the British Jews, the French Jews, and the American Jews." Recruits would come from Palestine (where he estimated 80,000 were available) and from "No Man's Land"—a term "unknown to geography, but in our days its meaning is so clear":

> No Man's Land, for us, is wherever Jewish refugees crowd, from
> Shanghai to Vilna and to the Danube, now also with the recent
> addition of many towns in France, and England where fugitives
> from Belgium and Holland have found temporary shelter; it in-
> cludes many of those whom British and French authorities call
> "enemy aliens" and keep in concentration camps. . . . There is
> manpower for several Jewish divisions scattered in No Man's
> Land; the appeal of a Jewish Army will reach them all. . . .

At the end of July, Jabotinsky decided to return to England, where he hoped to be re-united with his wife and to continue his efforts to form a Jewish army under British command.[93] On August 2, he signed a contract to publish a book on the Jewish problems that would follow the war.[94] On August 3, the *Times* reported that de Gaulle had been stripped

*Jabotinsky meeting Betar campers on Saturday, August 3, 1940, in Hunter, New York*

of his rank and condemned to death by the French collaborationist government because of his BBC radio addresses. In another article, the *Times*
reported that 20,000 Canadian troops had arrived in Britain—including
several hundred American volunteers. That evening, Jabotinsky traveled
128 miles north of New York City to the Catskill Mountains village of
Hunter, New York, to visit the Betar camp there. He had already visited
it once before, in July, but he wanted to go a second time.

## MONDAY MORNING, AUGUST 5, 1940

On Monday morning, August 5, 1940, *The New York Times* presented
its readers with front-page stories on three speeches. The first was by retired Gen. John J. Pershing, commander of the American forces in World
War I, who told his fellow citizens "it would be absolute folly even to
consider sending another expeditionary force" to Europe but supported
giving Britain some "over-age destroyers which are left from the days of
the World War." The second was a radio address by the Secretary of the
Navy, Frank Knox, supporting legislation for a draft, which was facing a
possible filibuster. He sought to rebut what he noted "many people" were
saying: "that military training is a step toward fascism, that it is against
all American traditions, that it would make us a militaristic nation." The

third was Charles Lindbergh's address in Chicago to 40,000 people at a rally of the "Citizens Committee to Keep America Out of War." Lindbergh called for cooperation with Germany if the Nazis won the war.[95] The *Times* printed the entire text of Lindbergh's speech:

## Text of Col. Lindbergh's Speech Appealing for Peace Plea to Europe

As readers continued reading through the *Times* that morning, they came to a page devoted to "Excerpts from Yesterday's Sermons"—a weekly feature with homilies typified by the one given by a guest pastor at Norman Vincent Peale's Marble Collegiate Church on Fifth Avenue, one of the oldest continuous Protestant congregations in North America, who "spoke in praise of [France's collaborationist Prime Minister] Marshal Petain, chief of the French State, saying that he had made no excuses for the defeat of his nation but instead had been thankful that there were many sacrificial years ahead to be used in France's reconstruction."

There were also lists that morning of new and best-selling books, including one by the *Times'* foreign correspondent, Otto D. Tolischus—a "close-up study of Hitler and his habits," which told, in the words of the *Times*, "the whole story of National Socialism as a political creed, a system of power dynamics, a military machine and a revolutionary force."

As readers reached page 13, they found a photograph and an article extending the full length of the page, with a headline that—at least for Jewish readers—was profoundly shocking:

# JABOTINSKY DEAD; LED NEW ZIONISTS

**Head of Revisionist Group Was Chief of Jewish Legion in Palestine During War**

---

**STRICKEN IN HUNTER, N. Y.**

---

**Succumbs in Youth Camp at 59 —Tried to Raise Army Here to Fight Italy and Reich**

**VLADIMIR JABOTINSKY**

Vladimir Jabotinsky, author, lecturer and world leader of the New Zionist Organization, died on Saturday night in the youth camp of the Zionist group at Hunter, N. Y., of a heart attack, according to word received here yesterday. He was 59 years old.

Mr. Jabotinsky, who had been living at 10 West Seventy-fourth Street since his arrival in this country from London on March 13, headed the Jewish Legion in Palestine during the World War. In recent weeks he had been working on a plan to raise a similar army to fight against Italy and Germany, and also had been conducting a drive for mass emigration of Jews to Palestine from Eastern and Central Europe.

He leaves a widow, Anna, who is in London, and a son, Eri, who is in prison in Palestine because of his nationalistic activities in behalf of the Jewish population of that country.

**Spoke to 5,000 Here**

Vladimir Jabotinsky, author, lecturer and world leader of the New Zionist Organization, died on Saturday night in the youth camp of the Zionist group at Hunter, N.Y., of a heart attack, according to word received here yesterday. He was 59 years old. Mr. Jabotinsky . . . headed the Jewish Legion in Palestine during the World War. In recent weeks he had been working on a plan to raise a similar army to fight against Italy and Germany, and also had been conducting a drive for mass emigration of Jews to Palestine from Eastern and Central Europe. . . . [He] had the multiple appeal of poet, soldier, orator and personal fire and magnetism. . . .

The *Times* reported that the funeral services for Jabotinsky would be held the following day at the Gramercy Park Memorial Chapel on Second Avenue in Manhattan.

## THE OUTPOURING AT JABOTINSKY'S FUNERAL

The morning of Jabotinsky's funeral, the *Times* carried a one-paragraph notice at the bottom of its Obituary page.

The *Jewish Daily Forward* carried a gracious editorial, written by Abraham Cahan himself, calling Jabotinsky's death "a national catastrophe."[96] But Cahan's staff—still adamant in their opposition to Jabotinsky's views—refused to cover the funeral.

**JABOTINSKY RITES TODAY**

**Veterans' Organizations to Take Part in Services for Zionist**

Funeral services for Vladimir Jabotinsky, leader of the New Zionist Organization who died Saturday, will be held at noon today at the Gramercy Park Memorial Chapel, 152 Second Avenue. Three rabbis, Morris M. Rose, N. Telushkin and H. F. Epstein, will officiate and a group of cantors will assist in the services.

Later that day, outside the Gramercy Park Chapel funeral hall, 12,000 people stood in the August heat, which reached 87 degrees in the shade. Inside the chapel, the 750 invitees sat without air-conditioning, including prominent Jewish leaders, as well as representatives of the British, Polish, and Czech consulates. Three rabbis officiated; 200 cantors chanted.[97] In accordance with Jabotinsky's wishes, as set forth in his will, the services followed the precedent of Herzl's 1904 funeral: there were no speeches, eulogies, or instrumental music.

The *Times* reported that the coffin, draped with a Zionist flag, was carried by an honor guard of fifty Betar youth, and that "many men and women wept as Martin Winnick, national bugler of the Jewish War Veterans, sounded taps." According to the *Times*, it was "one of the largest funerals on the East Side," with a "throng of 25,000 [that] followed the cortege or lined the route." Fifty patrolmen and five sergeants from the New York City Police were deployed to control the crowd. All traffic was stopped on lower Second Avenue, as the hearse and honor guard made its way north to 14th Street, then east to First Avenue and back to Second Avenue, and finally, as the *Times* reported:

# TRIBUTE BY 12,000 PAID JABOTINSKY

**They Stand Outside Chapel in Second Ave. During Funeral of Noted Zionist Leader**

**200 CANTORS SING RITUAL**

**Thousands Line Streets When Cortege Passes Through East Side After Service**

As more than 12,000 persons stood out in the street, a funeral service was held yesterday for Vladimir Jabotinsky, author, soldier and world leader of the New Zionist

Proceeding south on Second Avenue, where Jewish theatres and homes had hung out mourning drapes, the cortege stopped between Tenth and Ninth Streets in front of the funeral chapel, where the cantors sang a Jewish mourning song and the Jewish national anthem.

At Houston Street and Second Avenue, a salute of honor was given . . . and then a motorcade of fifty cars and eight buses left for the New Montefiore Cemetery [on Long Island] where a military service was held. Burial was in the cemetery's Nordau Circle.

*The crowd in front of the Second Avenue Chapel
for Jabotinsky's funeral*

*Crowds on both sides of Second Avenue awaiting the Jabotinsky funeral cortege*

*New Yorkers standing ten-deep at other locations along the cortege route*

## WEIZMANN AND BEN-GURION AT
## THE LONDON MEMORIAL SERVICE

The following day, the Jewish Agency held a memorial service for Jabotinsky in London, where both Weizmann and Ben-Gurion delivered eulogies. Ben-Gurion "said the great tragedy of Jabotinsky, as well as the Zionist movement, was that while he clearly saw the end, he failed to see the means to this end"—and "[t]his failure, I am afraid, largely destroyed a great career in Zionism."[98] Ben-Gurion's denigration alluded to Jabotinsky's withdrawal of his Revisionist Party from the Zionist Organization in 1935, and his founding of the New Zionist Organization, with its goal of establishing a Jewish state on both sides of the Jordan River as soon as possible. That goal had put Jabotinsky at odds with the more limited goals of Weizmann and Ben-Gurion, who did not clearly formulate a demand for a state until 1942.

For his part, Weizmann dwelled on his long relationship with Jabotinsky, going back to their joint efforts in 1916–17 to form the Jewish Legion. He said Jabotinsky had always been motivated by "one great idea, to bring about a solution of the Jewish problem as quickly as possible":

> The speed with which he wanted to achieve such a solution set Jabotinsky apart, Dr. Weizmann said. "History will judge whether Jabotinsky or the Zionist Organization was right," Dr. Weizmann said.
>
> "Jabotinsky was burned up by a sacred fire. In his opinion we had only a limited time in which our program could be realized. This may and may not be so. Factors and events independent of the desires of the Jewish people forced us to follow a path which may be difficult and above all slow."[99]

Weizmann implicitly rejected Jabotinsky's "opinion" that "we had only a limited time." Weizmann's remarks suggested he believed history would judge Jabotinsky wrong about the speed necessary to solve the Jewish problem, and would criticize what Weizmann believed was Jabotinsky's failure to appreciate that the process would be difficult—"and above all slow."[100]

There was, however, eventually no benefit—for most of the 7.7 million Jews then living in the Zone of Jewish Distress—from a Zionism resigned to a path "above all slow." Like Jabotinsky, six million of them would not live to see a Jewish state.

## THE WORLDWIDE JEWISH REACTION
## TO JABOTINSKY'S DEATH

Word of Jabotinsky's death stunned his followers around the world. His American colleagues were distraught.[101] A 15-year-old boy at the Betar camp in Hunter, New York, vividly recalled—in an interview conducted more than seventy years later—the reaction there the following day: "We were dumbfounded; we didn't think the movement could go on."[102] The boy's name was Moshe Arens, and he later served as foreign minister of the State of Israel and as its ambassador to the United States.[103] In 1940, Menachem Begin, later the Prime Minister of the State of Israel, was the 27-year-old head of the Polish Betar. He later recalled Jabotinsky's death as coming at a time when "catastrophe followed catastrophe" in Poland, and that:

> [I]n the midst of all these catastrophes, both private and na-
> tional, that befell humanity at large, Ze'ev Jabotinsky died. I am
> certain that if I filled whole pages I could not even attempt to ex-
> plain what the death of Rosh Betar [Head of Betar] meant to me.
> A stranger will not understand. The word "stranger" in this spe-

*Menachem Begin, in lower left corner, with Jabotinsky in Poland in 1939*

cial instance also includes some of my own people. . . . I felt that
the bearer of hope was gone, never to return; and with him—
perhaps never to return—hope itself.[104]

Begin recalled how his followers organized "all-night vigils . . . in
Vilna, Kovno and other Lithuanian towns to pay homage to the memory
of Ze'ev Jabotinsky," and "[w]e said a prayer and sang the song of *Rosh
Betar* . . . of faith that out of the 'decay and ashes' Israel would rise again."
Arthur Koestler, who had headed Jabotinsky's organization in Berlin
during the 1920s, and, in 1940, published *Darkness at Noon*, his powerful
anti-Stalinist novel, learned of Jabotinsky's death from a brief notice in a
local newspaper in Paris, where he was then living.[105] In his diary, Koestler wrote:

> Jabo is dead. Notice in Depeche de Toulouse: "Vichy, August 7th.
> M. Vladimir Jabotinsky, journalist and author, Chairman of the
> New Zionist Organization, died in New York at the age of fifty-
> nine. He had gone to America for the purpose of raising a Jewish
> Legion which was to fight on the side of England."
>
> Exit one of the great tragic figures of this century, unnoticed.
> Adored hero of the Jewish masses in Russia and Poland; creator
> of the first Jewish legion which helped conquer Palestine: sen-
> tenced to fifteen years hard labor for organizing Jewish resistance
> against Arab pogroms in Jerusalem; translated Dante and Shake-
> speare into modern Hebrew; wrote and spoke eight languages;
> most fascinating orator I ever heard. . . . One great friend less—
> there are not many left, at liberty, undamaged.[106]

In Palestine, there was a general work stoppage, while enormous crowds
gathered in the streets. Hebrew newspapers published editions bordered
in black.[107] In an editorial, *Haaretz* said that the "whole house of Israel
mourns the death of a proud, brave and highly-gifted son" and that "the
Zionist movement's history cannot be written without him."[108] *HaBoker*
editorialized that, "An eagle has fallen from the skies."[109] The New Zionist
Organization proclaimed a day of mourning throughout South America;
in Montevideo, the capital of Uruguay, 5,000 attended a memorial at the
Jewish Community House.[110]

On August 9, former British Prime Minister David Lloyd George wrote
that Jabotinsky was a "stout-hearted Jewish warrior worthy of the tradi-

*Kupat Holim nurses march in the Tel Aviv memorial procession for Jabotinsky,*
*August 6, 1940*

tions of the race which bred the Maccabees' spirit," and he predicted that
Jabotinsky's inspiration would "live on to nerve the forces of World Jewry
for the fight which is theirs as much as ours."[111]

In America, Rabbi Stephen S. Wise composed a tribute to Jabotinsky,
published in *OPINION—A Journal of Jewish Life and Letters,* a national
Jewish publication that Wise edited.[112] Like Ben-Gurion, Wise viewed
Jabotinsky as a person who had effectively exiled himself by leaving the
established Zionist Organization. In his monthly column, entitled "As I
See It," Wise wrote:

> The death of Vladimir Jabotinsky means a great sorrow to the
> Jewish world, the more so since those who differed from him never
> ceased to hope that someday the barriers would fall and he would
> find his way home again. . . . The current World War should have
> brought him to an unchallenging and unchallenged place beside
> the leadership of the Zionist movement. Alas, that it was not to be,
> that pride of will or contempt for caution or inhospitality and un-
> forbearance of antagonists kept him outside the gates!

Wise recognized, however, that Jabotinsky had been "electric in power,
dazzling in brilliance"—and that he ranked among the Jewish greats of
the century:

He was not only one of the most eloquent men of his time—and that in many tongues—but he was one of the bravest of men in setting out to make real his ideal. . . . He was one of the few men who, like Herzl and Brandeis, become legendary whilst yet they live.

Jabotinsky had generated a passionate response from American Jews. His efforts were even more remarkable because he had kept his private anxieties hidden from public view. In his final weeks, he appeared tired and gray to his colleagues, depressed at developments in Europe and Palestine, lonely in America without his wife, and concerned about his son in Palestine.[113] All summer he had worried about Joanna facing a Nazi assault on London without him; he had written to Lord Lothian seeking his help to obtain a visa for her to come to America, but his efforts had not succeeded: in August, she was still alone in London. His son Eri, 30, was a Betar leader in Palestine, and had been arrested by the British in February 1940 for assisting 2,000 Jews aboard the *SS Sakarya* to enter Palestine illegally. Six months later, on the day Jabotinsky died, he was still in prison.[114]

Jabotinsky's last words at the Betar camp were, "I am so tired, I am so tired."[115] He had worked for Zionism until the final moment of his life.

*Vladimir, Joanna, and Eri Jabotinsky, 1921*

In the autumn of 1940, with Weizmann in London and Jabotinsky tragically dead, it would fall to David Ben-Gurion—at age 53, the youngest of the three Zionist leaders—to travel to the United States, in the third mission of the year, seeking to generate support for a Jewish army, with the fate of the Jews of Europe growing increasingly dire.

# DAVID BEN-GURION

*October 1940–January 1941*

*During his trip to America, David Ben-Gurion received a letter referring to news reports of Britain's need for vessels and a British offer to pay the United States $3 million for twenty-six merchant ships. The letter writer suggested that "the Jewish People purchase these ships, and loan them to England for the duration of the war."[1]*

*Ben-Gurion replied, "Great historic problems cannot be solved merely with funds, and no amount of money we may collect for England will have any effect on our fate as a nation. The desired British victory will be won by fighting, and if we want to make this victory our own we must do our part in that fighting."[2]*

Six weeks after the memorial service for Jabotinsky in London, David Ben-Gurion left England for America.

He had moved to London from Palestine in May 1940, at Weizmann's invitation, and he now wrote to his wife, Paula—whom he had left in Palestine with their three children—that he would next travel to the United States. He told her, "I want to see with my own eyes what we can expect from America in wartime . . . I want to know the extent of the contribution America's Jews are prepared to make for the life of their own people."[3]

He would remain in America for more than four months. As with the visits of Weizmann and Jabotinsky, the trip would reveal a great deal not only about the Jews in America, but about their Zionist visitor as well.

The account that follows draws on the diary Ben-Gurion kept during his trip, written in Hebrew and translated into English for the first time for this book, as well as other contemporaneous documents from the trip, most of them previously unpublished.[4]

## BEN-GURION'S EARLY YEARS AND EMIGRATION TO PALESTINE

Ben-Gurion emigrated to Palestine in 1906, at the age of 19, when the Jewish population was 55,000. He was born David Gruen in 1886 in Plonsk, a small town in Western Russia with fewer than 8,000 inhabitants, thirty-six miles from Warsaw, where the local Jews worked selling small crafts, engaging in the timber trade, and living on farm produce. Although the town had four synagogues, it lacked a high school. His grandfather had read stories from the Bible to him each night, and Ben-Gurion would later boast that he had been born a Zionist.[5]

On the day in 1942 that his father died, Ben-Gurion wrote a long letter to his wife and children, reminiscing about his father, who had raised him alone after Ben-Gurion's mother had died when he was 11:

> From him I obtained my love for the Jewish people, the Land of Israel, the Hebrew language. In our small house in Plonsk, at the end of the town, next to the place Zion members used to meet when I was a child; and when Herzl's Zionist movement came into being, our home became the focal point of the Zionists in our town.
>
> After the Kishinev pogrom we young boys in Plonsk secretly founded a self-defense group and acquired some arms. I was the head of the group, and I hid the arms in our house. My father knew about this, but he didn't interfere with me, although he knew full well the danger to him and his position in the town if the guns were discovered.[6]

Ben-Gurion's father wanted him to study at a high school and graduate from a university, and Ben-Gurion recalled that "he was sorry when I told him I had decided to emigrate to Palestine in order to become a worker." His father was also disturbed that Ben-Gurion adopted socialism in addition to Zionism, but he did not attempt to argue with his headstrong son, nor to prevent him from leaving Plonsk.

On September 7, 1906, Ben-Gurion watched excitedly as his ship approached the harbor in the land of his ancestors. After landing in Jaffa, his elation turned to disgust. On seeing the desolate place, his first words were: "This is worse than Plonsk!"[7]

It was a reaction like that of many young Zionists on encountering the harsh realities of Palestine. But Ben-Gurion traveled on from Jaffa, went to work on a kibbutz, became involved in the socialist movement, helped establish trade unions and a national labor federation (the *Histadrut*), and would eventually become its representative in the Zionist Organization. At the outbreak of World War I, he believed—in contrast to Jabotinsky— that the Jews in Palestine should remain loyal to the Ottoman Empire, to avoid accusations of dual loyalty if Turkey emerged victorious. But he eventually came to support Britain, and in 1918, he served in Jabotinsky's Jewish Legion.

Ben-Gurion approached Zionism from a different perspective than either Weizmann or Jabotinsky. Unlike them, he never attended a univer-

*David Ben-Gurion in his Jewish Legion
uniform, 1918*

sity; he had spent his twenties as a worker in a hard land, without the re-
finements, exposure to European intellectuals, or higher education of the
other two.[8] He was mainly a self-educated man, a voracious reader who
eventually taught himself Greek in order to read the classics in the original. During his American trip in 1940, he spent days in bookshops pur-
chasing books in Greek, listing all the titles in his diary.[9]

The difference between Weizmann and Ben-Gurion was especially
stark. Weizmann was tall and dignified, spoke the understated language of the British upper class, and was infinitely patient in navigat-
ing the complex relationship between the British and the Jews. He op-
erated through personal relationships with British officials—in meetings
from which he often excluded other Zionist leaders, particularly David
Ben-Gurion.

Ben-Gurion, by contrast, was five feet tall, an impatient and pugna-
cious man who lacked Weizmann's sophisticated manner, and who combined dogmatic views with a tendency to take to his tent when others disagreed with him. In the words of the Israeli author, Amos Oz, Ben-Gurion
on the day he arrived in Palestine at age 19 was the person he "would re-

main all his life: a secular Jewish nationalist who combined Jewish Messianic visions with socialist ideals, a man with a fierce ambition for leadership, extraordinary tactical-political skills and a sarcastic edge rather than a sense of humor."[10] Ben-Gurion's two heroes were Theodor Herzl and Vladimir Lenin: he believed that an ideal leader would combine the qualities of both.[11]

In 1940, Ben-Gurion was the chairman of the Jewish Agency Executive (the leadership group that ran the Jewish Agency). He assumed that position in 1935, after heading the Labor Zionist movement from 1920 to 1935.[12] He dominated the nascent politics of the *Yishuv* (the Jewish community in Palestine); indeed, he "tyrannized" it, as even a sympathetic biographer noted.[13] He often threatened to resign from the Zionist leadership when his policies were not adopted. In 1938 alone, he threatened resignation no fewer than three times, and in 1939, the number of his ultimatums actually increased.[14]

Given their sharply contrasting natures, Weizmann and Ben-Gurion were, in the understated observation of Ben-Gurion's principal biographer, Shabtai Teveth, "not made to work in tandem."[15] Ben-Gurion's single-minded, stubborn self-confidence would lead to a break with Weizmann in 1940 and to Ben-Gurion's trip to America.

### BEN-GURION AND THE EVENTS IN PALESTINE IN 1939

Ben-Gurion's move to London in May 1940 resulted from events in Palestine after the issuance of the 1939 British White Paper—and from another of Ben-Gurion's resignations after his colleagues refused to follow his lead in responding to it. On May 23, 1939, Ben-Gurion told *The New York Times* in Palestine that the Jewish community there would fight Britain's new policy:

> The Jews who came to this country on the strength of British pledges that it would be a national home will suddenly find themselves . . . in a kind of ghetto. . . . [The British government] might have been misled by [their] Palestine administration that the Jews would take things lying down, but they won't.
>
> Anyone aware of the position of the Jews in Eastern and Central Europe today will not for one moment believe that they will cease coming to their homeland because some law terms it

illegal. . . . Jews who must choose between utter extinction and immigration to Palestine under conditions called illegal naturally will not waver for a moment in their choice.

Ben-Gurion warned that the new British White Paper, which would result in Arab rule over the Jews, could not be implemented without violence:

Neither will the imposition of Arab rule over the Jews in Palestine . . . be brought about without British bayonets. . . . The Jews will not have a Hitler regime in a country that was internationally pledged to them as a national home, whatever price they will have to pay for their opposition.

Later that week, Jewish demonstrators clashed with British police in Jerusalem, leaving 135 Jews injured, one British policeman dead, and another five officers injured, as the police faced 5,000 demonstrators in a three-hour battle. In Tel Aviv, a massive procession walked to the city's stadium for a three-hour meeting, chanting: "My heart for my people; my blood for my country; the Bible is our mandate; England cannot annul it." At the stadium, the mass meeting adopted this declaration:

[T]he betrayal policy [of the White Paper] will never materialize. Palestine Jewry will fight it with all its forces. . . . No power in the world can deter the natural right of our people to come home . . . and every Jew in Palestine will assist [Jews coming to Palestine] in opening the gates to them.

For their part, the Arab leaders in Palestine also rejected the new British policy, even though it was extraordinarily favorable to them. They refused to accept *any* Jewish immigration whatsoever; they demanded not merely its reduction to zero over five years, but also its immediate and complete cessation. They objected to giving Jews any right to live in Palestine, even as a one-third minority, and they demanded a definite date for the conversion of Palestine into an Arab state. Having rejected the Peel Commission's 1937 two-state proposal, with its generous borders for an Arab state covering most of Palestine, the Arabs now rejected even a single state under their control, if Jews were permitted to live in it.

After adopting the White Paper, the British now faced implacable opposition from both the Arabs and the Jews of Palestine.

BEN-GURION'S ACTIONS AGAINST THE WHITE PAPER

In November 1939, Ben-Gurion traveled to London for eight days to join an effort to have the British "tear up the decree" of the White Paper. During the course of this brief visit, he lost patience with Weizmann for not keeping him informed of his meetings with members of the British government.[16] The efforts to reverse the White Paper in the following months failed, and on February 28, 1940, the British issued new land regulations to implement their restrictions on Jewish immigration and land purchases.[17] In Palestine, Ben-Gurion circulated a statement castigating the regulations: "even land which the Arabs have no means of cultivating . . . is now being withheld from the Jews on the pretext of a shortage of land . . . [the regulations] confine [the Jews] to a Pale of Settlement in the country that is their national home."[18]

Ben-Gurion also wrote a letter to the British government and released it to newspapers throughout Palestine. Its message became a rallying cry for the Jews there: "The Jewish people will not submit to the conversion of the Jewish National Home into a ghetto."

> The effect of these regulations is that no Jew may acquire in Palestine a plot of land, a building, or a tree, or any rights in water, except in towns and in a very small part of the country. . . . They not only violate the terms of the Mandate but completely nullify its primary purpose. . . .
>
> [T]his attempt to frustrate the age-old aspirations of the Jewish people . . . is made at a time when millions of Jews are being mercilessly persecuted by a cruel enemy. This blow is being inflicted by the government of a great nation, which undertook to restore the Jewish people to their National Home.[19]

The day the letter was published, Jewish demonstrations swept through Palestine, lasting seven days. Three Jews were killed in clashes with the British. Ben-Gurion wanted the "disorder" in Palestine to continue until the British annulled their regulations, and he announced on February 29 his resignation as chairman of the Jewish Agency Executive because he could no longer work with the British:

> With the outbreak of the war I said that the war of England and France against the Nazis was our war too, and that we must lend

England and its army all the assistance that we, as Jews, can give
. . . But yesterday something happened, and we can no longer
live and act as we have done up till now. As of yesterday a Jewish ghetto was set up in Palestine. As of yesterday we Jews have
been put, as the Czechs were, in a "protectorate." . . . I cannot be
true to myself and continue holding this office, so I am stepping
down.[20]

Ben-Gurion's colleagues in Palestine refused to accept his resignation.
In the following months, he continued to press his position that, "We
must . . . determine that the war against the White Paper now takes first
priority," more important than working with the British in the new European war. He favored "fierce and prolonged disorder in Palestine." The
others opposed him: one called him "a zealot liable to drag us into the
abyss;" another said he did "not fear the injury to Britain at all [from Ben-
Gurion's proposal], rather the injury to *us*"; a third said that Ben-Gurion's
proposal could "harbor the danger of destruction."

Ben-Gurion was immune to these arguments, and when he failed to
persuade his colleagues of his position, he announced that he was retiring
to a kibbutz.[21] But Weizmann intervened to allow Ben-Gurion to extri-
cate himself from the corner into which he had painted himself: he invited
Ben-Gurion to come to London to "consult."[22] At the end of April, spared
from carrying out his resignation, Ben-Gurion left for London, arriving
on May 1, 1940.

## BEN-GURION IN LONDON

In London, Ben-Gurion found that Weizmann and his colleagues also
opposed his proposal for a more "active" resistance to the British. On
May 10, Chamberlain resigned as prime minister and was succeeded by
Winston Churchill, who was both a Zionist and a friend of Weizmann's.
Ben-Gurion decided to extend his stay in London to help raise what he
envisioned to be "a Jewish army in and for Palestine."[23] He wrote in his
diary, "Never before was there a prime minister more capable and inclined
to understand us, never before have there been in an English government
better and more sincere friends."[24]

On May 12, 1940, Weizmann published a proclamation in *The Times
of London* announcing the readiness of the Jewish people to assist Brit-

ain, urging that the Jews be allowed to fight as a nation. He proposed a 50,000-person volunteer force in Palestine, to be backed by Jewish chemists, engineers, doctors, and other scientists, as well as the conversion of Jewish businesses in Palestine to a war industry, producing goods and services to assist the British military effort. On May 13, Ben-Gurion wrote to Lord Lloyd at the Colonial Office, informing him that in Palestine there were "tens of thousands of young Jews who are eager to fight as the devoted allies of Britain" and who looked forward to "a new chapter in our relations." But Churchill's sympathy was insufficient to move the British bureaucracy to create a Jewish army. Anthony Eden in the War Office, Lord Halifax in the Foreign Office, and Lord Lloyd in the Colonial Office all remained staunchly pro-Arab and anti-Zionist.[25]

On July 2, 1940, the Washington philanthropist and business leader Edmund I. Kaufmann was elected president of the Zionist Organization of America, succeeding Rabbi Solomon Goldman. Rabbi Stephen S. Wise, Rabbi Abba Hillel Silver, and Louis Lipsky were elected vice presidents. Ben-Gurion cabled the new leaders:

> There is no time to lose. History will never forgive us if we fail to do in time whatever is humanly possible to give the Jewish community the chance of defending itself. I know the spirit of our people in Palestine. They are ready to die fighting and have proved it on numerous occasions.[26]

## BEN-GURION'S CONFLICT WITH WEIZMANN

On September 3, 1940, Weizmann had lunch with Churchill, who reiterated his support for the formation of Jewish combat units in Palestine. But less than a week later, Weizmann was summoned to the War Office, where the commander of the British force in Palestine, Lt. Gen. Sir R. H. Haining, outlined the practical and tactical problems with a Jewish force. It was a pattern that would repeat itself many times: the prime minister would assure Weizmann of his support for a Jewish force in principle, while those in charge of the British military and foreign policy bureaucracies made sure it did not come to pass.

Meanwhile, Ben-Gurion was growing increasingly frustrated by Weizmann's lack of success. One of Weizmann's friends wrote that Ben-Gurion was "behaving like Achilles and boycotting [meetings] for no ascertainable reason." Weizmann's assistant, Doris May, wrote in her diary that "David [Ben-Gurion] is simmering over with barely suppressed indignation against [Chaim], and [Chaim] is peevish and nervy about David." She described Ben-Gurion as a "fretful porcupine" whose quills could strike his friends and who was "making himself miserable and getting himself hated all round." In his diary entry for September 11, Ben-Gurion wrote caustically:

> I knew throughout these last four months that [Weizmann] doesn't understand the situation, is incapable of conducting any serious political negotiations whatsoever, and lacks the expertise and understanding necessary to discuss the Yishuv's defense. . . . We have never had such a justifiable demand as that for a Jewish army in Palestine (and abroad), never have the objective circumstances been so favorable to us, never has there been a prime minister more capable and inclined to understand us, never was an English cabinet made up of better and truer friends (along with a number of opponents and enemies)—and a special "talent" is needed to lose the battle under those conditions. Chaim, apparently, has this talent.[27]

On September 12, an angry Weizmann told Ben-Gurion, in response to his complaints, that he had gone out of his way to assure that Ben-Gurion was included in all discussions, other than meetings to which Weizmann had been invited to attend alone; that Weizmann was tired after working some forty-five years and was planning to step down at the next Zionist Congress, but that he rejected Ben-Gurion's "ultimatum" on how to proceed. Ben-Gurion responded that he had given no ultimatum, but had only observed that, "for the past four months I have seen, to my regret, that all my efforts to be of help failed."[28]

It was after this latest disagreement with Weizmann that Ben-Gurion decided to go to America, to "try to mobilize a Jewish unit to fight wherever the British high command might decide." He informed May, rather than Weizmann directly, of his decision, and on September 24 he left for the United States, resolving never to work with Weizmann again.[29] For his part, Weizmann wrote to his wife that "Ben-Gurion has gone off, and so—an irritant less."[30]

BEN-GURION ARRIVES IN AMERICA

Ben-Gurion traveled on the *SS Scythia*, a converted Cunard liner that had been requisitioned into service at the beginning of the war. Military vessels escorted the ship for the first two days of the trip before leaving it to proceed on its own through the hazardous waters of the Atlantic.[31] A week before, 284 people (including seventy-seven children) had drowned when the German Navy had torpedoed another British ship.[32]

Ben-Gurion arrived in New York on the morning of October 3, 1940, a month before the presidential election in which Franklin D. Roosevelt was seeking an unprecedented third term. It was a week after Japan had signed a tripartite pact with Germany and Italy, in which all three countries pledged to defend one another if any of them were attacked by a power not then involved in the European war. *The New York Times* reported that the pact was viewed as "a warning to the United States not to meddle in the affairs of Europe and Asia unless she was prepared to go to war with all three [members of the Axis]."[33]

October 3 was also Rosh Hashanah, the first day of the Jewish New Year. For this reason, there were no Jewish dignitaries at the dock to welcome Ben-Gurion, and he learned on his arrival that everyone was attending High Holiday services.[34] He had sent telegrams that morning to the American Zionist Federation and to *Poale Zion* ("Workers of Zion"), a Labor Zionist group, but the telegrams did not reach them until mid-afternoon.

Fortunately for Ben-Gurion, the director of Port Reception Services for the Hebrew Immigrant Aid Society (HIAS), Bernard Kornblith, was standing by to welcome Jewish travelers. The authorities told Kornblith there was a problem with one of the Jewish passengers, who refused to disclose the reason for his trip. Kornblith boarded the ship and recognized Ben-Gurion. Kornblith explained to the immigration official that it was David Ben-Gurion, the longtime Zionist leader, and that it would be embarrassing to have him detained at Ellis Island, especially on such a holy day. That explanation left the immigration official unmoved. Kornblith's memorandum to his files recorded what happened next:

> The inspector insisted that Mr. Ben Gurion reveal the reason for his coming, and he asked me to personally interview him. I took Mr. Ben Gurion aside, had quite a discussion with him and explained to him the rules and regulations in the United States,

that the inspector had the authority to determine admission and the inspector would be forced to send him to Ellis Island, so that if possible, he owned him some explanation.

Mr. Ben Gurion absolutely refused to discuss his purpose in coming. The inspector, being equally stubborn, ordered him to be held at Ellis Island until such time as a bond would be posted, and only then would Ben Gurion be released. . . . I reiterated to the inspector that it would be very embarrassing to send Mr. Ben Gurion to Ellis Island. . . . [But] Mr. Ben Gurion was ordered to [be taken there].[35]

Ben-Gurion's imperious personality had created yet another crisis. He had brought no documents with him to show the purpose of his trip. In a letter the following month to Justice Brandeis, responding to a request from Brandeis for substantiation of certain points Ben-Gurion had made at a Hadassah meeting, Ben-Gurion wrote that he did not have with him "a single document, report or letter on the question which interests you":

I deeply regret my inability to send you this material. . . . When I left Palestine [in May] I advisedly did not take with me a single paper or document, knowing that I would have to be examined on leaving the country, as well as at the various borders during my travel. When I left London [in September] I took with me only a few papers which I did not mind having examined by the censors.[36]

Faced with the obstinacy of both Ben-Gurion and the immigration inspector, Kornblith attempted to reach Rabbi Stephen S. Wise at home, but learned that he was conducting High Holiday services at Carnegie Hall. Kornblith left word that Ben-Gurion had arrived, gave the name of the ship and the pier, and asked Wise to intercede.[37] Ben-Gurion himself called Wise's home from the ship, learned he was conducting the service, and left the same message.

Wise received Kornblith's message and went directly to the pier at 2 p.m., where he assured the immigration authorities that he would personally guarantee that Ben-Gurion would present himself later to the immigration board.[38] On that basis, Ben-Gurion was permitted to leave the ship. He arrived at his hotel in Manhattan in late afternoon, and met with friends until after midnight.

ROSH HASHANAH SERMONS, 1940

As Jews attended High Holy Day services on October 3, much had changed in the seven months since Weizmann had left America, and even in the two months since Jabotinsky's death.

*The New York Times* reported that morning on the latest indiscriminate bombing of London; Britain announced it was suspending the evacuation of children to Canada and America, since German submarine warfare in the North Atlantic had rendered travel too dangerous; Italy was attacking British cruisers in the Mediterranean and striking British naval bases in Egypt and Libya, demanding control over Lebanon and Syria and the French naval bases there; the German High Command was planning a joint Axis drive across Egypt toward the Suez Canal. The Middle East was now a prime theater of war.[39] As they gathered to celebrate the new Jewish year, on one of the most holy days of the Jewish calendar, what did America's rabbis tell their congregants, in sermons the rabbis had prepared with special care, knowing that virtually all their congregants would be present to hear them?

Rabbi Wise's New Year's Day sermon was entitled "Chosen to Serve vs. Choosing to Enslave."[40] It was apparently not a sermon of lasting significance to him: he did not mention it, nor any of his other 1940 High Holiday sermons, in his memoirs.[41] But the sermons of two other distinguished Reform rabbis, and the sermon of the preeminent Conservative rabbi in the country, all illustrate the atmosphere within the American Jewish community that day.

Rabbi Harold I. Saperstein—a disciple of Rabbi Wise then in the seventh year of what would become a nearly half-century rabbinate at Temple Emanu-El in Lynbrook, New York—delivered a sermon entitled "Suffrage is the Badge."[42] In mid-1939, Rabbi Saperstein had taken a three-month trip to visit the Jewish communities of Poland, Romania, Palestine, and Egypt; he had attended the twenty-first Zionist Congress in Geneva from August 16–26, 1939; and he had returned on the *Queen Mary,* which made the Atlantic passage with its lights off at night to avoid German detection. He began his 1940 sermon by saying, "I shall not go into a catalogue of Jewish sorrows at the dawn of this New Year. God knows, if words are still needed, then words will never avail." Then he summarized what had transpired in the preceding year:

*Rabbi Harold I. Saperstein, circa 1940*
*(Photo courtesy Lexington Books and*
*Professor Marc Saperstein)*[43]

[T]he Jews of Europe today, with fewest exceptions, have no homes. Poland, once the center of traditional Jewish culture, is now a corpse picked clean by the Nazi and Russian vultures. Its three million Jews are homeless. The freedom-loving lands of Holland and Belgium, which once offered a haven for Jews driven from Spain, no longer proved a safe retreat for the Jewish refugees and residents who had escaped there from the Nazi tempest. Those who managed to find refuge in France had only a temporary breathing spell for their pains and for the risk of their lives. For within a few short weeks, the Nazi terror had again caught up with them. This is the fate of the Jews in the world today: to be harried, uprooted, as driven leaves blown in the wind.[44]

Rabbi Saperstein's Erev [Eve of] Rosh Hashanah sermon had contrasted the situation in America with that in Europe, but not as part of a prayer of gratitude to be "far from there," nor as a patriotic paean to "a land so fair." Instead, he used the comparison to emphasize the living hell of the European Jews:

While we are praying here, bombs are falling on the city of London, heroic citadel of human liberty and dignity. Jews in that city, if they can pray at all, must pray in bomb-proof shelters deep under the surface of the earth . . . I am here where men are free, the skies are peaceful, and a whole nation becomes concerned over the fate of one little kidnapped child.[45]

At Tifereth Israel in Cleveland, Rabbi Abba Hillel Silver delivered his Rosh Hashanah sermon on "Our Responsibility for Evil."[46] He told his congregation he had heard people ask, *Where is God?*—and that his answer was, "God has not forsaken the world . . . the world has forsaken God." He cited "the gross and unpardonable sins of our age . . . acts of betrayal, perfidy, and selfishness of governments, leaders, parties, and masses":

[Statesmen] did not see, because they would not see, that the same . . . barbarism which crushed and robbed the Jews of Germany . . . could someday crush and rob their own citizens . . . The Poles . . . thought that only Jews could be declared subhuman, branded as pariahs and forced to wear the yellow badge of serfdom. Frenchmen thought that only Czechoslovakia could be overrun and conquered. Englishmen never dreamed that their children might someday have to seek asylum in far distant places nor that the ships carrying their children to refuge would someday be sunk by the same Nazis whose fury and madness was scattering helpless Jewish children over the face of the earth. Each thought only of himself. And the God of nations . . . meted out to all of them a common cup of staggering confusion from which they must now drink.

Silver's message, however, was not one of despair. He said that God had created human beings free to fashion their own destiny:

We may not be at the end of this world war, but at its beginning. . . . We will be wise to gird ourselves morally for the great and long struggle ahead and be prepared to play a manly part in it. . . . This hour calls . . . for faith and valor and the buckling on of armor, both physical and spiritual. . . . The remaining free peoples of the earth must rally as one to slay the evil which threatens all mankind . . .

*Rabbi Abba Hillel Silver, circa 1940*

We Jews who fought all the savage and brutal gods of ancient days . . . we Jews who have suffered throughout the ages as we are suffering today . . . must again find our places in the vanguard of the free armies of mankind, and fight . . .

At the Brooklyn Jewish Center—dedicated in 1920 as a major new Conservative Jewish institution, with an imposing classical structure that housed not only a synagogue but also a gymnasium, a banquet hall, a swimming pool, classrooms, and a Hebrew academy—Rabbi Israel H. Levinthal gave a Rosh Hashanah sermon entitled "The Jew's Primary Duty Today."[47] He told his congregants the world was facing a tragedy of Biblical proportions, unprecedented in modern times, because:

There is a vast difference between the tragedy that we witness today and the human tragedies that have been enacted before. The world has always known suffering—but it was suffering endured by individuals, be they in the many thousands or millions. But the world as such was not crippled. . . . Today, however . . . Nations have been wiped out. It is not only a question of individual suffering; our tragedy is that whole peoples, nations, a world, are being threatened with annihilation.

And if we scan the Jewish scene, we note the same [thing].

. . . [Previously] the tragedy . . . came to individual Jews, or
to individual communities. When the Jews were driven from
Spain, Holland and Turkey extended to them a hand of welcome. When Jews were crushed in Germany, they could flee
to Poland and Russia. Today the curse . . . [threatens] all Jews
throughout the world. The Nazis are not content with annihi-
lating Jewish life in Germany; their aim is worldwide: to annihilate all Jews, everywhere. Their attack is directed against the
Jewish people, all of us, without any exception. Herein lies the
seriousness of the catastrophe that has befallen us.

Rabbi Levinthal asked, "How shall we meet this challenge to the very
existence of our faith and our people?" He said the first response was to
consider the European Jews as "our brothers":

If they suffer and we do not, it is simply because fate has been
kinder to us than to them. They missed the boat—that is all.
The hatred is directed against all of us, not only against them.
They are simply in the front ranks in the battle waged against us
all. Our tragedy lies in the fact that so many Jews have lost their
sense of kinship, their feeling of brotherliness.

The second response, he said, was to recall the Biblical promise of the
Land:

That land of Palestine is today the one great pride of our creative
achievement. We put into it our sweat and our blood. The eyes of
our enemies are today fixed upon it. They know that if they rob
us of that land they rob us of our heart, our life-blood. Today,
when all that we have created is threatened with annihilation
the words "V'ha-aretz Ezkor," "And I shall remember the land,"
must become a soul-stirring call to action to every Jew faithful to
his ancient heritage.

Rabbi Levinthal ended his sermon with a charge to his congregants: he
urged them to remember "our duty to our brethren throughout the world,
to our ancient Holy Land, and to our Faith."

These sermons, and others like them, show that by the final months of
1940, American Jews knew the situation facing the Jews of Europe; they
knew the threat was by no means confined to Europe; and they knew that

*Rabbi Israel H. Levinthal, circa 1940*
*(Photograph courtesy of the Brooklyn*
*Jewish Center Review)*

something must be done.[48] By the time Ben-Gurion arrived in October, the scale of the calamity, and the urgency of the situation, were apparent to all.

### BEN-GURION'S FIRST DAYS IN AMERICA

In Ben-Gurion's diary entry for the day after he arrived, he wrote candidly of the principal purpose of his trip: "the main action, in my opinion, is the establishment of the Jewish Army." Two days later, he recorded again that, "Only one thing occupies my mind right now: the effort to build a Jewish Army."[49]

Ben-Gurion had been unwilling to reveal the purpose of his trip to the U.S. immigration official, but once admitted to the country he did not hide his objective from the press. On October 6, he told the Jewish Telegraphic Agency (JTA) he expected that the center of the war would move from Europe to the Middle East, and that the future of Palestine would depend on the formation of a Jewish army.[50]

When a Jewish reporter from *The New York Times* came to his hotel to see him, Ben-Gurion wrote in his diary that, "When I told him about our plans to establish a Jewish Army, he said it was Jabotinsky's idea."

Ben-Gurion's chagrin at hearing Jabotinsky's name is palpable even on the page. Ben-Gurion's relationship with Jabotinsky, and the relations between their two movements, had long been contentious. In 1934, the two leaders had held sixteen meetings in London over the course of a month, seeking to negotiate agreements that would allow their respective movements to proceed on a unified basis. They signed three agreements to effectuate a renewed unity, but Ben-Gurion's followers voted them down, and the following year Jabotinsky left the Zionist Organization when it refused to adopt Jewish statehood as its immediate goal.

Ben-Gurion's Labor Zionists and Jabotinsky's Revisionists remained bitter political enemies, and Weizmann and his followers sided against Jabotinsky as well. The three leaders also differed over the ultimate Zionist goal: Ben-Gurion wanted a socialist Jewish entity; Weizmann championed a Jewish cultural homeland; Jabotinsky backed a democratic Jewish state not associated with any particular ideology.[51] All of them recognized, however, that a Jewish army was a necessary means to reach their goal.

Ben-Gurion recorded in his diary what his stream of visitors had told him about a Jewish army in the long discussions he held upon his arrival in the United States:

> In everyone's opinion, there is no hope in recruiting the young Jews in America to establish a Jewish Army. They are preoccupied with their own problems, they are afraid of what the Goyim are going to say, and that the new American military leadership will also be in the way. I cannot accept this verdict.[52]

One of Ben-Gurion's visitors that evening reiterated to him that Jewish youth in America "will not volunteer for [a Jewish] Army because of American patriotism and egotistical selfishness."[53] Ben-Gurion had spent the preceding four months in London witnessing the courage of the British people in their response to the German bombardment, and he knew that the Jews in Palestine were willing to fight in the war. It was inconceivable to him that American Jewish youth would not want to join that fight as well.

On October 2—the day before Ben-Gurion had arrived in America— *The New York Times* reported that two Jewish companies had been formed in Palestine and had begun infantry training, with a total of 400 Jews, in the hope that the British would permit the formation of further fighting units "for which many Jews are eager to volunteer."[54]

Weizmann had arrived in America during the "phony war" and chose to avoid discussing a Jewish army. Jabotinsky had brought the idea to the forefront on his trip and had sparked a flame, but his efforts had been cut short by his sudden death. Now that the fire was visible to all, it fell to Ben-Gurion to provide another clarion call.

## BEN-GURION MEETS WITH AMERICAN ZIONIST LEADERS

On October 5, Ben-Gurion met with the new leader of Zionist Organization of America (ZOA), Edmund I. Kaufman, and gained some insight into the social divide among American Jews, as well as their ambivalence toward Zionism. He noted in his diary that his impression of Kaufman was "not bad":

> His wish, he told me, was to attract the rich Jews to Zionism. They are standing afar from this—not because of a principled objection, but because there is a social divide between the lower and middle class of the Zionists and the upper class. He thinks that the approach to the rich Jews should be done in appropriate ways. There was bitterness in his words about the internal divisions within the Zionist movement and about the efforts to see him fail.[55]

The next day, Henry Montor, the executive vice chairman of the United Palestine Appeal, came to visit Ben-Gurion and provided a different perspective about Kaufman. Ben-Gurion recorded what Montor told him:

> [Montor said] Kaufman is ridiculous and insulting as a representative of the Zionists. He is uneducated and made money from interest (he used to sell jewelry—which came with high interest payments—to workers); he does not know anything about Zionism or about the Land of Israel; he has no political understanding; he has no ties to the Government. . . . He is being supported by Brandeis's people. The only person [Montor] did not complain about was [Abba Hillel] Silver. It looks like he would have liked to see him as the head of the Federation.[56]

That evening, Nahum Goldmann, a leading Zionist who later founded and served as the president, from 1948 to 1982, of the World Jewish Congress visited Ben-Gurion at his hotel to discuss the possibility of Jabotinsky's Revisionist Zionists re-joining the Jewish Federation in the wake of Jabotinsky's death. Ben-Gurion told him the Revisionists could come back—as long as they "gave real guarantees that they would eliminate their national military organization" and agreed to "stop all separate actions from the Haganah [the Jewish defense forces] and in the political arena."

Ben-Gurion effectively wanted the Revisionists to disband, renounce their allegiance to Jabotinsky's principles, and subject themselves instead to his leadership while giving up any right to dissent. Faced with Goldmann's suggestion of unity, Ben-Gurion demanded a surrender. The differences within the groups of American Zionists (typified by the hostility between Kaufman and Montor and competition between the followers of Brandeis and Wise) mirrored the differences among Ben-Gurion, Weizmann, and Jabotinsky and their own followers.

## BEN-GURION'S CONDITIONS FOR WORKING
### FOR A JEWISH ARMY IN AMERICA

Among the documents the American Zionists presented to Ben-Gurion on his arrival in America was a copy of the "Bardin memorandum," prepared by the educator Shlomo Bardin, who was close to Brandeis.[57] The memorandum argued that Arab agreement to Jewish settlement in Palestine could be effectuated by creating a Jewish-Arab federation and a joint army to fight Hitler. In his diary for October 9, Ben-Gurion wrote caustically that the plan was "excellent" and "original," but that Bardin "only forgot one small thing: how to deal with the objections of the Arabs." Ben-Gurion responded acerbically to the assertion in the memorandum that the plan might already have been implemented, but for a "failure of the Zionist leadership":

> I would be willing to take upon myself an effort to change the Zionist leadership if this nice program could exist . . . [but] Like many who think they have the "solution of solutions," Bardin thinks it is enough to prove to himself that the Jewish aliyah is good—so he assumes the Arabs will recognize it too. And he is proving it to them in a memorandum that was written in America to the Jews . . .
>
> Bardin sees difficulty only with the Jews. . . . He invents a new method of political rule: "both Jews and Arabs must assure

each other of the non-domination of one group by the other" . . .
[and concludes with] a very important warning that time is crucial and the "opportunity" might not return. . . .

Ben-Gurion thought that any efforts in America to promote the idea
of a Jewish army were inhibited by two other factors that required delay:
(1) the British had not yet approved a Jewish fighting unit; and (2) the impending American election made it unwise to raise the issue publicly, even
if the British did approve of the idea before Election Day. For Jabotinsky,
these had been the very reasons to move forward as quickly as possible: he
believed that (1) Britain would never approve a Jewish military unit unless
American public opinion pressured it to do so; and (2) the longer the delay,
the less likely Britain would ever give its assent. What for Jabotinsky were
reasons to proceed promptly were, for Ben-Gurion, roadblocks preventing
any action for the time being.

Ben-Gurion recorded in his diary that he had "serious doubts about
London's position" on a Jewish unit, and, as usual, he blamed Weizmann.
"Chaim did not understand," he wrote, how to present the question to
the British: "I am heavy with doubt about this point, but if there will be
a miracle and the decision will be positive . . . the establishment of the
Jewish Army will be the main focus of the Zionist movement at this time,
especially in America."[58]

Throughout his trip, Ben-Gurion continued to speak privately of the
importance of a Jewish army, but avoided making any public statements
before approval from London or a definitive electoral result in America.

## BEN-GURION'S SPEECHES TO AMERICAN GROUPS

On October 10, Ben-Gurion spoke to a meeting of Jewish organizations
at New York's Waldorf-Astoria Hotel, endorsing a future Jewish army. He
recorded in his diary that he had spoken about:

> a war by a Jewish Army against Hitler and for the defense of
> Eretz Israel; uprooting the fear that Hitler and his agents cause
> over the American Jews; consolidation of a brave Zionist leader-
> ship. . . .[59]

But Ben-Gurion's presentation that day produced not unity, but division. Some of his listeners wanted an army only for service in Pales-

tine; some wanted one only for a European war against Hitler; others thought Jewish fearfulness would preclude any action at all; and still others thought the whole idea impractical on the grounds that Zionist activists were too old to enlist. In his diary, Ben-Gurion wrote, "I am not a partner to the pessimism regarding the American Jews—but there is lack of leadership . . . [in] a group that should know what to do and act with courage."[60]

Ben-Gurion made a list of Zionist youth organizations in America and started meeting with their leaders.[61] He held meetings, gave talks, appeared at press conferences, wrote articles, and held interviews with reporters, but he was unable to win over Wise and Lipsky, who were Weizmann followers, or even the members of the more assertive Brandeis group. He spent a good deal of time with the leaders of Hadassah, the Women's Zionist Organization of America, which at that time was the largest Zionist group in the country. It had nearly twice as many members as the Zionist Organization of America.[62]

In mid-October, Ben-Gurion traveled by train to Washington for meetings with Brandeis and Felix Frankfurter, the Vienna-born associate justice of the U.S. Supreme Court (1939–1962). He met with another prominent figure who "spoke with worry about the elections" and told him (as Ben-Gurion recorded in his diary):

> The Republicans are spreading money like sand to make sure Roosevelt fails. They use every method, kosher and non-kosher, they divide the people with the war, and they also use anti-Semitic arguments (Roosevelt is surrounded by Jews). The Gallup Poll shows a rise in Willkie's popularity over the last few days.[63]

Ben-Gurion met Brandeis that afternoon and wrote later in his diary about the meeting:

> I told him what I saw in England during the four months of difficult defeats and failures—about the heroism of the English people and their moral stand. The old man was impressed . . . I told him that I was very bitter, like some among us during the period of the White Paper, but even during the most difficult days I differentiated between the passing policy of the government and the historical relationship with England itself. . . .

I told him, in brief, about my plans here—about the establishment of a Jewish Army, arranging an Air Training and pre-
Military Training for the young people here, and that I will only
start action on it after the election. The old man said little. He
expressed his regret that he is not my age anymore. He expressed
his agreement to the plan and asked me to come and visit again
after the elections.[64]

On October 18, at the suggestion of Nahum Goldmann, Ben-Gurion
met with Benjamin Akzin and Eliahu Ben-Horin, who were trying to
reorganize the Revisionist movement in the wake of Jabotinsky's death.
According to Ben-Gurion's diary, Akzin emphasized that Jews faced an
"emergency hour," and that the idea of a Jewish army could provide a
unifying objective around which all Jewish groups might coalesce. Ben-
Horin said that after Jabotinsky's death, "many were of the opinion that
the [Revisionist] movement was going to dissolve, but in reality it became
stronger. More members joined . . . revenue sources grew."

Ben-Gurion's response to Akzin and Ben-Horin dripped with disdain:

I told them that I will be frank . . . I do not value their movement. Revisionism was Jabotinsky. . . . I do not value Revisionism or any of their parties. But I am ready to do a lot to make it
easier on them [to rejoin the Zionist Organization] . . . if they
will accept, in this matter, absolute discipline.[65]

In his diary, Ben-Gurion recorded his impression that Akzin was "a
total idiot" who "does not have a lot of value," and that Ben-Horin was
"knowingly a total Nazi and a Revisionist and he enjoys it."[66] He wrote
that he did not think that they would be able to "deliver the goods"—a
commitment by the Revisionists to rejoin the Zionist Organization on the
terms Ben-Gurion had demanded as a condition of unity.

On October 26, Ben-Gurion flew to Chicago, where he spoke for an
hour at a Zionist conference in a large theater, and held day-long meetings and conversations there. On October 27, he spoke at a dinner in
New York marking the closing of the Palestine Pavilion at the World's
Fair, and proposed that 100,000 American Jews go to Palestine as soon
as possible, as a "living exhibit" of American Jewry's commitment to
their people.[67]

When Roosevelt won re-election on November 5, Ben-Gurion still had
no news from London about British approval of a Jewish military unit.
By then he was no longer certain that the decision "would be positive, or
soon." He wrote in his diary, "I can't really start the work even though I
intend to organize Air Training." He summarized the results of his trip
over the previous month:

> My coming to America on the eve of the election delayed the
> main part of the plan that I came here for: early preparation to
> establish a Jewish unit. It was clear that before the end of the
> election it would be impossible . . . to do anything real. I had
> nothing else to do but wait until after the elections. I used the
> time before the elections mainly to get familiar with the mood in
> America in general, and especially the situation among the Zion-
> ist Jewish youth groups.[68]

With the election over, Ben-Gurion wrote that there was now "a huge
role for America in this terrible struggle, maybe even crucial because in
the next four years it will all be decided (even though it could be that the
war could last more than four years)." And he saw evidence of the same
ideological conflict emerging in America that had consumed Europe:

> [T]he internal fighting in America is not very far from the fight-
> ing in Europe, because here too there are some fascist and Nazi
> forces . . . All of the anti-Semites and those that believe in Race
> Theory—and there are more than a few of them. . . . It is hard
> to describe the wild propaganda, the demagogy and the financial
> squandering that Willkie had, almost all of the capital newspapers
> . . . all the means of advertisement, commercials and propaganda,
> and tens of thousands of scripted speeches, the radio, the electric-
> ity, the means of transportation . . . boss pressure, bank manag-
> ers, heads of securities companies, etc. tried for weeks to ruin the
> reputation of Roosevelt in the eyes of the people and they praised
> Willkie like he was some kind of one-and-only savior.[69]

Ben-Gurion wrote a long letter to his wife, Paula, on November 9 that
included much of what he had written in his diary that day, with additional paragraphs that are striking not only in their detailed analysis but

also in the partisan fervor of a foreign observer. He castigated the Republican candidate in extraordinary terms, applying the kind of rhetorical venom he often deployed against his own Zionist adversaries:

> Willkie himself, who never in his life did anything for the good of America . . . was always busy chasing money and greed and catering to big corporations—was throwing promises left and right, promises that contradicted each other. . . . To England and to England's friends here he promised greater support and help than Roosevelt, and to Hitler and Hitler's friends here he promised that under no circumstances would America participate in the war . . . To the workers he promised to keep the social corrections that Roosevelt made, and to the wealthy he promised to cancel all the reforms. To the unemployed he promised work, to the rich he promised lower taxes, and to those that want a greater reinforcement of the America armed forces he promised a stronger Navy, a mighty Air Force, and a huge Army—and with it a smaller budget and elimination or reduction of the deficit.[70]

Ben-Gurion ended his post-election reflection by noting that he still awaited news from London about a Jewish fighting force, and that he would decide what to do in the coming week—but that "one thing was clear to me":

> The Jews of America are afraid. They are afraid of Hitler, they are afraid of Hitler's allies, they are afraid of war and they are afraid of peace. During the elections they were afraid that Willkie would be elected, and they were also afraid to openly support Roosevelt. The Zionists are afraid of the non-Zionists, and the non-Zionists are afraid of the non-Jews. Amongst the youth, a convenient exaggeration rules: pacifism or imperialism, internationalism, and the radicalism that does not obligate itself to anything.[71]

Ben-Gurion hoped, however, that this was "not the true expression of the American Jews," because in his view "The Zionist demand has not yet been heard and the conscience has not yet been touched":

> And there is a conscience, and there is ability, and there is a common destiny—and if we know what and how to demand it, I am sure we will be answered.[72]

With the election over, Ben-Gurion became increasingly outspoken in his speeches. On November 11, he addressed the Hebrew Federation Ball and recorded in his diary that, "I called upon the Hebrews to uproot the fear in the heart of the American Jews and to prepare for war against Hitler and to enlist a Jewish force." Two weeks later, however, he was once again noting the fear he had observed among American Jews:

> It is very difficult here, because America still has not clarified her policy, even though the elections were a success, but there are still a few hesitancies that are of course affecting the mood of the Jews. The Jewish public is in fear and totally lacking freedom of thought and action. Zionism must overcome these local difficulties. . . .

Ironically, even as Ben-Gurion grew increasingly pessimistic in his diary about the timidity of American Jews, the American Zionists were becoming more outspoken. In the November 15, 1940, issue of *The Congress Weekly*, the bi-monthly publication of the American Jewish Congress, ZOA Vice President Louis Lipsky wrote that Palestine had "over 500,000 Jews who occupy a strategic military position," ready to supply men and materiel for an army to repel the pending Italian invasion of Egypt, and were petitioning Britain "for the right to fight under the Jewish flag." Lipsky then asked:

> But what are we American Jews doing or proposing to do, in the way of registering our Jewish as well as our American patriotism in this connection? There has been little or no discussion of the problem. I have found in both Zionist and non-Zionist circles a definite fear of organizing any action by American Jews in their own name in any way at all. . . .
>
> It is important that we show that as Jews we are not satisfied to do only that which is expected of all Americans. . . . The defeat of Hitler means the victory of Jewish ideals as well as the defeat of the enemy of democracy. We should demand the right to make our own identifiable sacrifice to the cause of Jewish freedom and democracy. . . .
>
> When the time comes—and it may come soon—and a Jewish Army for service in the Near East is given public recognition, it may be possible to send American Jewish men of military age to join that army. . . . Let us not hesitate to do our duty also as Jews; in doing that we shall be making a significant contribution

to the idealism of America and at the same time help to restore
the honor of the Jewish people.[73]

## A NEW TRAGEDY CONFRONTS THE JEWS

On November 11, a horrific new agony was visited upon the Jews, as the
British intercepted two ships at sea headed to Palestine and transferred
the 1,771 Jewish refugees aboard to the *Patria*. Ben-Gurion received a cable from Weizmann a week later, informing him that the British intended
to turn away all ships carrying illegal immigrants to Palestine, because
the Nazis were allegedly using them to smuggle "*agents provocateurs*" into
Palestine. Because Weizmann thought a new public dispute with Britain
on this issue could only complicate the attempt to move forward with a
Jewish army, he directed Ben-Gurion to avoid making any negative statements in response to these actions.

Ben-Gurion replied that he understood the need to avoid embarrassing the British, but he believed that deporting all refugees was outrageous
and that there were other ways to ensure there were no German agents
among them. In contravention of Weizmann's directive, he helped organize a protest cable to the British Minister of Labour from the American
Federation of Labor. The American Zionists rejected Ben-Gurion's call to
organize protest rallies as well, however, and chose instead simply to send
a delegation to the British embassy to protest the British action.[74]

Meanwhile, in Palestine, the Haganah placed explosives on the *Patria*
to blow a hole in the ship, hoping to prevent a return voyage to Europe.
The explosion did more than blow a hole, however; it sank the ship, and
200 of the refugees on board drowned. The British permitted survivors
to remain in Palestine, but refused to make any changes to their depor-
tation policy.

Ben-Gurion again pressed for an active response at the December
meetings of the American Zionist groups, and again at a ZOA meeting in January. The only support he received was from Rabbi Abba Hillel Silver—the sole exception to what he asserted was "the all-pervasive
Jewish timidity in the United States." Exasperated once again with those
who would not follow his counsel, Ben-Gurion decided to leave America.
He concluded that his goal was "not to try to convert the non-Zionists
to Zionism, but rather to make Zionists out of the Zionists, their leaders
first of all."

### BEN-GURION'S PARTING MESSAGE TO AMERICAN JEWS

On January 13, 1941, Ben-Gurion flew to San Francisco, preparing to return to Palestine by traveling across the Pacific, since an Atlantic crossing was by then too hazardous. On January 16, from the St. Francis Hotel, he wrote a long letter to Tamar de Sola Pool, the 50-year-old national president of Hadassah. Hadassah was the organization that had most impressed him while he was in America.

*Tamar de Sola Pool in the 1940s*

In his letter, Ben-Gurion set forth his final thoughts about his American trip. He praised Roosevelt, who was beginning to mobilize public opinion in support of Britain after his re-election, and he contrasted FDR's actions with what he saw as the passivity of the Jews:

> I shall not . . . deny the distressing feeling which American Jewry has awakened in me. Even in Zionist circles I did not find an adequate awareness of the seriousness of this desperate and tragic hour in the history of Israel. Does the fate of millions of their kin in Europe concern Jewry in America less than the fate of England affects the people of America? Is Palestine less dear to the five million Jews in the United States than Britain is to the 130 million people in America?

Ben-Gurion urged Mrs. de Sola Pool to inspire American Zionists to rise to the occasion:

> What is demanded of American Jewry? Who is mobilizing its national, traditional and financial resources for the salvation of the Jewish Homeland and the Jewish People, struggling for their very existence, and threatened with extinction everywhere in Europe? . . . I fear that American Zionists have not yet fully grasped the tremendous and weighty responsibility which history has imposed upon them in the present fateful hour.
>
> . . . If only Zionism in America will find itself, and draw inspiration from its great achievement in Palestine . . . and will find a way of presenting the great Zionist ideal to the masses of Jewry and the American people—only then will Jews rally to the call, just as the Americans respond to the call of Roosevelt.

Two days later, on January 18, 1941, Ben-Gurion departed the United States. He arrived in Palestine in early February, nine months after he had left for Britain and America.

## THE IMPACT OF BEN-GURION'S VISIT

The practical results of Ben-Gurion's trip were no greater than Weizmann's. He lacked Weizmann's international stature and Jabotinsky's oratorical power; he gave speeches in English, but he had neither Weizmann nor Jabotinsky's fluency in that language.[75] While more forceful than Weizmann, he nonetheless exhibited Weizmann's same caution, declining to call publicly for a Jewish army before either the British or the American governments gave their approval for the idea.

As with Weizmann's trip, the fault was not entirely, or perhaps even mainly, with the American Jews. Ben-Gurion did not publicly challenge them to support a Jewish army, and he did not produce the emotional response that Jabotinsky had generated in his two Manhattan Center speeches. Like Weizmann, Ben-Gurion would later downplay his 1940 trip: in his 862-page book, *Israel: A Personal History* (1971), Ben-Gurion devotes only a single sentence to it.[76]

Perhaps the combined efforts of Weizmann, Jabotinsky, and Ben-Gurion in 1940, however, had a delayed effect. With the three visits, there was continuously a world Zionist leader in America for the entire year, giving speeches both public and private, holding meetings, introducing themselves to American Zionist leaders, forming connections that would play out in future years. The three missions contributed to a dawning awareness on the part of American Jews that their own future was tied to that of the Jews in Europe and Palestine, and that awareness only deepened over time. In the following years, American Zionists would play an increasingly important role in international Jewish affairs, and their assistance was instrumental in the eventual United Nations and American recognition of the Jewish state.[77]

The most important part of Ben-Gurion's visit may have been the historic charge he left for American Jews in his farewell letter to Hadassah's president. At the end, he urged Mrs. de Sola Pool to:

> Impress upon the Jews in America the extent of the catastrophe which has befallen our people in Europe. Tell them what we have accomplished in Palestine. I am confident that American Jewry will respond to the call, for it is not inferior to other peoples in America.
>
> And to the American people, too, you should present our lofty ideal . . . Americans will lend an ear to a great ideal. . . . Insignificant projects will not interest them and will not merit their attention.
>
> This is a moment pregnant with significance and every historic hour has its vision. And now the time has come for great and far-reaching Zionist achievement. My blessings to you—may you live up to the demands of the present times.[78]

Mrs. de Sola Pool read Ben-Gurion's letter aloud to the National Board meeting of Hadassah, and copies of it were sent to the Hadassah members throughout the country.[79]

As 1941 began, however, there was still no Jewish army on the horizon.

# EPILOGUE: 1948

The Jewish army that Weizmann, Jabotinsky, and Ben-Gurion hoped would join the fight against Hitler never came to be.[1]

In September 1944—in the final months of the war—Britain permitted the formation of a single Jewish brigade. With its 5,000 soldiers, mainly from Palestine, it served in Italy under the command of a Canadian-born Jew, Brigadier Ernest F. Benjamin.[2] The British disbanded the brigade in 1946. After the war, most of the Jewish Brigade migrated to Palestine, and many of its members joined the ranks of the Jewish underground military forces, the Haganah and the Irgun. Eventually, thirty-five veterans of the Jewish Brigade rose to the level of General in the Israel Defense Forces (IDF).[3] In 1948, the first chief of staff of the IDF, Lt. Gen. Yaacov Dori, was a veteran of Jabotinsky's World War I Jewish Legion.[4]

ON NOVEMBER 29, 1947, the United Nations General Assembly adopted Resolution 181 to partition Palestine into an Arab and a Jewish state, with the heart of Palestine allocated to the Arabs and the Jewish State relegated to a narrow strip along the Mediterranean Sea, and the Negev desert.[5]

The resolution, supported by both the United States and the Soviet Union, passed by a vote of 33–13, with ten abstentions.[6] Every Arab state (Egypt, Iraq, Lebanon, Saudi Arabia, Syria, and Yemen) voted against the resolution, joined by every Muslim state (Afghanistan, Iran, Pakistan, and Turkey), as well as Greece and India. The next day, Arab pogroms swept through Palestine, and Arab violence against the Jews continued throughout the following months. The Arab war against the Jewish state began not with Israel's Declaration of Independence on May 14, 1948, but rather six months earlier, as the murderous reaction to the UN resolution that recommended two states for two peoples.[7]

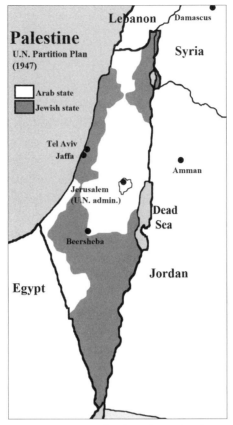

*UN Partition Plan for Palestine (1947)*
*(map produced by U.S. Central*
*Intelligence Agency)*

In 1948, Weizmann, Ben-Gurion, and Jabotinsky (through Menachem Begin, his successor) all played critical roles, as the Jewish community in Palestine faced an existential question: whether to declare a state in the middle of the ongoing terror war against them, with five Arab states poised to invade Palestine if the declaration were made, or whether to heed the warnings from the Department of State of the United States, as well as some prominent American Jews.

As we will see, the diplomatic, political, and military foundations necessary for the declaration were the result of the actions and influence of the three Zionist leaders, and it is unlikely a state could have been declared, much less have survived, without the efforts of all three.

## WEIZMANN

At the end of World War II, Weizmann was 70 years old and in poor health. He had failed to win re-election as president of the Zionist Organization in 1946, and Ben-Gurion succeeded him as its new leader.[8] As 1948 dawned, the United States State Department—unenthusiastic about a Jewish state and faced with unremitting Arab opposition to Jewish sovereignty even in a small part of historic Palestine—began to develop a new plan: a United Nations "trusteeship" for Palestine, a scheme that would effectively end the prospects for a Jewish state.[9]

American Zionists were eager to meet with President Truman, but he refused to see them. He had been dealing with the issue of displaced persons in Europe ever since he became president three years earlier, and had been lobbied by all sides within and outside the government. He described the Jews as "so emotional," the Arabs as "so difficult," and the British as "exceedingly non-cooperative."[10] In his memoirs, he later wrote that:

> Individuals and groups asked me, usually in rather quarrelsome and emotional ways, to stop the Arabs, to keep the British from supporting the Arabs, to furnish American soldiers, to do this, that, and the other. . . . As the pressure mounted, I found it necessary to give instructions that I did not want to be approached by any more spokesmen for the extreme Zionist cause.[11]

In desperation, the Zionists turned to Weizmann in London, where he and his wife, Vera, were on the eve of their departure for Palestine: indeed, they had already sent their luggage in advance of their arrival. Nonetheless, the Zionists begged him to travel to America to meet with the President. Weizmann was reluctant at his age to undertake an arduous winter trip to America, and neither he nor Vera was in good health.[12] Many Zionists telephoned him from New York, however, in calls that became, Weizmann later recalled, "more numerous and more urgent."[13] Aubrey Eban (later known as Abba Eban) cabled him on January 23, impressing upon him the importance of "your presence, advice, activity, influence" as the "most crucial phase of all now approaches."[14] Weizmann insisted that the appeal be made officially by the Jewish Agency Executive in New York, and, after it was, he agreed.[15]

As a result, in late January 1948, the 73-year-old Weizmann and his 66-year-old wife, Vera, boarded the *Queen Mary* for the trip to New York, arriving on February 4, 1948. It was a difficult passage across the ocean, and the ship arrived two days late. Weizmann thought the trip would involve a few weeks. It ended up consuming the next four months, and would involve, Vera wrote later, "a round of political activities of such intensity and complexity as my husband and I had never before experienced." It would be "the most hectic period of our lives."[16]

The trip began inauspiciously: exhausted by the voyage and subjected to New York's piercing weather, Weizmann developed a fever. His physicians ordered him to rest for a week.[17] In the following weeks, he was mainly confined to his bed.[18]

Then Truman refused to meet with him. Weizmann had learned that Truman would be leaving Washington shortly for a trip to the Caribbean, and he wrote to the President on February 10, in a letter drafted for him by Felix Frankfurter and others, and which was flown by a colleague to Washington to be delivered personally to the White House. Opening with, "My dear Mr. President," the letter read in part as follows:

> I was on the eve of leaving for Palestine last week from London when I received an urgent call to return to the United States in view of the crisis which had developed in the affairs of Palestine. . . . I was largely swayed by the hope that it might be possible for me to have an opportunity of meeting with you. . . . I would not venture to intrude on you at this moment were not the situation, in my opinion, so serious. . . . I am emboldened to ask you respectfully to receive me . . . and to spare me a few minutes of your precious time.[19]

Two days later Truman's personal secretary responded, telling Weizmann that Truman's schedule for the eight days before his Caribbean trip was completely full. In his memoirs, Truman wrote that he had decided to "put off" seeing Weizmann. Weizmann wrote on March 10 to his secretary, Doris May, that for more than a month he had "not been able to do anything at all, and so far my trip has been . . . rather useless."[20]

The Zionists appealed to the one person they thought might possibly persuade the President to agree to a meeting—his old friend and one-time business partner in Missouri, Eddie Jacobson.[21] Jacobson traveled to Washington and went directly to the White House, without an appointment, and was ushered in by Truman's aides, who warned him not to discuss Palestine. He raised the issue anyway, and Truman launched into a tirade about pressure from American Jewish leaders. Jacobson responded with a single request: that Truman meet with "a hero, a man I never met, but who is, I think, the greatest Jew who ever lived":

> [H]e is a gentleman and a great statesman as well, I am talking about Chaim Weizmann; he is a very sick man, almost broken in health, but he travelled thousands and thousands of miles just to see you and plead the cause of my people. Now you refuse to see him because you were insulted by some of our American Jewish leaders, even though you know that Weizmann had absolutely nothing to do with these insults. . . . If you will see him, you will be properly and accurately informed on the situation as it exists in Palestine. . . .[22]

Truman reluctantly agreed, but only as a courtesy to Jacobson, and instructed his aides to grant Weizmann an appointment with no public announcement and no press coverage.[23] On March 18, Weizmann traveled from New York to Washington, was brought into the White House through a side gate, and met for forty-five minutes with the President. During that conversation, Truman told him he would continue to support partition of Palestine.[24]

The next day, contrary to the President's assurance to Weizmann, the American ambassador to the UN, Warren Austin, told the Security Council that the United States would propose a UN "trusteeship" that would allegedly be "temporary"—it would end, Austin said, "whenever Arabs and Jews agreed on future government of their country."[25] Later that day, the State Department officially announced the new policy.[26]

Weizmann was outraged; he believed Truman had misled him.[27] But Truman had himself been blindsided by the action of his own State Department, which had failed to notify him of Austin's speech. Truman wrote in his diary that he had been put in the position of a "double-crosser," and that Weizmann "must think I'm a plain liar."[28]

As the discussions between the White House and the State Department continued over the following weeks, Weizmann remained in contact with Truman. He wrote to him on April 9, warning of the dire consequences of the withdrawal of American support for a Jewish state:

> The clock cannot be put back to the situation which existed before November 29. I would also draw attention to the psycholog-

ical effects of promising Jewish independence in November and attempting to cancel it in March. . . . The choice for our people, Mr. President, is between Statehood and extermination. History and providence have placed this issue in your hands, and I am confident that you will yet decide it in the spirit of the moral law.[29]

As May 15 approached—the date the British had announced they would withdraw from Palestine—the American delegation to the UN proposed a mediator for Palestine, in another attempt to preclude the declaration of a Jewish state. On May 13, Weizmann wrote Truman a last letter, delivered by night train to the White House from New York.[30] He informed the President that an independent Jewish state would be declared the following day:

> I deeply hope that the United States, which under your leadership has done so much to find a just solution, will promptly recognize the Provisional Government of the new Jewish state. The world, I think, would regard it as especially appropriate that the greatest living democracy should be the first to welcome the newest into the family of nations.[31]

When Truman received the letter, on May 14, 1948, he summoned several members of his administration to discuss it, and later the same day Truman recognized the Jewish State of Israel, eleven minutes after Ben-Gurion read the Declaration of Independence in Tel Aviv.[32] On April 23, Truman had told Samuel Rosenman, a prominent New York attorney, judge, and senior adviser to both Presidents Roosevelt and Truman, that "I have Dr. Weizmann on my conscience." As he issued the American recognition of Israel on May 14, Truman told his staff, "The old Doctor will believe me now."[33] The next day, he sent Weizmann a personal note saying he had "appreciated very much your letter of May thirteenth."[34]

A week and a half later, the "old Doctor" stood by the President's side, representing Israel as its first president, and presented him with a Torah to mark the occasion.[35]

We can never know whether Truman would have acted as he did on May 14 if Weizmann had not made his last-minute trip to America, nor been able to meet with the President, nor met him fortuitously just one day before the State Department sought to implement a new policy for

*President Truman and President Weizmann at the White House, May 25, 1948*

Palestine, nor followed his meeting with letters to Truman marked by eloquence and moral urgency, nor sent the final one to be delivered to the President by night train from Manhattan for his immediate consideration the following day.

We can say with some certainty, however, that at a critical point in history, there was no other Zionist figure who could have had the impact that Chaim Weizmann did.

### BEN-GURION

While Weizmann was working in the United States to generate American support for a Jewish state, the situation in Palestine was also fraught with uncertainty.

On May 11, 1948—four days before the British were to leave—Ben-Gurion's own party, the *Mapai* (the Workers' Party of the Land of Israel), was deeply divided. Its leaders had increasing doubts about declaring independence; several were unalterably opposed to doing so. Of the four *Mapai* representatives in the provisional government, only Ben-Gurion actively supported a declaration. The others—knowing a Jewish state would be attacked from all sides, and having been warned by the State Department that a declaration would be dangerous—counseled caution. In any event, it was clear that no arms or other military assistance would be forthcoming from the United States government.[36]

The debate within Ben-Gurion's party extended, inconclusively, far into that night.[37] The next day, May 12, the Arab Legion launched a large-scale attack on a bloc of Jewish settlements near Jerusalem.[38] Ben-Gurion spent the day in an eleven-hour meeting, deliberating how to proceed. Jewish military commanders warned him that the Arabs held a considerable military advantage, with heavy weapons exceeding those then available to Jewish forces. The group split 6–4 on statehood. That night, the Mapai Central Committee met for a third time, and finally decided to declare a state.

On May 13, the provisional government held its final meeting to draft a Declaration, to be released on Friday, May 14, before the Sabbath began. On the evening of May 13, Ben-Gurion rewrote the draft, substituting more powerful language. The 1,000-word Declaration read in part:

> The Land of Israel . . . was the birthplace of the Jewish people. Here their spiritual, religious and political identity was shaped. Here they first attained to statehood, created cultural values of national and universal significance and gave to the world the eternal Book of Books. . . . In recent decades they returned in their masses . . . made deserts bloom, revived the Hebrew language, built villages and towns, and created a thriving community controlling its own economy . . .
>
> WE APPEAL—in the very midst of the onslaught launched against us now for months—to the Arab inhabitants of the State of Israel to preserve peace and participate in the up-building of the State . . .
>
> WE APPEAL to the Jewish people throughout the Diaspora to rally round the Jews of Eretz-Israel . . . in the great struggle for the realization of the age-old dream—the redemption of Israel.[39]

The Declaration ended with this sentence: "*Placing our trust in the 'Rock of Israel,' we affix our signatures to this Proclamation.*" [Emphasis added.] It was the final compromise that permitted all the Zionist groups to sign the Declaration. The reference to "Rock of Israel" satisfied both the ultra-

*Ben-Gurion reading the Declaration of Independence under a portrait of Herzl,*
*May 14, 1948*

secularists, who opposed any reference in the document to God, and the ultra-religious, who insisted on one. One group was satisfied with "Rock of Israel" as a synonym for the Lord, while the other accepted the same phrase as simply a metaphor for Jewish strength.[40]

Many historians believe that, but for the political will, forceful personality, and relentless efforts of David Ben-Gurion, there would have been no decision on May 14, 1948, to declare a state.[41] Yigael Yadin (whom Ben-Gurion named as the second IDF chief of staff) contended that "the decision on the proclamation was solely due" to Ben-Gurion.[42] The Declaration was in fact the result of the efforts of many, but we can say with some certainty that there was no other Zionist leader, at that time and in that place, who could have provided such decisive leadership.[43]

## JABOTINSKY

In late 1942, Menachem Begin arrived in Palestine from Poland as Jabotinsky's successor. The following year, at the age of 30, he assumed control of the Irgun, the military force that had split from the Haganah in the belief that, in addition to a defense force against the Arabs, offensive action should be taken against the British. On February 1, 1944, the Irgun published its "Proclamation of the Revolt," written by Begin. It noted that the World War was in its fourth year, and yet:

> [The Jews] have not been accorded international status, no Jewish Army has been set up, the gates of the community have not been opened. The British regime has sealed its shameful betrayal of the Jewish people and there is no moral basis whatsoever for its presence in Eretz Israel. . . . The fighting youth . . . will not surrender until they have renewed our days as of old, until they have ensured for our people a Homeland, freedom, honor, bread and justice.

Long after the war, Begin described his thinking at the time:

> It was really a decision whether to fight or not. The official leadership—the Jewish Agency, the Haganah, [and others] told us, "wait until after the war." To remember this advice is to say outright that it was monstrous. Wait until after the war to create a Jewish state? Only then will we start to think about a Jewish state? To wait another two years, until every Jew in Europe is dead?[44]

Begin worked underground for more than five years, disguised as a rabbi, coordinating attacks against British institutions in Palestine, ultimately including their military headquarters at the King David Hotel in Jerusalem.[45] The Irgun revolt and the attacks on the symbols of British authority were instrumental in causing Britain to decide to leave Palestine.[46] On May 15, 1948, as Israel faced an invasion by the surrounding Arab states, with the Israel Defense Forces still being formed from the combined forces of the Haganah and the Irgun, Begin gave a radio address broadcast carried throughout Israel:[47]

> The Hebrew Revolt of 1944–48 has been blessed with success— the first Hebrew revolt since the Hasmonean insurrection that has ended in victory. . . . And yet, even before our State is able to set up its normal national institutions, it is compelled to fight— or to continue to fight satanic enemies and blood-thirsty mercenaries. . . .
>
> [D]o you remember how we started? With what we started?

You were alone and persecuted, rejected, despised . . . you were tortured but you did not surrender; you were cast into prison but you did not yield; you were exiled from your country but your spirit was not crushed. . . .

[As we fight], we shall be accompanied by the spirit of those who revived our Nation—Herzl, Nordau, Trumpeldor, and the father of resurrected Hebrew heroism, [Vladimir] Ze'ev Jabotinsky.[48]

## JABOTINSKY'S RETURN

A decade and a half after Jabotinsky's death, long after he had been proven right on what the European Jews faced, and how much time was left to them, Louis Lipsky—one of the Zionist leaders who had joined Rabbi Stephen S. Wise in the June 17, 1940, trip to Washington to inform Lord Lothian that they wanted to disassociate themselves from Jabotinsky's Manhattan Center rally—wrote a poignant tribute:

[Jabotinsky] never lived in the regular time of day. He had his own time. While we Zionists saw the clock at six, he saw it at twelve. He did not know what was meant by premature; whatever was true was timely. . . . He came to the United States when it was frozen in the spirit of isolation, and died before American isolation became defense and aid for England. He preached to his last days for a Jewish army and Jewish flag (Jews as allies of the fighters against Hitler). . . .

He was dazzled by a Light. He saw his people once more like the other peoples of the earth, at home in freedom, the masters of their own land, no longer suppliants and pariahs, no longer enduring inferiority, but bravely and courageously fighting for their freedom. That Light never got out of his eyes. . . . He was a bold, imaginative, brave man. Practically alone, he marched ahead. He was sure the army would follow him some day.[49]

Jabotinsky's body remained at the Long Island cemetery until 1964.[50] Prime Minister Ben-Gurion refused to let it be re-buried in Israel, telling Jabotinsky's followers that Israel needed "live Jews, not dead ones."[51] But after Ben-Gurion's retirement in 1963, his successor as prime minister, Levi Eshkol—a member of Ben-Gurion's party and a veteran of Jabotinsky's Jewish Legion—ordered Jabotinsky's remains to be moved to Israel and reburied on Mount Herzl in Jerusalem, in the section reserved for the "Great Men of the Nation."[52]

On July 6, 1964, Times Square was renamed "Jabotinsky Square" for the day, and the remains of Jabotinsky and his wife, Joanna, were exhumed, with the caskets borne through Manhattan in a hearse drawn by four white horses, followed by marchers carrying the flags of the United States and Israel, to a memorial service led by forty cantors, and then on to John F. Kennedy International Airport for a flight to Israel.[53]

The JTA reported that "[h]uge crowds participated" in the funeral procession as Jabotinsky's casket was brought to the Young Israel Synagogue in Manhattan:

> The memorial service at the synagogue was led by rabbis and cantors including Moshe Kussevitzki. Ambassador Katriel Katz, Israel's Consul-General in New York, represented President [Zalman] Shazar, and read the Israel Government's order for the re-internment internment. . . . Leaders of [Menachem Begin's] Herut Party . . . who came to the funeral services from Israel, were also present.
>
> Many Jewish dignitaries and representatives of Latin Ameri-

*Jabotinsky's casket borne through Manhattan, July 6, 1964*

can Jewish communities participated in the service, which cul-
minated in the reciting of the Kaddish by Professor Eri Jabotinsky, the son of the late Zionist-Revisionist leader. An impressive
rendition of the "Kol Berama Nishma" (Jeremiah 31:15) [Rachel's
Lament for Her Children], by 40 New York cantors, highlighted
the service.[54]

Prime Minister Eshkol was in France on an official visit at the time and
met the plane on its re-fueling stop, accompanied by French officials, in a
hangar decorated with hundreds of Israeli and French flags. The aircraft
then continued to Israel, escorted by two jet planes.[55] In Tel Aviv, it was
a hero's homecoming.[56] Prime Minister Ehud Olmert later recalled it in a
2007 address to the Knesset:

> I clearly remember the immense funeral procession in the streets
> of Tel Aviv, which was unparalleled; I remember the tremen-
> dous emotion, sometimes tearful, of students and admirers,
> headed by the Chairman of the Herut Movement, Menachem
> Begin, who accompanied the coffin. A huge audience . . . came
> to pay their respects to the great Zionist leader; a bit late but
> wholeheartedly.[57]

*Procession transferring caskets of Vladimir and Joanna Jabotinsky*
*from Tel Aviv to Jerusalem*

*Jabotinsky's grave on Mt. Herzl, Jerusalem (Photo credit: Deror Avi)*

Among those also watching the procession that day was a 14-year-old boy, whose father had been Jabotinsky's executive assistant in 1940. Five decades later, that boy, Benjamin Netanyahu, would become the longest-serving Israeli prime minister after Ben-Gurion. In 2009, he told the Knesset that the Jabotinsky homecoming in 1964 had "made a tremendous impact on me."[58] Knesset Speaker Reuven Rivlin later remarked that

*Benzion Netanyahu and his son, Benjamin Netanyahu, Election Eve,*
*February 9, 2009*
*(Photo © Michal Fattal, http://www.michalfattal.com)*

Benjamin Netanyahu had "learned the pure Zionism from a man [his fa-
ther] who was so close to Jabotinsky."[59]

The unity that had eluded the Zionists in 1940 finally arrived—if only
symbolically—with Jabotinsky's reburial. Three years later, it had an important practical effect: Eshkol included Begin and his party—excluded
by Ben-Gurion from every coalition government from 1948 to 1963—in a
government of national unity. That government successfully defended the
Jewish state in the 1967 Six-Day War.[60]

## RACING AGAINST HISTORY

In 1879—before Leo Pinsker wrote *Auto-Emancipation* (1882); before Theodor Herzl published *The Jewish State* (1896); before the Jewish Legion and
the Balfour Declaration (1917); before the League of Nations Mandate for
Palestine (1922) and all that followed—the British novelist George Eliot
published an essay that, more than 135 years later, would still strike Zionist
readers as "remarkable" and "amazing."[61]

Eliot's essay was the result of a prodigious study she had made of Jewish
history and Jewish literature. Her essay was published as the final chapter

of her final book.[62] In it, she envisioned the restoration of a Jewish state, "planted on the old ground, as a center of national feeling, a source of dignifying protection, a special channel for special energies which may contribute some added form of national genius, and an added voice in the councils of the world."

Eliot questioned why people dismissed "the notion of a renovated national dignity for the Jews, whose ways of thinking and whose very verbal forms are on our lips in every prayer which we end with an Amen." She concluded that the "hinge of possibility" for a Jewish state was:

> . . . simply the existence of an adequate community of feeling
> as well as widespread need in the Jewish race, and the hope that
> among its finer specimens there may arise some men of instruc-
> tion and ardent public spirit, some new Ezras, some modern
> Maccabees, who will know how to use all favoring outward con-
> ditions, how to triumph by heroic example, over the indifference
> of their fellows and the scorn of their foes, and will steadfastly set
> their faces towards making their people once more one among
> the nations.

Weizmann, Jabotinsky, and Ben-Gurion—new Ezras and modern Maccabees—did not win the race against history in 1940, but their missions to America were part of a larger Zionist chronicle, one that had begun more than half a century earlier, and one that would continue throughout World War II, culminating eight years later in the founding of the modern State of Israel.

David Ben-Gurion became its first prime minister; Chaim Weizmann its first president; and Jabotinsky's successor, Menachem Begin, its first leader of the loyal opposition. Begin ran in election after election for nearly three decades, until in 1977 he too became prime minister.[63] Two-thirds of a century after its re-creation, Israel remains a vibrant democracy, one of the leading economies in the world, a vital center of the arts, sciences, and technology. It is the home of more than six million Jews.

In that sense, the race against history was won, after all.

# BIBLIOGRAPHY

## PRIMARY SOURCES

### Documents

Adler, Cyrus, ed. *The Voice of America on Kishineff*, (Philadelphia: The Jewish Publication Society of America, 1904)

"A Survey of Palestine," prepared in December 1945 and January 1946 for the Anglo-American Committee of Inquiry (Washington: The Institute of Palestine Studies, 1991)

The Balfour Declaration, November 2, 1917, http://www.jewishvirtuallibrary.org/text-of-the-balfour-declaration

Churchill, Winston. The Churchill Society, "The War Situation, January 20th, 1940, BBC Broadcast, London," http://churchill-society-london.org.uk/Joybells.html

Churchill, Winston. The Churchill Society, "Be ye men of Valour," broadcast May 13, 1940, http://churchill-society-london.org.uk/BeYeMofV.html

Churchill, Winston. "Moses—The Leader of a People," reprinted in the *Brooklyn Jewish Center Review*, February 1941, 5–7, 23 http://brooklynjewishcenter.org/cr1941.php

Declaration of Independence of the State of Israel, May 14, 1948, www.mfa.gov.il/MFA/ForeignPolicy/Peace/Guide/Pages/Declaration%20of%20Establishment%20of%20State%20of%20Israel.aspx

Kraines, Oscar, and Rafael Medoff, "Jabotinsky's Campaign in America: A Previously Unpublished Interview," *The Journal of Israeli History*, Vol. 15, No. 2 (1994)

Lindbergh, Charles. Des Moines speech, September 11, 1941, www.charleslindbergh.com/americanfirst/speech.asp

Rifkind, Simon H., et al. *The Basic Equities of the Palestine Problem* (New York: Arno Press, 1977), a reprint of the 1947 edition

Zola, Gary Phillip, and Marc Dollinger, eds., *American Jewish History: A Primary Source Reader* (Waltham: Brandeis University Press, 2014)

The League of Nations Mandate for Palestine (1922), www.jewishvirtuallibrary.org/jsource/History/PalestineMandate.html

"Munich Agreement [Europe] 1938," www.britannica.com/event/Munich-Agreement

Palestine Royal Commission Report ("Peel Commission Report"), July 1937, https://

www.scribd.com/document159990119/Peel-Commission-Reportpassia.org/
    publications/bookmaps/page1.htm
The Pittsburgh Platform, http://ccarnet.org/rabbis-speak/platforms/guiding-
    principles-reform-judaism/

*Newspaper Articles*

"Jews Face Crisis in Eastern Europe," *The New York Times*, February 7, 1937
Vladimir Jabotinsky, "A White Paper Against Diaspora Jewry," *The Jewish Herald*,
    June 23, 1939
"War, Executions, Disease Wiped Out 250,000 Jews in Nazi Poland, 'White Book'
    Charges," Jewish Telegraphic Agency (JTA), December 18, 1939
"'Nazi Spy' Picture Best of the Year," *The New York Times*, December 25, 1939,
    http://query.nytimes.com/mem/archive/pdf?res=9C05E1D8153EE432A25756C2
    A9649D946894D6CF
"Among Those Who Arrived from Europe on the Liner Rex Last Night," *The
    New York Times*, January 13, 1940, http://query.nytimes.com/mem/archive/
    pdf?res=9F0DE1DE113EE23ABC4B52DFB766838B659EDE
"Weizmann Set for 6-week Speaking Tour; Stresses U.S. Jewry's Refugee-aid Role,"
    JTA, January 15, 1940
"Weizmann Confers with Brandeis—Meeting Their First in 21 Years," JTA,
    February 7, 1940, www.jta.org/1940/02/07/archive/weizmann-confers-with-
    brandeis-meeting-their-first-in-21-years
"Zionist at White House/Dr. Weizmann Reports President Hopeful on Palestine
    Issue," *The New York Times*, February 9, 1940
"Palestine Curbs Jews' Land Buying—Britain Bans Purchases in Big Area, Limits
    Them in Another—Jewish Agency Defiant," *The New York Times*, February 29,
    1940
"Share in U.P.A. Funds for Palestine Revisionists Urged by Jabotinsky," JTA,
    April 4, 1940, www.jta.org/1940/04/04/archive/share-in-u-p-a-funds-for-palestine-
    revisionists-urged-by-jabotinsky
"Polish Leaders Seek Views of Jewish Groups on Future Status in Poland," JTA,
    May 12, 1940, www.jta.org/1940/05/12/archive/polish-leaders-seek-views-of-
    jewish-groups-on-future-status-in-poland
"Zionist Leaders Here Frown on Jabotinsky's Army Plan," JTA, June 19, 1940
"Jabotinsky, at Rally Here, Predicts Jewish Army Fighting at Britain's Side," JTA,
    June 20, 1940
"British and Nazi Armies," *The New York Times*, June 28, 1940
"Estimate of Losses Made by De Gaulle," *The New York Times*, June 30, 1940
"Zionists Make Plea for Broad Support," *The New York Times*, July 3, 1940
"Irving Berlin Song to Aid Our Youth," *The New York Times*, July 11, 1940
S. J. Woolf, "What Makes a Song: A Talk with Irving Berlin," *The New York Times*,
    July 28, 1940
"Vladimir Jabotinsky Dies of Heart Attack at 59; Was Visiting Youth Camp," JTA,
    August 5, 1940

"Palestine Mourns Jabotinsky; Work Stoppage Called; Son Freed from Jail," JTA, August 6, 1940

"Weizmann Pays Tribute at London Meeting," JTA, August 8, 1940, http://www.jta .org/1940/08/08/archive/weizmann-pays-tribute-at-london-meeting

"5,000 Attend Memorial in Montevideo," JTA, August 11, 1940

"Tributes in London," JTA, August 11, 1940

Stephen S. Wise, "Vladimir Jabotinsky," column in 1940, reprinted in *As I See It* (New York: Marstin Press, 1944)

"Berlin Composition Chosen," *The New York Times*, August 29, 1940

"London Views Pact as Warning to U.S.—Intimidate on Meddling in Europe or Asia Is Read Into Axis Alliance With Japan," *The New York Times*, September 28, 1940

*Time Magazine*, "Badgered Ballad," September 30, 1940

"Nazi-Led Drive in Egypt Foreseen . . . German Officers Said to Be in 'De Facto' Charge of Africa Campaign, Suez Is Held Objective," *The New York Times*, October 3, 1940

"Jews Fight for Britain—Palestine Recruiting Already Above Quota and Closed," *The New York Times*, October 3, 1940

"Ben-Gurion Here en Route to Palestine," JTA, October 7, 1940 (published originally as "Palestine's Future Depends on Jewish Army—Says David Ben-Gurion"), http://www.jta.org/1940/10/07/archive/ben-gurion-here-en-route-to-palestine

"Mr. Ben-Gurion Suggests 'Living Exhibit' of American Jewry," JTA, October 27, 1940

"Falsehood Cry in Movie Hearing," *The New York Times*, September 26, 1941, http://query.nytimes.com/mem/archive/pdf?res=9D0CE2DB163AE233A25755 C2A96F9C946093D6CF

Associated Press, "Only 100 Tanks in Britain at First, Churchill Reveals," December 16, 1942

"Brigadier Benjamin, Commander of Jewish Brigade, Comes from Family Active in Jewish Life," JTA, October 25, 1944

"Weizmann, Other Prominent Jewish Leaders in England Marked by Gestapo for 'Extermination,'" JTA, September 16, 1945, www.jta.org/1945/09/16/archive/ weizmann-other-prominent-jewish-leaders-in-england-marked-by-gestapo-for-extermination

"Truman's Palestine Views," *The New York Times*, March 26, 1948

"Huge Crowds Participate in Jabotinsky Funeral Procession in New York," JTA, July 7, 1964

"Dr. Edgar Romig, a Pastor Here, 74: Senior Minister of Four Collegiate Churches Dies," *The New York Times*, November 13, 1963

"Israel to Bury Jabotinsky, American Zionist Leader," *The New York Times*, June 14, 1964

"Mourners Pay Homage to Jabotinsky; Funeral Procession Set for Today," JTA, July 6, 1964

"Eshkol Pays Respects to Remains of Jabotinsky at Paris Airport," JTA, July 8, 1964

"Thousands in Tel Aviv View Jabotinsky Coffin," *The New York Times*, July 8, 1964

Drew Middleton, "At 'Their Finest Hour': Churchill's Confidence in Dark Days of 1940 Inspired the British People," *The New York Times*, January 24, 1965

"Kate Smith, All-American Singer, Dies at 79," *The New York Times*, June 18, 1986, www.nytimes.com/learning/general/onthisday/bday/0501.html Max Colchester, "French Remember de Gaulle on Day of Historic Address," *Wall Street Journal*, June 18, 2010

"Benzion Netanyahu to be Laid to Rest in Jerusalem," *The Jerusalem Post*, May 1, 2012, www.jpost.com/National-News/Benzion-Netanyahu-to-be-laid-to-rest-in-Jerusalem

## Autobiographies, Memoirs, and Diaries

Arens, Moshe. *Flags Over the Warsaw Ghetto: The Untold Story of the Warsaw Ghetto Uprising* (Jerusalem: Gefen Publishing House, 2011)

Begin, Menachem. *White Nights: The Story of a Prisoner in Russia* (New York: Harper & Row, 1957)

Begin, Menachem. *The Revolt: The Story of the Irgun* (New York: Henry Schuman, 1951)

Ben-Ami, Yitzhaq. *Years of Wrath, Days of Glory: Memoirs from the Irgun*, Second Expanded Edition (New York: Shengold Publishers Inc., 1983)

Ben-Gurion, David. Private diary for October 1, 1940, to December 31, 1940, collected for this book by Avi Shilon and translated into English by Aliza Perl Klaiman and Ophir Klainman

Ben-Gurion, David. *The Eternity of Israel* (Jerusalem: The Government Yearbook, 1954)

Ben-Gurion, David. *Israel: A Personal History* (New York and Tel Aviv: Funk & Wagnalls and Sabra Book, 1971)

Ben-Gurion, David. *Memoirs* (New York and Cleveland: The World Publishing Co., 1970)

Berlin, Isaiah. "Zionist Politics in Wartime Washington: A Fragment of Personal Reminiscence," a lecture delivered in Jerusalem in 1972, reprinted in Henry Hardy, ed., *Flourishing: Isaiah Berlin Letters 1928–1946* (Cambridge: Cambridge University Press, 2004), 665–666

Cahan, Abraham. *The Education of Abraham Cahan* (Philadelphia: The Jewish Publication Society, 1969)

Hertzberg, Arthur. *A Jew in America*: *My Life and a People's Struggle for Identity* (New York: HarperCollins, 2002)

Horowitz, Brian, and Leonid Katsis, eds., *Vladimir Jabotinsky's Story of My Life* (Detroit: Wayne State University Press, 2016)

Jabotinsky, Vladimir. *The Story of the Jewish Legion* (New York: Bernard Ackerman Inc., 1945)

Jabotinsky, Vladimir. *The War and the Jew* (New York: Altalena Press, 1987)

Jabotinsky, Vladimir. *The Five*, translated by Michael R. Katz (Ithaca: Cornell University Press, 2005)

Koestler, Arthur. *Scum of the Earth* (New York: The Macmillan Co., 1941)

Lowdermilk, Walter C. *Palestine, Land of Promise* (New York and London: Harper & Brothers Publishers, 1944)

McDonald, James G. *My Mission in Israel, 1948–1951* (New York: Simon and Schuster, 1951)

Patterson, Lt. Col. J. H. *With the Judaeans in the Palestine Campaign* (Hutchinson & Co: London, 1922)

Patterson, Lt. Col. J. H. *With the Zionists in Gallipoli* (London: Hutchinson & Co., 1916)

Peres, Shimon. *The Imaginary Voyage: With Theodor Herzl in Israel* (New York: Arcade Publishing, 1998)

Philipson, David. *My Life as an American Jew* (Cincinnati: John G. Kidd & Son Inc., 1941)

Podhoretz, Norman. *My Love Affair with America: The Cautionary Tale of a Cheerful Conservative* (New York: The Free Press, 2000)

Podhoretz, Norman. *Why Are Jews Liberals?* (New York: Vintage, 2010)

Weizmann, Chaim. *Trial and Error: The Autobiography of Chaim Weizmann* (New York: Harper & Brothers, 1949)

Weizmann, Vera. *The Impossible Takes Longer: The Memoirs of Vera Weizmann, Wife of Israel's First President, as told to David Tutaev* (New York and Evanston: Harper & Row, 1967)

### Correspondence

Barzilay, Dvorah, and Barnet Litvinoff, eds., *The Letters and Papers of Chaim Weizmann, Vol. VIII, Series A, November 1917–October 1918* (Jerusalem: Transaction Books, 1977)

Ben-Gurion, David. Letter to Justice Louis D. Brandeis, November 8, 1940

Ben-Gurion, David. Letter to Mrs. David de Sola Pool, January 15, 1941

Ben-Gurion, David. *Letters to Paula* (London: Vallentine, Mitchell & Co., 1971)

Cohen, Michael J., ed., *The Letters and Papers of Chaim Weizmann, Vol. XX, Series A (July 1940–January 1943)* (Jerusalem: Transaction Books, Rutgers University, Israel Universities Press, 1979)

Gordon, Louis. "'An Old Jewish Journalist to Another': The Private Correspondence of Ze'ev Jabotinsky and Ab. Cahan," *The Forward*, May 26, 2000

Jabotinsky, Vladimir. Letter as president of the New Zionist Organization, to Prime Minister Neville Chamberlain, September 4, 1939, Letter No. 4115, Reference Code A-1 2/29/2, The Jabotinsky Institute in Israel

Jabotinsky, Vladimir. Letter to Lt. Col. John Patterson, April 14, 1940, Letter Number, 4232, Reference Code A-1 2/30/1, The Jabotinsky Institute in Israel

Litvinoff, Barnet, ed. *The Letters and Papers of Chaim Weizmann*, Vol. II, Series B, December 1931–April 1952 (Rutgers University, New Brunswick, N.J., and Jerusalem: Transaction Books and Israel Universities Press, 1984), 384–392

Rose, Norman A., ed. *The Letters and Papers of Chaim Weizmann, Volume XIX, Series A, January 1939–June 1940* (New Brunswick, N.J., and Jerusalem: Transaction Books, Rutgers University, and Israel Universities Press, 1979)

Stein, Leonard, ed. *The Letters and Papers of Chaim Weizmann, Series A, Letters, Volume I, Summer 1885–29 October 1902* (London: Oxford University Press, 1968)

*Sermons from 1940*

Goldstein, Israel. *Toward a Solution* (New York: G. P. Putnam's Sons, 1940)

Levinthal, Israel Herbert. *A New World is Born: Sermons and Addresses* (New York and London: Funk & Wagnalls Co., 1943)

Lindbergh, Charles. "Des Moines Speech: Delivered in Des Moines, Iowa, September 11, 1941," http://www.charleslindbergh.com/americanfirst/speech.asp

Saperstein, Harold I. *Witness from the Pulpit: Topical Sermons 1933–1980*, edited by Marc Saperstein (Lanham, Md.: Lexington Books, 2000)

Saperstein, Marc. *Jewish Preaching in Times of War, 1800–2001* (Oxford and Portland, Or.: Littman Library of Jewish Civilization, 2008)

Silver, Abba Hillel. *Therefore Choose Life: Selected Sermons, Addresses, and Writings of Abba Hillel Silver, Volume One*, ed. Herbert Weiner (Cleveland: The World Publishing Company, 1967)

Wise, Stephen S. 1940 High Holiday Sermons, Jacob Rader Marcus Center of the American Jewish Archives, Stephen S. Wise Collection, Manuscript Collection 49, Box 21, Folder 10, and Box 21, Folders 1–4, Cincinnati, Ohio, http://collections.americanjewisharchives.org/ms/ms0049/ms0049.html

*Memoranda*

Memorandum dated October 4, 1940, entitled "David Ben-Gurion's Arrival in the United States," by Bernard Kornblith, Director of Port Reception Services, from the files of the YIVO Institute for Jewish Research, New York, New York

*Historical Background*

Bialik, Chaim Nachman. "In the City of Slaughter," http://faculty.history.umd.edu/BCooperman/NewCity/Slaughter.html, in Israel Efros, ed. *Complete Poetic Works of Hayyim Nahman Bialik*, Vol. I (New York: Histadruth Ivrith of America, 1948)

Eliot, George. "The Modern Hep! Hep! Hep!" www.online-literature.com/georgeeliot/theophrastus-such/18/

Hess, Moses. *Rome and Jerusalem: A Study in Jewish Nationalism* (New York: Bloch Publishing Company, 1918), originally written in German in 1862

"History of the Jewish Agency for Israel," http://jafi.org/JewishAgency/English/About/History

"History of Revisionist Zionism," www.knesset.gov.il/vip/jabotinsky/eng/Revisionisteng.html

"In Our Own Backyard: Resisting Nazi Propaganda in Southern California: 1933–1945," http://digital-library.csun.edu/Backyard/anti-semitism.html

"Lt. Gen. Yaacov Dori (1947–49)," https://www.idfblog.com/about-the-idf/past-chiefs-of-staff/lt-gen-yaacov-dori-1947–49/

Lewis, Sinclair, *It Can't Happen Here* (New York: Signet Classics, 1970)

Pinsker, Leo. *Road to Freedom: Writings and Addresses* (Westport, Conn.: Greenwood Press, 1944)

Remarque, Erich Maria. *The Night in Lisbon* (United States: Harcourt, Brace & World, 1964)

"The Scope of Jewish Dictatorship in the U.S.," *Dearborn Independent*, December 11, 1920, excerpted in Gary Phillip Zola and Marc Dollinger, eds., *American Jewish History: A Primary Source Reader* (Waltham: Brandeis University Press, 2014)

"World Zionist Organization," http://en.wikipedia.org/wiki/WorldZionist Organization

## Government Reports

*A Report of the Commissioners of Immigration Upon the Causes Which Incite Immigration to the United States* (Washington, D.C.: Government Printing Office, 1892)

*Propaganda in Motion Pictures*, Hearings before a Subcommittee of the Committee on Interstate Commerce, United States Senate, Seventy-Seventh Congress, First Session, September 9 to 26, 1941 (U.S. Government Printing Office, Washington, D.C.: 1942)

## Speeches and Addresses

"Charles de Gaulle: Great Speeches of the 20th Century," at www.guardian.co.uk/theguardian/2007/apr/29/greatspeeches1

Vladimir Jabotinsky, "The Fate of Jewry," address at the Manhattan Center, New York City, March 19, 1940, The Jabotinsky Institute in Israel, Reference Code A-1 8/59

Vladimir Jabotinsky, "Rosh Betar's Speech," address at the Capitol Hotel, March 31, 1940, The Jabotinsky Institute in Israel, Reference Code A-1 8/58

Vladimir Jabotinsky, "The Second World War and a Jewish Army," address at the Manhattan Center, June 19, 1940, The Jabotinsky Institute in Israel, Reference Code A-1 8/60

Vladimir Jabotinsky, "Lublin or Palestine, Which?" 1940 address to the Brooklyn-Queens Council and American Friends of a Jewish Palestine, http://collection.mjhnyc.org/index.php?g=detail&objectid=1886

Max Nordau, "Address at the First Zionist Congress" (1897), http://www.jewishvirtualibrary.org/address-by-max-nordau-at-the-first-zionist-congress; *Zionism and Anti-Semitism—Zionism by Nordau; and Anti-Semitism by Gottheil* (Amazon Digital Services LLC)

Max Nordau, Address at the Sixth Zionist Congress (1903), http://www.jewishvirtuallibrary.org/address-by-max-nordau-at-the-sixth-zionist-congress

Chaim Weizmann, "A Vision of the Future," Address to Mass Meeting, New York City, January 16, 1940, in Litvinoff, Barnet, ed. *The Letters and Papers of Chaim Weizmann*, Vol. II, Series B, December 1931–April 1952 (Rutgers University, New Brunswick, N.J. and Jerusalem: Transaction Books and Israel Universities Press, 1984), 384–392

SECONDARY SOURCES

*Books*

Acher, H., ed. *Zionism and the Jewish Future* (New York: The Macmillan Company, 1916)

Arens, Moshe. *Flags Over the Warsaw Ghetto: The Untold Story of the Warsaw Ghetto Uprising* (Jerusalem: Gefen Publishing House, 2011)

Atkinson, Rick. *An Army at Dawn* (New York: Henry Holt & Co., 2000)

Avner, Yehuda. *The Prime Ministers: An Intimate Narrative of Israeli Leadership* (New Milford, Conn.: The Toby Press, 2010)

Bardin, Shlomo, ed. *Self-Fulfillment Through Zionism: A Study in Jewish Adjustment* (Freeport, N.Y.: Books for Libraries Press, 1943)

Barzilay, Dvorah and Barnet Litvinoff, eds. *The Letters and Papers of Chaim Weizmann, Vol. VIII, Series A, November 1917–October 1918* (Jerusalem: Transaction Books, 1977)

Bar-Zohar, Michael. *Ben-Gurion: A Biography* (New York: Delacorte Press, 1978)

Beckman, Morris. *The Jewish Brigade: An Army with Two Masters 1944–1945* (New York: The History Press, 2008)

Ben-Ami, Yitshaq. *Years of Wrath, Days of Glory: Memoirs from the Irgun*, Second Expanded Edition (New York: Shengold Publishers Inc., 1983)

Begin, Menachem. *White Nights: The Story of a Prisoner in Russia* (Harper & Row: New York, 1957)

Begin, Menachem. *The Revolt: The Story of the Irgun* (New York: Henry Schuman, 1951)

Ben-Gurion, David. *Israel: A Personal History* (New York and Tel Aviv: Funk & Wagnalls and Sabra Book, 1971)

Ben-Gurion, David. *Memoirs* (New York and Cleveland: World Publishing Co., 1970)

Ben-Gurion, David. *The Eternity of Israel* (Jerusalem: The Government Yearbook, 1954)

Ben-Gurion, David. *Letters to Paula* (London: Valentine Mitchell, 1968)

Berg, Scott. *Lindbergh* (New York: G. P. Putnam's Sons, 1998)

Berlin, Isaiah. *Letters 1928–1946*, edited by Henry Hardy (Cambridge: Cambridge University Press, 2004)

Beevor, Antony. *The Second World War* (New York: Little, Brown & Co., 2012)

Birdwell, Michael E. *Celluloid Soldiers: Warner Bros.'s Campaign against Nazism* (New York: New York University Press, 1999)

Brandeis, Louis Dembitz. *The Jewish Problem; How to Solve it* (New York: The Zionist Essays Publication Committee, 1915)

Breitman, Richard, and Allan J. Lichtman. *FDR and the Jews* (Cambridge: Harvard University Press, 2013)

Brook, Vincent. *Driven to Darkness: Jewish Émigré Directors and the Rise of Film Noir* (New Brunswick, N.J.: Rutgers University Press, 2009)

Cahan, Abraham. *The Education of Abraham Cahan* (Philadelphia: The Jewish Publication Society, 1969)

Churchill, Winston S. *The Second World War, Volume I, The Gathering Storm* (Boston: Houghton Mifflin, 1948)

Cohen, Eliot A. *Supreme Command: Soldiers, Statesmen, and Leadership in Wartime* (New York: Anchor Books, 2003)

Cohen, Naomi W. *The Americanization of Zionism, 1897–1948* (Hanover and London: Brandeis University Press, 2003)

Cohen, Naomi W. *American Jews and the Zionist Idea* (United States of America: KTAV Publishing House Inc., 1975)

Crossman, Richard H. S. *A Nation Reborn* (New York: Atheneum, 1960)

Dinnerstein, Leonard. *Anti-Semitism in America* (New York and Oxford: Oxford University Press, 1994)

Doherty, Thomas. *Hollywood and Hitler, 1933–1939* (New York: Columbia University Press, 2013)

Duggan, Christopher. *The Force of Destiny: A History of Italy Since 1796* (London: Penguin Books, 2008)

Fachler, Yanky. *6 Officers, 2 Lions, and 750 Mules* (Baltimore: Publish America, 2006)

Friedrich, Otto. *City of Nets: A Portrait of Hollywood in the 1940s* (New York: Harper Perennial, 1987)

Gal, Allon. *David Ben-Gurion and the American Alignment for a Jewish State* (Indianapolis: Indiana University Press, 1991)

Gelernter, David. *Americanism: The Fourth Great Western Religion* (New York: Doubleday, 2007)

Gilbert, Martin. *The Second World War: A Complete History* (New York: Henry Holt & Co., 1989)

Gilder, George. *The Israel Test* (New York and London: Encounter Books, 2012)

Glinert, Lewis. *The Story of Hebrew* (Princeton and Oxford: Princeton University Press, 2017)

Goldstein, Israel. *Toward a Solution* (New York: G. P. Putnam's Sons, 1940)

Gordis, Daniel. *Menachem Begin: The Battle for Israel's Soul* (New York: Nextbook Schocken, 2014)

Gurock, Jeffrey S. *American Jewish History, Vol. 8, American Zionism: Mission and Politics* (New York and London: Routledge, 1998)

Hardy, Henry, ed. *Flourishing: Isaiah Berlin Letters 1928–1946* (Cambridge: Cambridge University Press, 2004)

Halpern, Ben. *A Clash of Heroes: Brandeis, Weizmann, and American Zionism* (New York and Oxford: Oxford University Press, 1987)

Hertzberg, Arthur. *A Jew in America: My Life and a People's Struggle for Identity* (New York: HarperCollins, 2002)

Herzog, Chaim. *The Arab-Israeli Wars: War and Peace in the Middle East from the War of Independence through Lebanon* (New York: Vintage Books, 1984)

Heller, Daniel Kupfert. *Jabotinsky's Children: Polish Jews and the Rise of Right-Wing Zionism* (Princeton and Oxford: Princeton University Press, 2017)

Himmelfarb, Gertrude. *The Jewish Odyssey of George Eliot* (New York: Encounter Books, 2009)

Hoffman, Bruce. *Anonymous Soldiers: The Struggle for Israel, 1917–1947* (New York: Alfred A. Knopf, 2015)

Jabotinsky, Vladimir. *The War and the Jew* (New York: Altalena Press, 1987)

Jabotinsky, Vladimir. *The Story of the Jewish Legion* (New York: Bernard Ackerman, Incorporated 1945)

Kaplan, Eran. *The Jewish Radical Right: Revisionist Zionism and Its Ideological Legacy* (Madison, W.I.: The University of Wisconsin Press, 2005)

Kaskowitz, Sheryl. *God Bless America: The Surprising History of an Iconic Song* (Oxford: Oxford University Press, 2013)

Katz, Samuel, *Days of Fire* (Jerusalem, Tel Aviv, and Haifa: Steimatzky's Agency Ltd., 1966)

Katz, Shmuel. *Lone Wolf: A Biography of Vladimir (Ze'ev) Jabotinsky* (New York: Barricade Books, 1996)

Kelly, John. *Never Surrender: Winston Churchill and Britain's Decision to Fight Nazi Germany in the Fateful Summer of 1940* (New York: Scribner, 2015)

Kochanski, Halik. *The Eagle Unbowed* (Cambridge: Harvard University Press, 2012)

Kurzman, Dan. *Ben-Gurion: Prophet of Fire* (New York: Simon & Schuster, Inc., 1983)

Langword, ed. *Churchill by Himself*

Landau, David. *Ben-Gurion: A Political Life* (New York: Nextbook Schocken, 2011)

Laqueur, Walter. *A History of Zionism* (New York: Schocken Books, 1976)

Levinthal, Israel Herbert. *A New World is Born: Sermons and Addresses* (New York: Funk & Wagnalls, 1943)

Lipsky, Louis. *Memoirs in Profile* (Philadelphia: Jewish Publication Society, 1975)

Lipsky, Seth. *The Rise of Abraham Cahan* (New York: Schocken Books, 2013)

Litvinoff, Barnet. *Ben-Gurion of Israel* (New York: Praeger, 1954)

Litvinoff, Barnet, ed. *The Letters and Papers of Chaim Weizmann, Volume II, Series B, December 1931–April 1952* (Jerusalem: Transaction Books, Rutgers University, 1984)

Lowdermilk, Walter Clay. *Palestine, Land of Promise* (New York and London: Harper & Brothers, 1944)

McDonald, James G. *My Mission in Israel, 1948–1951* (New York: Simon and Schuster, 1951)

MacDonnell, Francis. *Insidious Foes: The Axis Fifth Column and the American Homefront* (New York: Oxford University Press, 1995)

Medoff, Rafael. *Militant Zionism in America: The Rise and Impact of the Jabotinsky Movement in the United States, 1926–1948* (Tuscaloosa: The University of Alabama Press, 2002)

Merlin, Samuel. *Millions of Jews to Rescue* (Washington, D.C.: The David S. Wyman Institute for Holocaust Studies, 2011)

Moorhouse, Roger. *The Devils' Alliance: Hitler's Pact with Stalin, 1939–1941* (New York: Basic Books, 2014)

Netanyahu, Benzion. *The Founding Fathers of Zionism* (Jerusalem: Gefen Publishing House Ltd. and Balfour Books, 2012)

Nordau, Max, and Richard Gottheil. *Zionism and Anti-Semitism Zionism by Nordau; and Anti-Semitism by Gottheil* (Amazon Digital Services LLC)

Oney, Steve. *And the Dead Shall Rise: The Murder of Mary Phagan and the Lynching of Leo Frank* (New York: Vintage Books, 2004)

Oren, Michael B. *Power, Faith, and Fantasy: America in the Middle East, 1776 to the Present* (New York: W. W. Norton & Co., 2007)

Oren, Michael B. *Six Days of War: June 1967 and the Making of the Modern Middle East* (Oxford: Oxford University Press, 2002)

Patterson, John. *With the Judaeans in the Palestine Campaign* (London: Hatchenson & Co., Paternoster Row, 1922)

Penkower, Monty Noam. *The Jews Were Expendable: Free World Diplomacy and the Holocaust* (Champaign: University of Illinois Press, 1983)

Peres, Shimon, in conversation with David Landau. *Ben-Gurion: A Political Life* (New York: Nextbook Schocken, 2011)

Peres, Shimon. *The Imaginary Voyage: With Theodor Herzl in Israel* (New York: Arcade Publishing, 1998)

Pinsker, Leo. *Road to Freedom: Writings and Addresses* (Westport, Conn.: Greenwood Press, 1944)

Podhoretz, Norman. *Why Are Jews Liberals?* (New York: Vintage, 2010)

Podhoretz, Norman. *My Love Affair with America: The Cautionary Tale of a Cheerful Conservative* (New York: The Free Press, 2000)

Rabinowicz, Oskar K. *Fifty Years of Zionism: A Historical Analysis of Dr. Weizmann's "Trial and Error"* (London: Robert Anscombe & Co. Ltd., 1950)

Radosh, Allis, and Ronald Radosh. *A Safe Haven: Harry S. Truman and the Founding of Israel* (New York: HarperCollins, 2009)

Ravitzky, Aviezer. *Messianism, Zionism, and Jewish Religious Radicalism* (Chicago: The University of Chicago Press, 1996)

Reinharz, Jehuda, and Anita Shapira, eds. *Essential Papers on Zionism* (New York: New York University Press, 1996)

Reinharz, Jehuda. *Chaim Weizmann: The Making of a Statesman* (New York: Oxford University Press, 1993)

Rifkind, Simon H., et al. *The Basic Equities of the Palestine Problem* (New York: Arno Press, 1977, a reprint of the 1947 edition)

Roberts, Andrew. *The Storm of War: A New History of the Second World War* (New York: Harper, 2012)

Rosbottom, Ronald C. *When Paris Went Dark: The City of Light Under German Occupation, 1940–1944* (New York: Little Brown and Co., 2014)

Rose, Norman. *Chaim Weizmann: A Biography* (New York: Viking Penguin Inc., 1986)

Rose, Norman A., ed. *The Letters and Papers of Chaim Weizmann, Volume XIX, Series A, January 1939–June 1940* (Jerusalem: Transaction Books, Rutgers University, 1979)

Rosenbaum, Ron, ed. *Those Who Forget the Past: The Question of Anti-Semitism* (New York: Random House, 2004)

Rosenzweig, Laura B. *Hollywood's Spies: The Undercover Surveillance of Nazis in Los Angeles* (Goldstein-Goren Series in American Jewish History) (New York: NYU Press, 2017)

Ross, Steven J. *Hitler in Los Angeles: How Jews Foiled Nazi Plots Against Hollywood and America* (New York: Bloomsbury USA, 2017)

Sachar, Howard M. *A History of Israel: From the Rise of Zionism to Our Time* (New York: Alfred A. Knopf, 1976)

Saperstein, Harold I. *Witness from the Pulpit: Topical Sermons 1933–1980*, edited by Marc Saperstein (Lanham, Md: Lexington Books, 2000)

Saperstein, Marc Eli. *Jewish Preaching in Times of War, 1800–2001* (Oxford: Littman Library of Jewish Civilization, 2008)

Sarna, Jonathan D. *American Judaism: A History* (New Haven: Yale University Press, 2004)

Scammell, Michael. *Koestler: The Literary and Political Odyssey of a Twentieth-Century Skeptic* (New York: Random House, 2009)

Schneer, Jonathan. *The Balfour Declaration: The Origins of the Arab-Israeli Conflict* (New York: Random House, 2010)

Schechtman, Joseph B. *Fighter and Prophet: The Vladimir Jabotinsky Story: The Last Years* (New York: Thomas Yoseloff, 1961)

Schechtman, Joseph B. *Rebel and Statesman: The Vladimir Jabotinsky Story: The Early Years* (New York: Thomas Yoseloff, 1956)

Shapira, Anita. *Israel: A History* (Waltham, Mass.: Brandeis University Press, 2012)

Shavit, Yaacov. *Jabotinsky and the Revisionist Movement, 1925–1948* (London: Frank Cass & Co. Ltd., 1988)

Shindler, Colin. *The Rise of the Israeli Right: From Odessa to Hebron* (New York: Cambridge University Press, 2015)

Silberman, Charles E. *A Certain People: American Jews and Their Lives Today* (New York: Summit Books, 1985)

Silver, Abba Hillel. *Therefore Choose Life: Selected Sermons, Addresses, and Writing of Abba Hillel Silver, Volume One*, ed. Herbert Weiner (Cleveland: The World Publishing Company, 1967)

Snow, Nancy. "Confessions of a Hollywood Propagandist: Harry Warner, FDR and Celluloid Persuasion," in *Warners' War: Politics, Pop Culture & Propaganda in Wartime Hollywood,* Martin Kaplan and Johanna Blakley, eds. (Los Angeles: Norman Lear Center Press, 2004)

Silverberg, Robert. *If I Forget Thee O Jerusalem: American Jews and the State of Israel* (New York: William Morrow and Co., 1979)

Stanislawski, Michael. *Zionism and the Fin de Siècle: Cosmopolitanism and Nationalism from Nordau to Jabotinsky* (Berkeley: University of California Press, 2001)

Stanislawski, Michael. *Autobiographical Jews: Essays in Jewish Self-Fashioning* (Seattle: University of Washington Press, 2004)

Stein, Leonard, ed. *The Letters and Papers of Chaim Weizmann, Series A, Letters, Volume I (Summer 1885–29 October 1902* (London: Oxford University Press, 1968)

Tedesche, Rabbi Sidney D. *A Set of Holiday Sermons, 5701–1940* (Cincinnati: The Tract Commission, 1940)

Teveth, Shabtai. *Ben-Gurion: The Burning Ground 1886–1948* (Boston: Houghton Mifflin Company, 1987)

Urwand, Ben. *The Collaboration: Hollywood's Pact with Hitler* (Cambridge: Harvard University Press, 2013)

Urofsky, Melvin I. *A Voice that Spoke for Justice: The Life and Times of Stephen S. Wise* (Albany: State University of New York Press, 1981)

Urofsky, Melvin I. *American Zionism: From Herzl to the Holocaust* (Lincoln and London: University of Nebraska Press, 1975)

Urofsky, Melvin I. *Louis D. Brandeis: A Life* (New York: Alfred A. Knopf, 2009)

Walzer, Michael, and Menachem Lorberbaum, Noam J. Zohar, eds. *The Jewish Political Tradition: Volume One: Authority* (New Haven and London: Yale University Press, 2000)

Walzer, Michael. *The Paradox of Liberation: Secular Revolutions and Religious Counterrevolutions*, (New Haven and London: Yale University Press, 2015)

Wasserstein, Bernard. *Britain and the Jews of Europe: 1939–1945* (Oxford: Oxford University Press, 1979)

Wasserstein, Bernard. *On the Eve: The Jews of Europe Before the Second World War* (New York: Simon & Schuster, 2012)

Webster, Charles. *The Art and Practice of Diplomacy* (London: Chatto & Windus, 1961)

Weisgal, Meyer W., and Joel Carmichael, eds., *Chaim Weizmann: A Biography by Several Hands* (New York: Atheneum, 1963)

Welky, David. *The Moguls and the Dictators: Hollywood and the Coming of World War II* (Baltimore: Johns Hopkins University Press, 2008)

Wisse, Ruth R. *Jews and Power* (New York: Nextbook Schocken, 2007)

Wisse, Ruth R. *The Modern Jewish Canon: A Journey Through Language and Culture* (New York: The Free Press, 2000)

Wyman, David S., and Rafael Medoff. *A Race Against Death: Peter Bergson, America, and the Holocaust* (New York: The New Press, 2002)

## Articles

Appel, John J. "*The Trefa Banquet*," *Commentary Magazine*, February 1, 1966

Applebaum, Diana Muir. "The First War of National Liberation," *Jewish Ideas Daily*, December 12, 2012

Corbett, Anne. "A Certain June 18," *History Today* 50, no. 7 (July 2000), www.history today.com/anne-corbett/certain-june-18th

Decter, Midge. "A Jew in Anti-Christian America," in Richard John Neuhaus, *The Chosen People in an Almost Chosen Nation* (Grand Rapids, Mich.: William B. Eerdmans Publishing Co., 2002)

Decter, Midge. "Return and Exile," a review of Shmuel Katz's biography of Jabotinsky, *Commentary Magazine*, July 1996

Denby, David. "Hitler in Hollywood: Did the Studios Collaborate?" *The New Yorker*, September 16, 2013

Eban, Abba. "Chaim Weizmann and the Personality of Power," *The Jerusalem Post*, International Edition, November 18, 1989

Fivel, T. R. "Weizmann and the Balfour Declaration," in Meyer W. Weisgal and Joel Carmichael, eds., *Chaim Weizmann: A Biography by Several Hands* (New York: Atheneum, 1963)

Gordon, Louis A. "Arthur Koestler and His Ties to Zionism and Jabotinsky," *Studies in Zionism* 12, no. 2 (1991)

Halkin, Hillel. "Sacrifices," *The New Republic*, December 18, 2005, https://new republic.com/article/62680/sacrifices

Hayes, Richard K. "God Bless America, Land That I Love," http://katesmith.org/gba.html

Hutchinson, Lydia. "*Irving Berlin's 'God Bless America*,'" http://performingsongwriter .com/god-bless-america/

Kaplan, Martin, and Johanna Blakley, eds. (Los Angeles: Norman Lear Center Press, 2004), www.learcenter.org/pdf/WWRoss.pdf

Holocaust Encyclopedia, "Kristallnacht: A Nationwide Pogrom, November 9–10, 1938," www.ushmm.org/wlc/en/article.php?ModuleId=10005201

Jewish Virtual Library. Yad Vashem, "The Jewish Brigade," http://www.yadvashem .org/yv/en/exhibitions/thismonth/march/13.asp

Jewish Virtual Library. "Max Nordau," www.jewishvirtuallibrary.org/jsource/ judaica/ejud0002015014907.html

Jewish Virtual Library. "Shlomo Bardin," www.jewishvirtuallibrary.org/jsource/ judaica/ejud0002000300231.html

KCET, "From Contract to Blacklist: Hollywood Exile Experience," www.kcet.org/ arts/artbound/counties/los-angeles/blacklist-hollywood-exile-experience-warner-brothers.html

Kristol, William. "The Jewish State at 60," *The New York Times*, May 12, 2008, at A19, www.nytimes.com/2008/05/12/opinion/12kristol.html?r=0

Lieberman, Anne. "Six Days Remembered," *The Jewish Press*, June 1, 2005, www .jewishpress.com/indepth/front-page/six-days-remembered/2005/06/01/

Lieberman, Anne. "Two Jews," *American Thinker*, September 27, 2009, http://www .americanthinker.com/articles/2009/09/twojews.html

Lipsky, Seth. "Abraham Cahan Speaks," *Tablet Magazine*, July 7, 2012

Mahross. "The Jewish Brigade," January 1, 2004, www.ww2f.com/topic/8959-the-jewish-brigade/

Medoff, Rafael. "Who Fought for the 'Right to Fight'? A Response to Arye Bruce Saposnik's Article on the Campaign for a Jewish Army, 1939–1944," *The Journal of Israeli History* 18, no. 1 (Spring 1997)

Middleton, Drew. "At 'Their Finest Hour,'" *The New York Times*, January 24, 1965, 70

Oz, Amos. "David Ben-Gurion," *Time Magazine*, April 13, 1998, http://content.time .com/time/magazine/article/0,9171,988160,00.html

The Prime Minister's Office. "Levi Eshkol," http://www.pmo.gov.il/English/ Memorials/PrimeMinisters/Pages/LeviEshkol.aspx

Radosh, Allis, and Ronald Radosh. "Lowdermilk Makes the Case," a description of Lowdermilk's book, *Palestine, Land of Promise* (New York: Harper & Bros., 1944), http://www.jbooks.com/interviews/index/IPRadosh.htm

Raphael, Chaim. "The Letters and Papers of Chaim Weizmann, Vols. III–VII," *Commentary Magazine*, October 1975

Richman, Rick. "Jabotinsky Then and Now," *Commentary Magazine,* https://www
.commentarymagazine.com/culture-civilization/history/jabotinsky-then-and-now/

Richman, Rick. "Why Jabotinsky Still Matters," *The Tower Magazine* (June 2014),
http://www.thetower.org/article/why-jabotinsky-still-matters/

Richman, Rick. "Jabotinsky's Lost Moment: June, 1940," *The Tower Magazine* (December 2013), http://www.thetower.org/article/jabotinskys-lost-moment-june-1940/

Rosenzweig, Laura. "Hollywood's Anti-Nazi Spies," *Jewish Review of Books* (Winter 2014)

Ross, Steven J. "Confessions of a Nazi Spy: Warner Bros., Anti-Fascism and the Politicization of Hollywood," in *Warners' War: Politics, Pop Culture & Propaganda in Wartime Hollywood*

Stansky, Peter. "80 Days that Saved the World: The Duel 10 May–31 July 1940," *The New York Times*, March 3, 1991

Schoffman, Stuart. "Hollywood and the Nazis," *Jewish Review of Books*, Winter 2014

Saposnik, Arye Bruce. "Advertisement or Achievement? American Jewry and the Campaign for a Jewish Army, 1939–1944: A Reassessment," *The Journal of Israeli History* 17, no. 2 (1996)

Sussman, Lance. "The Myth of the Trefa Banquet: American Culinary Culture and the Radicalization of Food Policy in American Reform Judaism," *American Jewish Archives Journal* (2005)

Harry S. Truman Library & Museum. "Creation of the State of Israel, 1948, Torah Scroll," www.trumanlibrary.org/israel/torah.htm

United States Holocaust Museum. Holocaust Encyclopedia, "United States Policy and Its Impact on European Jews," http://www.ushmm.org/wlc/en/article.php?
ModuleId=10007652

Wolpe, David. "The Changing Face of Anti-Semitism," *Los Angeles Review of Books,* December 11, 2015

## Videos

"Remarks of Bob Cohen and Truman-Jacobson Video," shown at the 2016 AIPAC Policy Conference in Washington, D.C., March 20, 2016, https://www.youtube
.com/watch?v=P7f5p42r0rg

"The Evolution of the Israeli Right: From Jabotinsky to Begin to Netanyahu," Children of Jewish Holocaust Survivors, August 23, 2012, https://www.youtube.com/
watch?v=u4tM27r3cbg

# NOTES

*Preface*

1. See "World Zionist Organization," http://www.wzo.org.il/world-zionist-organization. As of 1940, the name of the organization was the "Zionist Organization." In 1960, it changed its name to the "World Zionist Organization."

2. See the summary of the Revisionist Movement at the website of the Israeli Knesset: https://www.knesset.gov.il/vip/jabotinsky/eng/Revisionisteng.html. Jabotinsky's Revisionist Party was the forerunner of the Herut Party formed by Menachem Begin in 1948, which became the Likud Party in 1973. The Likud has been headed since 2009 by Benjamin Netanyahu.

3. See "History of the Jewish Agency for Israel," http://jafi.org/JewishAgency/English/About/History. The League of Nations Mandate for Palestine in 1922 provided in part as follows:

> Whereas the Principal Allied Powers [Great Britain, France, Italy, and Japan] have agreed . . . to entrust to a Mandatory selected by the said Powers the administration of the territory of Palestine, which formerly belonged to the Turkish Empire . . . ; and

> Whereas the Principal Allied Powers have also agreed that the Mandatory should be responsible for putting into effect the [Balfour] declaration originally made on November 2nd, 1917 . . . and adopted by the said Powers [in 1920 at San Remo], in favor of the establishment in Palestine of a national home for the Jewish people . . . ; and

> Whereas recognition has thereby been given to the historical connection of the Jewish people with Palestine and to the grounds for reconstituting their national home in that country; . . .

> \* \* \*

> ARTICLE 4. An appropriate Jewish agency shall be recognized as a public body for the purpose of advising and cooperating with the [British] Administration of Palestine in such economic, social and other matters as may affect the establishment of the Jewish national home . . .

The full text of the Mandate for Palestine is at: http://www.jewishvirtuallibrary.org/jsource/History/PalestineMandate.html.

4. In his address to Congress on April 2, 1917, seeking a declaration of war against Germany, President Woodrow Wilson had told Congress that:

> The world must be made safe for democracy. Its peace must be planted upon the tested foundations of political liberty. We have no selfish ends to serve. We desire no conquest, no dominion. We seek no indemnities for ourselves, no material compensation for the sacrifices we shall freely make. We are but one of the champions of the rights of mankind. . . .
>
> [W]e shall fight for the things which we have always carried nearest our hearts—for democracy, for the right of those who submit to authority to have a voice in their own governments, for the rights and liberties of small nations, for a universal dominion of right by such a concert of free peoples as shall bring peace and safety to all nations and make the world itself at last free.

See "Making the World 'Safe for Democracy': Woodrow Wilson Asks for War," http://historymatters.gmu.edu/d/4943/. By 1939 that view of the war had long since soured.

5. More than 116,000 Americans died in World War I. See U.S. Department of Veterans Affairs, "America's Wars," https://www.va.gov/opa/publications/factsheets/fsamericaswars.pdf. The vast majority of Americans, watching a new European war begin, wanted no repetition of the high-minded experience into which President Wilson had led them.

6. Chaim Weizmann devoted only three pages to his 1940 trip in his autobiography, Chaim Weizmann, *Trial and Error: The Autobiography of Chaim Weizmann* (New York: Harper & Brothers, 1949), 418–421. For reasons noted in the chapter on Weizmann in this book, he did not tell the full story. Norman Rose's excellent 520-page biography devotes a single sentence to it. See Norman Rose, *Chaim Weizmann: A Biography* (New York: Viking Penguin Inc., 1986), 358. Jehuda Reinharz's magisterial two-volume biography ends with the adoption of the Balfour Declaration in 1917 and its aftermath, and thus does not cover the 1940 trip at all. See Jehuda Reinharz, *Chaim Weizmann: The Making of a Statesman* (New York: Oxford University Press, 1993).

David Ben-Gurion, in *Israel: A Personal History* (New York and Tel Aviv: Funk & Wagnalls and Sabra Book, 1971), mentioned his 1940 trip only in passing, devoting only a single page of the 862-page book to it—for reasons we will also explore. Allon Gal covers the trip in *David Ben-Gurion and the American Alignment for a Jewish State* (Indianapolis: Indiana University Press, 1991), 118 *et seq.*, and Shabtai Teveth covers it in *Ben-Gurion: The Burning Ground 1886–1948* (Boston, Houghton Mifflin Company, 1987.)

Vladimir Jabotinsky, for reasons beyond his control, never wrote a memoir about his 1940 trip, but the trip has been described in the two magisterial biographies of him, Shmuel Katz, *Lone Wolf: A Biography of Vladimir (Ze'ev) Jabotinsky*, Vol. 2 (New York: Barricade Books, 1996), 1754–1783, and Joseph B. Schechtman, *Fighter and Prophet: The Vladimir Jabotinsky Story: The Last Years* (New York: Thomas Yoseloff, 1961), 384–398, and by Rafael Medoff in *Militant Zionism in America: The Rise and Impact of the Jabotinsky Movement in the United States, 1926–1948* (Tuscaloosa: The University of Alabama Press, 2002), 45–64; see also David S. Wyman and Rafael Medoff, *A Race Against Death: Peter Bergson, America, and the Holocaust* (New York: The New Press, 2002), 16–19.

*Introduction: The World in 1940*

1. See Roger Moorhouse, *The Devils' Alliance: Hitler's Pact with Stalin, 1939–1941* (New York: Basic Books, 2014), xxiii–xxvi.

2. Martin Gilbert, *The Second World War: A Complete History* (New York: Henry Holt & Co., 1989), 9. Roger Moorhouse, *The Devils' Alliance: Hitler's Pact with Stalin, 1939–1941* (New York: Basic Books, 2014), 301–303.

3. Antony Beevor, *The Second World War* (New York: Little, Brown & Co., 2012), 35.

4. After meeting with Hitler's Army chief of staff on September 9, a week into the German invasion, a Nazi colonel wrote in his diary that it was Hitler's intention "to destroy and exterminate the Polish nation. More than that cannot even be hinted at in writing." Gilbert, *The Second World War: A Complete History*, 6.

On September 10, the head of the German Secret Intelligence Service traveled to the front line and was told of "an orgy of massacre." *Ibid.*, 8. On September 13, the German SS began the arrest and shooting of large numbers of "suspicious elements, plunderers, Jews and Poles," in more than thirteen Polish towns and villages. Warsaw was bombed on the Jewish New Year, Rosh Hashanah, September 14. *Ibid.* On September 21, SS commanders were summoned to Berlin and told that Polish Jews were to be concentrated in several large cities, with Western Poland to be "cleared completely of Jews." *Ibid.*, 12.

In December 1939, the World Jewish Congress issued a fifteen-page "Jewish White Book" that the *Jewish Telegraphic Agency* reported was "the darkest narration ever known in Jewish history." The report charged that "a quarter of a million [Polish] Jews have been wiped out by military operations, executions, disease and starvation . . . [and] at least 80% of the remained have been reduced to complete beggary." The report stated further that:

The White Book estimates that a majority of the 40,000 Jews who attempted to escape from Warsaw during the Nazi bombardment were killed by Nazi bombs in the suburbs of the former Polish capital. This is in addition, the document states, to 30,000 who perished in Warsaw during and after the Nazi occupation.

The White Book charges that cities populated chiefly by Jews were burned down completely, that Nazis executed 400 Jews in the public market place of the township of Lukow, that a similar execution took place in Kalushin and other Jewish populated towns, and that uncounted numbers of Jews died as a result of torture inflicted by Gestapo agents while working on forced labor projects. The document dwells lengthily on the Nazi plan to set up ghettos and on the Lublin "reservation."

*"War, Executions, Disease Wiped out 250,000 Jews in Nazi Poland, 'White Book' Charges,"* JTA, December 18, 1939.

5. Roger Moorhouse, *The Devils' Alliance: Hitler's Pact with Stalin, 1939–1941, supra* at 46.

6. Antony Beevor, *The Second World War*, 51.

7. Halik Kochanski, *The Eagle Unbowed* (Cambridge: Harvard University Press, 2012), xxx. The Poles were highly anti-Semitic and their army in exile was of no help to Polish Jews. It was heroic from a Polish perspective, but not from a Jewish one.

8. Obligated under the 1922 League of Nations Mandate to facilitate the establishment of a Jewish national homeland, Britain had progressively reneged on that obligation, restricting Jewish immigration to Palestine to 29,727 in 1936, 10,536 in 1937, and 12,868 in 1939 before issuing its new "White Paper." *American Jewish Yearbook*, 1940 *"Statistics of Jews,"* 632.

9. *Ibid.*, 601.

10. In *Never Surrender: Winston Churchill and Britain's Decision to Fight Nazi Germany in the Fateful Summer of 1940* (New York: Scribner, 2015), 49, John Kelly notes that a Gallup poll in October 1939 found Americans favored neutrality by 95 to 5 percent, with Americans resentful that they had suffered 116,708 dead in the previous war and still had $10 billion in unpaid European debt:

> Beyond that, every American had his or her own personal reasons for supporting isolationism: German and Irish Americans because of a historic enmity toward Britain; Midwestern isolationists from the conviction that the only country an American should defend was his own; businessmen because a world war would disrupt the international economy; and the parents of draft-age sons, such as Ambassador Kennedy, for fear that American boys would be dragged back into the European abattoir.

11. Antony Beevor, *The Second World War*, 22. See "The World at War: History of World War II, 1940–1945," www.euronet.nl/users/wilfried/ww2/1940.htm.

12. Rick Atkinson, *An Army at Dawn* (New York: Henry Holt & Co., 2000), 8.

13. *Ibid.*

14. Martin Gilbert, *The Second World War: A Complete History*, 4. President Roosevelt issued Proclamation No. 2349 on September 5, 1939, noting a state of war between Germany, France, Poland, the United Kingdom, India, Australia, and New Zealand, and admonishing U.S. citizens not to export arms to any of those countries. In November 1939, Congress allowed sales of arms to belligerents as long as they paid cash and transported the arms in non-American ships. On November 4, 1939, Roosevelt issued an updated proclamation. Franklin D. Roosevelt: "Proclamation 2374—Neutrality"; see Gerhard Peters and John T. Woolley, *The American Presidency Project*, www.presidency.ucsb.edu/ws/?pid=15831.

15. Winston S. Churchill, *The Second World War, Volume I, The Gathering Storm*: (Boston: Houghton Mifflin, 1948), 461.

16. The Maginot Line consisted of an elaborate set of modern fortresses, bunkers, and other fortifications that France constructed along its border with Germany af-

ter World War I, named after the French Minister of War, André Maginot. It was thought to be impenetrable, but proved useless when German troops invaded France in May 1940. See "Maginot Line," www.britannica.com/topic/Maginot-Line.

17. See "Munich Agreement [Europe] 1938," www.britannica.com/event/Munich-Agreement.

18. Winston S. Churchill, *The Second World War*, Volume I, *The Gathering Storm*, *supra* at 307. On March 31, 1939, Prime Minister Chamberlain told Parliament that:

"[I]n the event of any action which clearly threatened Polish independence . . . His Majesty's Government would feel themselves bound at once to lend the Polish Government all support in their power. They have given the Polish Government an assurance to this effect. I may add that the French Government has authorized me to make it plain that they stand in the same position in this matter."

*Ibid.*, 310. See Antony Beevor, *The Second World War*, 9 ("British outrage forced Chamberlain to offer guarantees to Poland as a warning to Hitler against further expansion").

19. Winston S. Churchill, *The Gathering Storm*, 353.

20. *Ibid.*, 354.

21. *Ibid.*, 423.

22. *Ibid.*, 425 and 430.

23. *Ibid.*, 428.

24. See Ronald C. Rosbottom, *When Paris Went Dark: The City of Light Under German Occupation, 1940–1944* (New York: Little Brown and Co., 2014), 19–20:

After declaring war on Germany . . . both nations almost desultorily began preparations for a European war. The French . . . moved cautiously a few kilometers into Germany, where they met little resistance, for the Luftwaffe and the panzers of the Wehrmacht were firmly engaged in Poland. Thus began nine months of the "phony war" on the Western Front, as Hitler bided his time before taking on the combined Allied forces of Holland, Belgium, France, and the United Kingdom.

25. Winston S. Churchill, 422.

26. *Ibid.*, 429–430.

27. *Ibid.*, 430–431.

28. *Ibid.*, 405, 407, 410. In a September 18, 1939, note to Chamberlain, Churchill wrote that the French should be told of the British intention to build up an army of fifty-five divisions in twenty-four months, but that the actual construction of such an army might take thirty to forty months.

29. See Martin Gilbert, *The Second World War*, 18:

British bombers flew over Berlin itself. They dropped, not bombs, but leaflets, telling the German public that whereas they were forced to go to war 'with hunger rations', their leaders had secreted vast sums of money overseas. . . .

After one month of war, ninety-seven million leaflets had been printed, of which thirty-one million had already been dropped. A joke popular at that time told of an airman who was rebuked for dropping a whole bundle of leaflets still tied up, in its brick-like packet: "Good God, you might have killed someone!"

30. Andrew Roberts, *The Storm of War: A New History of the Second World War* (New York: Harper, 2012), 35.

31. Winston S. Churchill, *The Gathering Storm*, 434.

32. Andrew Roberts, *The Storm of War,* 35. Churchill called the period from September 3, 1939, to May 10, 1940, the "Twilight War." Winston S. Churchill, *The Gathering Storm*, 359.

33. Andrew Roberts, *The Storm of War,* 46.

34. *Ibid.*

35. Langword, ed., *Churchill by Himself,* 16, quoted in Andrew Roberts, *The Storm of War,* at 46.

36. Broadcast, London, January 20, 1940, http://www.winstonchurchill.org/learn/speeches/speeches-of-winston-churchill/1940-finest-hour/98-the-war-situation-house-of-many-mansions.

37. The Churchill Society, "The War Situation, January 20th, 1940, BBC Broadcast, London," http://churchill-society-london.org.uk/Joybells.html. The final paragraph of Churchill's broadcast read as follows:

In the bitter and increasingly exacting conflict which lies before us we are resolved to keep nothing back, and not to be outstripped by any in service to the common cause. Let the great cities of Warsaw, of Prague, of Vienna banish despair even in the midst of their agony. Their liberation is sure. The day will come when the joy bells will ring again throughout Europe, and when victorious nations, masters not only of their foes but of themselves, will plan and build in justice, in tradition, and in freedom a house of many mansions where there will be room for all.

38. Winston Churchill, first broadcast as prime minister to the British people, http://www.winstonchurchill.org/learn/speeches/speeches-of-winston-churchill/1940-finest-hour/92-blood-toil-tears-and-sweat.

39. The Churchill Society, "*Be ye men of Valour,*" broadcast May 13, 1940, http://churchill-society-london.org.uk/BeYeMofV.html.

40. See Diana Muir Appelbaum, "The First War of National Liberation," *Jewish Ideas Daily,* December 12, 2012. In an essay published in 1932, entitled "*Moses—The Leader of a People,*" reprinted in the February, 1941, issue of the *Brooklyn Jewish Center Review,* Churchill recounted the story of Moses and the wanderings of the Hebrew people, which he treated not simply as a story, but as literal history:

We may be sure that all these things happened just as they are set out according to Holy Writ. We may believe that they happened to people not so very different from ourselves, and that the impressions those people received were faithfully recorded and have been transmitted across the centuries with far more accuracy than many of the telegraphed accounts we read of the goings on of today. In the words of a forgotten work of Mr. Gladstone, we rest with assurance upon "The impregnable Rock of Holy Scripture."

http://brooklynjewishcenter.org/cr1941.php. To view the February issue of the *Brooklyn Center Review*, with the Churchill article, readers can click on the white arrows at the bottom of the screen to move through the twenty-five pages of the January issue to reach the February issue.

41. The remaining one million European Jews were spread out in smaller numbers among the other countries on the continent. See Bernard Wasserstein, *On the Eve: The Jews of Europe Before the Second World War* (New York: Simon & Schuster, 2012), 11. *The American Jewish Yearbook* for 1940, Table at pp. 602 and 605 shows slightly different figures: Poland (3,113,900); Soviet Union (3,020,141); Germany (240,000); France (240,000); United Kingdom (300,000).

About 365,000 Jews left Germany or areas controlled by the Reich between 1933 and 1939. About 57,000 went to America; 53,000 to Palestine; about 50,000 to Britain; 40,000 to France; 25,000 to Belgium; and 10,000 to Switzerland. The total number of Jewish immigrants to Palestine between 1933 and 1939 was 215,232. Bernard Wasserstein, *Britain and the Jews of Europe: 1939–1945* (Oxford: Oxford University Press, 1979), 7, 12.

42. *American Jewish Yearbook*, 1940 *"Statistics of Jews,"* 600.

43. *Ibid.*, 601.

44. The report is at http://ajcarchives.org/AJCDATA/Files/194019419AJCAnnual Report.pdf.

45. Bernard Wasserstein, *On the Eve,* xvii.

46. *Ibid.* See David Wolpe, "The Changing Face of Anti-Semitism," *Los Angeles Review of Books*, December 21, 2015, https://lareviewofbooks.org/article/changing-face-antisemitism/.

47. Bernard Wasserstein, *On the Eve,* xvii.

48. A March 21, 1937, article in *The New York Times* reported that the American Jewish Joint Distribution Committee (JDC) was holding a national campaign to raise $4,650,000 to aid overseas Jews, with its chairman noting that "millions" of European Jews were living in "unspeakable degradation and misery" and "making a desperate attempt to survive." The JDC statement, however, opposed "mass migration" of Jews from Eastern European countries, because it was "neither a practical nor a desirable solution" and would only result in Jews "torn up by the roots and transplanted to some foreign soil." The statement noted that "[m]eanwhile . . . *the 400,000 Jews remaining in Germany face extermination*." [Emphasis added.]

49. *Brooklyn Jewish Center Review* XXI, no. 6 (October 1939), 3, http://brooklyn jewishcenter.org/cr1939.php. To view the October issue of the *Brooklyn Center Review*, readers can click on the white arrows at the bottom of the screen to move through the months of the year to reach the October issue.

50. See Midge Decter, *"A Jew in Anti-Christian America,"* in Richard John Neuhaus, *The Chosen People in an Almost Chosen Nation* (Grand Rapids, Mich.: William B. Eerdmans Publishing Co., 2002), 21:

In the comfort of our American existence we were aware that Hitler was doing evil things to Jews, first in Germany and next in Central and Eastern Europe; we would not for a few years—in some cases not till the end of the war
in Europe—know just exactly how evil, but what we already knew by the later
1930s was bad enough.

51. The first Jews to immigrate to America arrived in New Amsterdam (present-day
New York) in 1654—they included some twenty refugees from Brazil, expelled when
the Portuguese captured it from the Dutch. Jonathan D. Sarna, *American Judaism:
A History* (New Haven: Yale University Press, 2004), 1.

President George Washington, in his 1790 letter to the Jews of Newport, Rhode
Island, responding to their congratulations on his election, noted that "happily the
government of the United States, which gives to bigotry no sanction, to persecution
no assistance, requires only that they who live under its protection should demean
themselves as good citizens in giving it on all occasions their effectual support." *Ibid.*,
38–39. In a lecture published in 1806, a Jewish leader described America as a "second
Jerusalem" and a "promised land." *Ibid.*, 51–52.

52. The plight of the Jews in Russia from 1880–1905 attracted significant attention
in America from both the government and the public. In 1892, the U.S. Treasury Department appointed a commission to investigate immigration to the United States
and sent the commissioners to Europe to ascertain the "principal causes which oper-
ate in the several countries of Europe to incite emigration to the United States." *A Report of the Commissioners of Immigration Upon the Causes Which Incite Immigration
to the United States* (Washington, DC: Government Printing Office, 1892), 1–2. The
commissioners visited many towns and hamlets in the Pale of Settlement and prepared reports such as this one, about their visit to the village of Samokvalovich near
Minsk:

The conditions of affairs as related to us were serious to these people and would
have been much more so had there not been an emigration to America. . . . It
was difficult to see how these people live, as they are not permitted to till the
soil outside the limits of the little town, there being only a small patch of ground
connected with each dwelling. The houses are low, one-story buildings, but
much more neat in appearance than those occupied by the Russian families
passed by us in our journey out. . . .

[In one house], they looked upon us with undisguised wonder, and it was stated
that we were the first foreigners who had ever visited the place. We examined
some of the books on the shelves, and found a copy of the Bible, an atlas, with
maps of the globe, a French reader, and others printed in the Russian and Hebrew languages. . . . Here, as everywhere else in the Pale visited by us, the su-
perior intelligence and cultivation of the Jew over the Russian was plain and
unmistakable.

. . . Aside from a small proportion of Jews who look longingly and hopefully toward Palestine next to their religion and their persistent eagerness for education,

America is the present hope and goal of their ambition, toward which their gaze is directed as earnestly as that of their ancestors toward the promised Land.

*Ibid.*, 71.

After the brutal Russian pogrom in Kishinev in 1903, there was an outcry in America. Virtually every major American newspaper published editorials severely criticizing the Czar and the Russian government. Speeches and rallies were held across the United States. The speeches, editorials, resolutions, and sermons were collected in a 491-page book, *The Voice of America on Kishineff*, edited by Cyrus Adler (Philadelphia: The Jewish Publication Society of America, 1904). *The New York Times* alone ran a total of sixteen editorials in May, June, and July 1903. *Ibid.*, 390–416.

53. Charles E. Silberman cites the following statistics: 3,000 in 1818; 15,000 in 1840; 50,000 in 1850, reaching 150,000 during the 1850s. Charles E. Silberman, *A Certain People: American Jews and Their Lives Today* (New York: Summit Books, 1985), 42.

54. The Union of Reform Judaism contains this summary of Rabbi Wise's early years:

Rabbi Isaac Mayer Wise, widely known as the founder of Reform Judaism in North America, was a native of Bohemia who came to the United States in 1846. As the rabbi of Congregation Beth Emet in Albany, NY, he introduced many reforms in worship services, such as the seating of men and women together and choral singing. These changes were not universally welcome, leading to his dismissal on Rosh Hashanah in 1850.

Four years later, Rabbi Wise went to Cincinnati's congregation Beth Eichim, where he remained for the rest of his life. It was in Cincinnati that Wise founded the three major arms of the Reform Movement: an umbrella organization of synagogues, a seminary and a rabbinic conference . . . [which by 1875] had grown to 72 congregations. . . .

See https://urj.org/history

55. Charles E. Silberman, *A Certain People*,, 43.

56. *Ibid.*, 46.

57. The descriptions of the Trefa Banquet are primarily from two major profiles of the event: John J. Appel, "The Trefa Banquet," *Commentary Magazine*, February 1, 1966; and Lance J. Sussman, "The Myth of the Trefa Banquet: American Culinary Culture and the Radicalization of Food Policy in American Reform Judaism," *American Jewish Archives Journal* (2005). A replica of the menu for the banquet can be found at: http://www.clevelandjewishhistory.net/res/cyber-gems-trefa-dinner.htm.

58. Lance J. Sussman, "The Myth of the Trefa Banquet," argues that the absence of pork was significant, since it indicated a less-than-total rejection of the kosher laws. But in response to the criticism he received for the menu, Rabbi Wise launched a broad attack on such laws: they were, he asserted, part of a "kitchen and stomach" religion that "wasted" religious and moral sentiments in "small and insignificant observances" that "cheapened" Judaism.

59. Moshe D. Sherman, "A Short History of Orthodox Judaism in America:

A History from Colonial Times to World War II," reprinted by My Jewish Learning, www.myjewishlearning.com/article/a-short-history-of-orthodox-judaism-in-america/. While there was a significant Orthodox movement in America, with hundreds of rabbis moving there, other Eastern European rabbis warned against moving to the land where "desecration of the Torah" was rampant, and they sometimes argued that Jews who wanted "to live properly before God" should move back to Poland and Russia. See Jeffrey S. Gurlock, "Religious Dilemmas of a Treif Land," Project Muse, https://muse.jhu.edu/chapter/389364.

60. The text of the Pittsburgh Platform is at http://ccarnet.org/rabbis-speak/platforms/guiding-principles-reform-judaism/.

61. Steve Oney, *And the Dead Shall Rise: The Murder of Mary Phagan and the Lynching of Leo Frank* (New York: Vintage Books, 2004), 12.

62. From the *Central Conference of American Rabbis Yearbook*, 7 (1987–98), x–xii, as excerpted in Gary Phillip Zola and Marc Dollinger, eds., *American Jewish History: A Primary Source Reader* (Waltham: Brandeis University Press, 2014), 166.

63. See generally, Aviezer Ravitzky, *Messianism, Zionism, and Jewish Religious Radicalism* (Chicago: The University of Chicago Press, 1996). Ravitzky writes that "[t]he Zionist movement has from its inception appeared to the Orthodox religious leadership as a threatening paradox":

> The Zionists were eager to bring about a human, worldly redemption for their people. Their goal was to render the "Eternal People" a historical people, temporally and spatially bound; to transform the "Chosen People" into a "normal people," like other nations. Moreover, they claimed to offer national salvation against the background of the deepest spiritual rebellion (Enlightenment, reform, secularization) in Jewish exilic history. Did not Zionism thus threaten to breach into the holy sanctum?

*Ibid.*, 10.

64. "Jews Eager to Enlist—Enthusiasm at Recruiting Offices in Jerusalem and Jaffa," *The New York Times*, August 17, 1918.

65. "American Rabbis Object—Central Conference Opposes Nationalization of Palestine," *The New York Times*, July 5, 1918.

66. As historian Michael B. Oren has noted, anti-Zionism was by no means restricted to Reform Jews, but also found support among Orthodox and socialist Jews, as well:

> Orthodox Jews also opposed the movement—not because of its emphasis on Jewish nationhood but rather because of its secularism. Zionists represented "the most formidable enemy ever to have arisen among the Jewish people," according to the Orthodox association Agudath Israel. "Their entire desire . . . is to remove the burden of Torah . . . and to uphold only their nationalism," claimed Shalom Dov Ber Schneerson, the revered Lubavitcher rebbe. For the broadening ranks of socialist Jews who saw themselves not as members of a distinct people but as workers in an international proletariat, Zionism was also anathema. Indeed,

antipathy to the Zionist idea was one of the few positions around which, in the early 1900s, most of American Jewry could rally.

Michael B. Oren, *Power, Faith, and Fantasy: America in the Middle East, 1776 to the Present* (New York: W. W. Norton & Co., 2007), 351–352.

67. See "The American Jewish Committee," http://www.myjewishlearning.com/article/the-american-jewish-committee/.

68. See "Stephen S. Wise (1874–1949)," United States Holocaust Memorial Museum, Holocaust Encyclopedia, https://www.ushmm.org/wlc/en/article.php?ModuleId=10007309.

69. Isaiah Berlin—who in 1940 was a thirty-one-year attaché to the British embassy in Washington—described the American Jewish Committee, in an August 16, 1940, letter to his parents, as "the rich Jews' anti-Zionist organization." *Isaiah Berlin: Letters 1928–1946*, Henry Hardy, ed. (Cambridge: Cambridge University Press, 2004), 333.

70. In 1898, Rabbi Philipson chaired a committee that reported a resolution to the Union of American Hebrew Congregations, opening with the words, "We are unalterably opposed to political Zionism." More than forty years later, he wrote that this had been his consistent stand and that he "rather imagine[s] that this will thus continue until the end." David Philipson, *My Life as an American Jew* (Cincinnati: John G. Kidd & Son Inc., 1941), 140. In 1922, he appeared before the House Foreign Relations Committee as "the Rev. Dr. David Philipson" to protest a resolution calling for U.S. recognition of the Balfour Declaration. He testified that he opposed it on two grounds: "first, as a follower of liberal or Reform Judaism, and secondly, as an American citizen." In his 1941 autobiography, he called the Balfour Declaration an "ill-advised" statement that was "a matter of Old-World politics." *Ibid.*, 489 and 303.

71. David Philipson, *My Life as an American Jew,* 139.

72. *Ibid.*, 138.

73. *Ibid.*, 304–305.

74. See Richard K. Hayes, "God Bless America, Land That I Love," http://katesmith.org/gba.html. The *Kate Smith Hour,* which aired weekly from 1937–45, was the nation's most popular radio variety hour. "Kate Smith's Biography," http://katesmith.org/katebio.html. See also "Kate Smith, All-American Singer, Dies at 79," *The New York Times*, June 18, 1986, http://www.nytimes.com/learning/general/onthisday/bday/0501.html:

> She recorded almost 3,000 songs—more than any other popular performer. She introduced more songs than any other performer—over a thousand, of which 600 or so made the hit parade. She made more than 15,000 radio broadcasts and, over the years, received more than 25 million fan letters. . . .

> Kate Smith had been a national singing star almost from the outset of her broadcasting career in 1931. But her identification with patriotism and patriotic themes dates from the night of Nov. 11, 1938, when, on her regular radio program, she introduced a new song written expressly for her by Irving Berlin— "God Bless America."

In a short time, the song supplanted "The Star-Spangled Banner" as the nation's most popular patriotic song. There were attempts—all unsuccessful—to adopt it formally as the national anthem. For a time, Kate Smith had exclusive rights to perform "God Bless America" in public. She relinquished that right when it became apparent the song had achieved a significance beyond that of just another new pop tune.

Mr. Berlin and Miss Smith waived all royalties from performances of "God Bless America." The royalties continue to be turned over to the Boy and Girl Scouts of America.

75. See generally, Sheryl Kaskowitz, *God Bless America: The Surprising History of an Iconic Song* (Oxford: Oxford University Press, 2013).

76. S. J. Woolf, "What Makes a Song: A Talk with Irving Berlin," *The New York Times*, July 28, 1940.

77. *Ibid; see* Lydia Hutchinson, "Irving Berlin's 'God Bless America,'" http://performingsongwriter.com/god-bless-america/.

78. "Berlin Composition Chosen," *The New York Times*, August 29, 1940.

79. See Holocaust Encyclopedia, *Kristallnacht: A Nationwide Pogrom, November 9–10, 1938*, http://www.ushmm.org/wlc/en/article.php?ModuleId=10005201.

80. See "Dr. Edgar Romig, a Pastor Here, 74: Senior Minister of Four Collegiate Churches Dies," *The New York Times*, November 13, 1963, quoting Rev. Romig's 1940 sermon.

81. Quoted in Sheryl Kaskowitz, *God Bless America,* 65.

82. *Time Magazine*, "Badgered Ballad," September 30, 1940; "Irving Berlin Song to Aid Our Youth," *The New York Times*, July 11, 1940.

83. Sinclair Lewis decided to stage his novel through the Federal Theatre Project, rather than on Broadway, so that he could attract the widest possible audience for the play. On one day—October 27, 1936—twenty-two productions opened in eighteen cities. Nearly 500,000 people saw the play during its run. Library of Congress, "Coast to Coast: The Federal Theatre Project, 1935–1939," entry on *It Can't Happen Here* by Sinclair Lewis," https://www.loc.gov/exhibits/federal-theatre-project/modern-drama.html.

84. See Francis MacDonnell, *Insidious Foes: The Axis Fifth Column and the American Homefront* (New York and Oxford: Oxford University Press, 1995), 30–31 ("In February 1936, Metro-Goldwyn Mayer generated a national sensation when it backed out of plans to produce [the film].") MGM had assigned a Pulitzer Prize-winning writer to produce the screenplay and Lionel Barrymore to star.

85. David Welky, *The Moguls and the Dictators: Hollywood and the Coming of World War II* (Baltimore: Johns Hopkins University Press, 2008), at 27–29 and 144–146.

86. David Denby, "Hitler in Hollywood: Did the Studios Collaborate?" *The New Yorker*, September 16, 2013, summarizing findings in recent books: Thomas Doherty, *Hollywood and Hitler, 1933–1939* (New York: Columbia University Press, 2013) and Ben Urwand, *The Collaboration: Hollywood's Pact with Hitler* (Cambridge: Harvard University Press, 2013). Breen wrote to MGM's president, Louis B. Mayer, with a seven-page letter proposing sixty cuts in the screenplay for *It Can't Happen Here* and

warned that, even with the cuts, production of the film "may result in enormous difficulty to your studio."

87. See Vincent Brook, *Driven to Darkness: Jewish Émigré Directors and the Rise of Film Noir* (New Brunswick, N.J.: Rutgers University Press, 2009). The book is a study of the seminal influence of Jewish émigré directors from Germany and Austria: Fritz Lang, Billy Wilder, Otto Preminger, Edgar G. Ulmer, Fred Zinnemann, Robert Siodmak, Curtis Bernhardt, Max Ophuls, Anatole Litvak, and John Brahm. The title of Brook's book is a reference to Isa. 8:22 ("And they shall look unto the earth / and behold trouble and darkness / dimness of anguish / and they shall be driven to darkness").

*See also* Otto Friedrich, *City of Nets: A Portrait of Hollywood in the 1940s* (New York: Harper Perennial, 1987), 67–68:

> Anti-Semitism in America in 1940 was widespread and strong, far more so than is now remembered. . . . Jews were totally excluded from many executive jobs and from many of the best places to live. There were quotas limiting Jews in many universities, clubs, corporations. Ordinary Americans . . . generally regarded them as an alien people, avaricious, scheming, and dishonest. "What [people] seem to resent," Raymond Chandler wrote to his English publisher in a fairly typical expression of the common view, "is the feeling that the Jew is a distinct racial type, that you can pick him out by his face, by the tone-quality of his voice, and far too often by his manners. In short, the Jews are to some extent still foreigners. . . . I've lived in a Jewish neighborhood, and I've watched one become Jewish, and it was pretty awful." . . .
>
> In Hollywood, stars assumed neutral names like Fairbanks or Howard or Shaw; actresses underwent plastic surgery; some made a point of going to Christian churches or donating money to Christian charities. This was not so much a denial of Jewishness—though it was also that—as an effort to make Jewishness appear insignificant, too unimportant to be criticized, or even noticed.

88. See Laura Rosenzweig, "Hollywood's Anti-Nazi Spies," *Jewish Review of Books* (Winter 2014) at 5–6. Starting in 1934, Jewish studio heads such as Louis B. Mayer (MGM), Emanuel Cohen (Paramount Studios), and Jack Warner (Warner Bros.) secretly funded informants to infiltrate Nazi groups operating in Los Angeles. The "Friends of New Germany" (FNG) had opened the Aryan Bookstore in downtown Los Angeles to sell pro-Nazi, anti-Semitic literature on the Jewish-Bolshevik threat in the United States and the "Hitler Miracle" in Germany. That year 50,000 people attended an FNG rally at Madison Square Garden, and a private, brown-shirted militia group was training in the Hollywood Hills. The head of the Anti-Defamation League approached a group he referred to as "the moneyed men" of Jewish Los Angeles— successful bankers, real estate developers, doctors, and others—to help fund investigations, but they raised only a negligible amount.

On March 13, 1934, a special dinner meeting of entertainment moguls, including Louis B. Mayer, Irving Thalberg, and community leaders such as Rabbi Edgar Magnin and Judge Lester Roth, was held at Hillcrest Country Club. The studio heads formed the Los Angeles Jewish Community Committee (LAJCC) and raised $22,000 (the 2015 equivalent of about $400,000) to fund further investigations, and provided Congress with evidence of Nazi propaganda activities in Los Angeles. According to Rosenzweig, the work of the LAJCC was never made public.

Two recent books describe the private efforts of Jews in Hollywood to discover Nazi activities and provide information to the government, usually through a non-Jewish organization. Steven J. Ross, in *Hitler in Los Angeles: How Jews Foiled Nazi Plots Against Hollywood and America* (New York: Bloomsbury USA, 2017), writes that attorney Leon Lewis ran a spy operation that infiltrated every Nazi and fascist group in Los Angeles and foiled plans to kill the city's Jews and sabotage its military installations. Laura B. Rosenzweig, in *Hollywood's Spies: The Undercover Surveillance of Nazis in Los Angeles* (Goldstein-Goren Series in American Jewish History) (New York: NYU Press, 2017), describes the efforts of the LAJCC. She writes that there were similar activities in other American cities, but almost always *sub rosa*, and that the American Jewish Committee discontinued its fact-finding operations out of fear that their disclosure would "give credence to the charge of underhanded Jewish strategy and corrupt use of Jewish money. . . ."

89. The three-minute 1939 preview of the movie can be seen on YouTube: https://www.youtube.com/watch?v=Y4M0BW1GLnw. The entire movie can be seen on YouTube: https://www.youtube.com/watch?v=S4tkNhyQofc. The background relating to the release of the film is recounted by Steven J. Ross in "*Confessions of a Nazi Spy*: *Warner Bros., Anti-Fascism and the Politicization of Hollywood*," http://www.learcenter.org/pdf/WWRoss.pdf. Ross writes that:

> "The evening of April 27, 1939," declared film critic Welford Beaton, "will go down in screen history as a memorable one. It marked the first time in the annals of screen entertainment that a picture ever really said something definite about current events, really took sides and argued for the side with which it sympathized." . . . Not everyone was enamored with the film. Nazi sympathizers in Milwaukee burned down the local Warner Bros. theatre shortly after the movie opened. Angry citizens in other cities picketed theatres, slashed seats and threatened exhibitors. In Poland, anti-Semitic audiences hanged several theater owners in their movie houses for exhibiting the film. Nazis banned the film everywhere they could exert pressure.

90. In 1937 Warner Bros. produced its first attempt at a serious historical movie. *The Life of Emile Zola*, starring Paul Muni (formerly a star of the Yiddish theatre), told the story of the French writer and the Dreyfus affair. The film was nominated for ten Academy Awards. The word "Jew" is never spoken in it. See David Denby, "Hitler in Hollywood: Did the Studios Collaborate?," *The New Yorker*, September 16, 2013. Denby wrote that the film was "a perfect example of the half-boldness, half-cowardice, and outright confusion that marked [the 1930s]":

> In that decade, the industry produced a generally good-hearted and liberal cinema that celebrated such democratic virtues as easy manners, tolerance, heroic

individualism, and loathing of mob violence—all of which can be seen as a de-facto rebuke to Nazism. At the same time, the studios cancelled several explicitly anti-Nazi films planned for production, and deleted from several other movies anything that could be construed as critical of the Nazis, along with anything that might be seen as favorable to the Jews.

91. "'Nazi Spy' Picture Best of the Year," *The New York Times*, December 25, 1939, http://query.nytimes.com/mem/archive/pdf?res=9C05E1D8153EE432A25756C2 A9649D946894D6CF.

92. In August 1939, Adolf Zukor told a reporter, "I don't think that Hollywood should deal with anything but entertainment. The newsreels take care of current events." Michael E. Birdwell, *Celluloid Soldiers: Warner Bros.'s Campaign against Nazism* (New York: New York University Press, 1999), 3 and 32. In 1936 Harry Warner issued an order stating that Warner theaters would not exhibit any newsreels glorifying Hitler. *Ibid.*, 29–30. But Jack Warner did not share his brother's rage and urged him not to try to fight the Nazis single-handedly. In a note dated October 5, 1939, he said, "The less you, I or any Warner talks at this time, the better." *Ibid.*, 31. But see Steven J. Ross, "Warners' War: Politics, Pop Culture & Propaganda in Wartime Hollywood," https://learcenter.org/pdf/WWRoss.pdf (quoting Jack Warner as saying that efforts had been made "to persuade us to call off these pictures" such as *Confessions of a Nazi Spy*, "but that "[w]e do not intend to heed them").

93. Harry M. Warner, "*United We Survive, Divided We Fall*," a fifteen-page pamphlet in which the June 6, 1940, speech was subsequently printed, quoted in Nancy Snow, "Confessions of a Hollywood Propagandist: Harry Warner, FDR and Celluloid Persuasion." Warner told his employees that he was worried about "the enemy within," and he cited the fact that "right in our very studio here, in my own car, I have found literature sowing the seeds of intolerance and advocating the overthrow of American democracy." A flier distributed in Hollywood, available in the USC Libraries, Jack L. Warner Collection, read as follows:

> "*Boycott the Movies! Hollywood is the Sodom and Gomorrah [sic] where international Jewry controls vice, dope, gambling—where young gentile girls are raped by Jewish producers, directors, casting directors who go unpunished . . .*"

Fliers were reportedly dropped from the roof of the Taft Building on Hollywood Boulevard to "snowstorm" pedestrians below. http://digital-library.csun.edu/cdm/singleitem/collection/InOurOwnBackyard/id/155. Similar material is collected at http://digital-library.csun.edu/Backyard/hollywood.html.

94. See KCET, Anne-Marie Gregg, "From Contract to Blacklist: Hollywood Exile Experience," October 30, 2013, http://www.kcet.org/arts/artbound/counties/los-angeles/blacklist-hollywood-exile-experience-warner-brothers.html.

95. Michael E. Birdwell, *Celluloid Soldiers: The Warner Bros. Campaign against Nazism* (New York: New York University Press, 1999), 83. According to Birdwell:

> Harry personally donated $25,000 to the International Red Cross to purchase twenty ambulances for hospitals in Britain and France. In July of 1940 he initi-

ated a program to rescue the children of Warner employees in Britain from the blitz. In an incredible outpouring of largess, arrangements were made to transport two thousand children to the United States, where they would be cared for in the homes of Warner executives and employees. Not only that, but Warner Bros. agreed to pay for their education and guaranteed all other financial needs.

*Ibid.*, 83–84. Harry Warner's efforts were not popular among other Jewish film executives:

MGM's Louis B. Mayer, the Cohn brothers of Columbia, and Carl Laemmle of Universal downplayed their Jewishness, trying to assimilate into American society. The last thing they wanted was for Harry Warner to purposely draw attention to the Jewishness of the film community; they opposed his desire to expose Nazism abroad, much less at home." *Ibid.*, 37.

96. U.S. Congress, Senate, *Propaganda in Motion Pictures*, Hearings before a Subcommittee of the Committee on Interstate Commerce, September 9 to 26, 1941, 77th Cong., 1st Session, (U.S. Government Printing Office, Washington, DC: 1942), 379.
   97. *Ibid.*, 17.
   98. The witness was James M. Fidler, a Hollywood radio commentator, whose column, "Jimmie Fidler in Hollywood," was carried at the time by about 140 newspapers. Fidler rated various movies for the subcommittee as either (a) "propaganda," (b) "medium propaganda," or (c) "definitely propaganda." *Ibid.*, 138, 172.
   99. *Ibid.*, 379.
   100. *Ibid.*, 380.
   101. None of the other witnesses was challenged as directly as was Harry Warner. For example, Senator Clark and Barney Balaban, president of Paramount Pictures Corporation, had the following colloquy:

Senator CLARK of Idaho. How many of these alleged propaganda pictures has your company produced?

Mr. BALABAN. None.

Senator CLARK of Idaho. None?

Mr. BALABAN. No, sir; our pictures have been listed in various newspaper reports that I have seen, and I saw one in which one of our pictures was called medium propaganda. I don't know how to define "medium propaganda," but that is what was said.

Senator CLARK of Idaho. Can you give any reason, Mr. Balaban, why Paramount has not produced so-called propaganda or anti-Nazi films, or whatever designation it may be?

Mr. BALABAN. Very frankly, our studio did not have the manpower or actors required to make serious dramatic pictures. This was way back [*sic*] in 1939, when they started to offer a number of these to us. But we were doing well with the type we were doing. . . .

Senator CLARK of Idaho. So, you have not gone in for making that kind of picture?

Mr. BALABAN. That's right.

102. See "Falsehood Cry in Movie Hearing," *The New York Times*, September 26, 1941, http://query.nytimes.com/mem/archive/pdf?res=9D0CE2DB163AE233A25755 C2A96F9C946093D6CF.

103. Quoted in Leonard Dinnerstein, *Anti-Semitism in America* (New York and Oxford: Oxford University Press, 1994), 123–124. Dinnerstein notes that Jews often reacted to the anti-Semitism by hiding what would otherwise be identifying Jewish characteristics:

> [S]everal reporters at *The New York Times* believed that publishers Adolph Ochs and Arthur Hays Sulzberger were so sensitive to anti-Semitism that they encouraged newcomers to use initials instead of their given name of Abraham in bylines. Thus readers noted stories by A. H. Raskin, and in later years by A. H. Weiler and A. M. Rosenthal, without becoming aware of their Jewish-sounding given names. . . . [T]he young Mel Israel gladly accepted the advice of CBS radio officials [and] changed his surname to Allen and went on to a lengthy career broadcasting New York Yankees baseball games.

> In 1936, the editors of *Fortune Magazine* published a book entitled *Jews in America*. Its opening paragraph asserted that "[t]he apprehensiveness of American Jews has become one of the important influences in the social life of our time." See Stuart Schoffman, "Hollywood and the Nazis," *Jewish Review of Books*, Winter 2014, 17.

104. See "The Scope of Jewish Dictatorship in the U.S.," *Dearborn Independent*, December 11, 1920, excerpted in Gary Phillip Zola and Marc Dollinger, eds., *American Jewish History: A Primary Source Reader* (Waltham: Brandeis University Press, 2014), 219. See "The Dearborn Independent," https://www.adl.org/education/resources/backgrounders/the-international-jew-1920s-anti-semitism-revived-online#the-dearborn-independent:

> At the peak of its popularity, the Dearborn, Michigan paper, owned by auto magnate Henry Ford Sr., boasted a circulation of 700,000. The Dearborn Independent first attacked Jews in its May 22, 1920 issue and continued to do so in 91 subsequent editions.

> Many of the paper's anti-Semitic articles were reprinted by the Dearborn Publishing Company in four paper-bound volumes: *The International Jew, the World's Foremost Problem* (November 1920); *Jewish Activities in the United States* (April, 1921); *Jewish Influences in American Life* (November, 1921); and *Aspects of Jewish Power in the United States* (May, 1922). Collectively known as *The International Jew: The World's Foremost Problem*, these volumes were later published in a variety of languages and disseminated widely in the United States and abroad.

105. See Vincent Brook, *Driven to Darkness: Jewish Émigré Directors and the Rise of Film Noir* (New Brunswick, N.J.: Rutgers University Press, 2009), 6. Brooks recounts that:

A letter in *Life* magazine of 1940, titled "Refugees De Luxe," descried the "well-to-do-refugees taking over expensive hotels, filling fashionable resorts, and dining in expensive restaurants, displaying assertive and flamboyant behavior." Articles in *American Magazine*, with headings such as "Refugees—Burden or Asset?" "Spies Among Refugees," and "Refugee Gold Rush," "all contributed to the impression that refugees were a problematic issue in America."

106. Leonard Dinnerstein, *Anti-Semitism in America,* 127.

107. See the collection of pamphlets in the exhibit "*In Our Own Backyard: Resisting Nazi Propaganda in Southern California: 1933–1945,*" http://digital-library.csun.edu/Backyard/anti-semitism.html. Deed provisions commonly provided that "None of the said lands, interests therein or improvements thereon shall be sold, resold, conveyed, leased, rented to or in any way used, occupied or acquired by any person of Negro blood, or to any person of the Semitic race, blood, or origin, which racial description shall be deemed to include Armenians, Jews, Hebrews, Persians or Syrians." See Jewish Historical Society of Greater Washington, https://www.jhsgw.org/exhibitions/online/jewishwashington/exhibit-images/restrictive-covenants-shelley-kramer.

108. "Restrictive Covenant Language from Deed," Jewish Historical Society of Greater Washington, https://www.jhsgw.org/exhibitions/online/jewishwashington/exhibit-images/restrictive-covenants-shelley-kramer.

109. Leonard Dinnerstein, *Anti-Semitism in America*, 127.

110. An even clearer indication of the atmosphere and tensions in America as of 1940 can be gleaned from Charles Lindbergh's speech at an America First rally in Des Moines, Iowa, on September 11, 1941—a large portion of which consisted of assertions about a process he alleged had been going on from "that day in September 1939, until the present moment." Lindbergh told the rally that the American people had been solidly opposed to entering the war from the start:

Why shouldn't we be? We had the best defensive position in the world; we had a tradition of independence from Europe; and the one time we did take part in a European war left European problems unsolved, and debts to America unpaid. National polls showed that when England and France declared war on Germany, in 1939, less than 10 percent of our population favored a similar course for America . . .

Jewish groups in this country should be opposing [war] in every possible way for they will be among the first to feel its consequences. . . . Their greatest danger to this country lies in their large ownership and influence in our motion pictures, our press, our radio and our government. . . . We cannot allow the natural passions and prejudices of other peoples to lead our country to destruction.

Charles Lindbergh, "Des Moines Speech: Delivered in Des Moines, Iowa, September 11, 1941," http://www.charleslindbergh.com/americanfirst/speech.asp.

## WEIZMANN

1. Quoted in Allon Gal, *David Ben-Gurion and the American Alignment for a Jewish State* (Indianapolis: Indiana University Press, 1991), 76–77.

2. Norman A. Rose, ed., *The Letters and Papers of Chaim Weizmann,* 40, Letter to Doris May in London, from Rehovot, dated April 23, 1939, and note 1 to Letter No. 44. Credit Yad Chaim Wezmann, Rehovot, Israel.

3. *Ibid.*, 5, note 2 to Letter No. 6. Weizmann had already received a substantial advance from Hamish Hamilton (London) and Harper Brothers (New York).

4. Weizmann, Chaim. *Trial and Error,* 420. Credit Yad Chaim Weizmann, Rehovot, Israel.

5. The Balfour Declaration, signed November 2, 1917, by British Foreign Minister Arthur Balfour on behalf of the British government, set forth a commitment to "the establishment in Palestine of a national home for the Jewish people" in Palestine.

The Declaration was, Weizmann later wrote, the "Magna Carta of Jewish Liberty," because it recognized the Jewish people as not simply a religious group, but a national one. Dvorah Barzilay and Barnet Litvinoff, eds., *The Letters and Papers of Chaim Weizmann, Vol. VIII, Series A, November 1917–October 1918* (Jerusalem: Transaction Books, 1977) no. 1, November 2, 1917, 2; see "The Letters and Papers of Chaim Weizmann, Vols. III–VII," review by Chaim Raphael in *Commentary Magazine*, October 1, 1975.

**PALESTINE FOR THE JEWS.**

**OFFICIAL SYMPATHY.**

Mr. Balfour has sent the following letter to Lord Rothschild in regard to the establishment of a national home in Palestine for the Jewish people :—

I have much pleasure in conveying to you, on behalf of his Majesty's Government, the following declaration of sympathy with Jewish Zionist aspirations which has been submitted to and approved by the Cabinet :—

His Majesty's Government view with favour the establishment in Palestine of a national home for the Jewish people, and will use their best endeavours to facilitate the achievement of this object, it being clearly understood that nothing shall be done which may prejudice the civil and religious rights of existing non-Jewish communities in Palestine, or the rights and political status enjoyed by Jews in any other country.

I should be grateful if you would bring this declaration to the knowledge of the Zionist Federation.

*The Balfour Declaration as published in the Times of London, November 9, 1917*

Historians credit Weizmann, more than any other individual, for the Declaration. Walter Laqueur states that the "Balfour Declaration was essentially the work of one man—Chaim Weizmann." Richard Crossman, a British official intimately involved with Palestine in the late 1940s, wrote that it was "one of the very rare cases where one can assert with confidence that one man's personality changed the course of history." Jonathan Schneer, in his book-length study of the Declaration, describes Weizmann's role as that of a "genius."

See Walter Laqueur, *A History of Zionism* (New York: Schocken Books, 1976); Richard H. S. Crossman, *A Nation Reborn* (New York: Atheneum, 1960), 47; Jonathan Schneer, *The Balfour Declaration: The Origins of the Arab-Israeli Conflict* (New York: Random House, 2010), 369; see also Charles Webster, *The Art and Practice of Diplomacy* (London: Chatto & Windus, 1961), 114 ("No one will dispute that Dr. Weizmann was the main creator of the National Home"); T. R. Fivel,

"Weizmann and the Balfour Declaration," in Meyer W. Weisgal and Joel Carmichael, eds., *Chaim Weizmann: A Biography by Several Hands* (New York: Atheneum, 1963), 143; Abba Eban, "Chaim Weizmann and the Personality of Power," *The Jerusalem Post,* International Edition, November 18, 1989, 8.

6. The official name of the commission was the Palestine Royal Commission. It was known as the "Peel Commission" after its chairman, William Robert Wellesley Peel, Lord Peel. It held hearings in 1936–1937 and then published an extensive report. The map showing its recommendations can be found in the Palestine Royal Commission Report ("Peel Commission Report"), July 1937, https://www.scribd.com/document159990119/Peel-Commission-Reportpassia.org/publications/bookmaps/page1.htm.

7. "British White Paper of June 1922," http://avalon.law.yale.edu/20thcentury/brwh1922.asp.

8. Norman A. Rose, ed., *The Letters and Papers of Chaim Weizmann,* Letter No. 43, 39–40.

9. Richard Breitman and Allan J. Lichtman, *FDR and the Jews* (Harvard University Press, 2013), 240; Melvin I. Urofsky, *Louis D. Brandeis: A Life* (New York: Alfred A. Knopf, 2009), 740.

10. The cable continued with a description of "tragedies . . . enacted every day":

Boats, overloaded with refugees from German concentration camps, are floating about for weeks on end in the Mediterranean, their passengers starved and afflicted with the diseases of hunger and exhaustion, among them women and children of tender age. . . . Can you visualize the feeling of the Jews of this country in witnessing these ghastly spectacles, when they know all the time that these unfortunate people could be productively absorbed in Palestine without any harm being done to the Arabs?

11. Norman Rose, ed., *The Letters and Papers of Chaim Weizmann,* Letter No. 51, 52.

12. Norman A. Rose, ed., *The Letters and Papers of Chaim Weizmann,* Letter No. 59, 65 (Churchill) and Letter No. 6, 67 (Chamberlain).

13. In the note on the conversation in the Central Zionist Archives, the exchange is described as follows:

Dr. Weizmann [said] that there was really nothing he had to tell Mr. MacDonald, except that everything he had done, and the way in which he had done it, had aroused their uncompromising hostility . . .

Mr. MacDonald said that the Jews had made many mistakes in the past, to which Dr. Weizmann replied: "Oh, yes, certainly we have made mistakes; our chief mistake is that we exist at all . . ."

The conversation reached its crisis when Dr. Weizmann . . . said that at least in Hitler one found the virtue of an absolutely frank brutality, whereas Mr. MacDonald was covering up his betrayal of the Jews under a semblance of legality. He added that Mr. MacDonald was handing over the Jews to their assassins.

Mr. MacDonald showed great indignation and said that it was of no use to talk to him like that. He said he knew that the Jews had been calling him a hypocrite and a coward. Dr. Weizmann replied: I have never called you a coward. . . .

[Dr. Weizmann] then said that the Government would have to use troops against the Jews, and the troops would have to shoot. Their masters would certainly be delighted. Mr. MacDonald asked: "Who are our masters?" And Dr. Weizmann replied: "The Mufti and his friends."

Bernard Wasserstein, *Britain and the Jews of Europe: 1939–1945* (Oxford: Oxford University Press, 1979), 21, quoting from CZA [Central Zionist Archives] S25/7563.
    14. *Ibid.*, 22.
    15. Norman A. Rose, ed., *The Letters and Papers of Chaim Weizmann,* Letter No. 71, 74.
    16. Barnet Litvinoff, editor, *The Letters and Papers of Chaim Weizmann, supra,* Paper 41, 364–370. Credit Yad Chaim Weizmann, Rehovot, Israel.
    17. Chaim Weizmann, *Trial and Error,* 411–412. Churchill invited Weizmann to lunch on the day of the debate. Weizmann wrote that:

There were present at the lunch, besides Mr. Churchill and myself, Randolph Churchill and Lord Cherwell. . . . Mr. Churchill was thoroughly prepared. He produced a packet of small cards and read his speech out to us; then he asked me if I had any changes to suggest. I answered that . . . [my points] were so unimportant that I would not bother him with them. As everyone now knows, Mr. Churchill delivered against the White Paper one of the great speeches of his career.

    18. Norman A. Rose, ed., *The Letters and Papers of Chaim Weizmann,* Letter No. 80.
    19. In his speech, Churchill referred to the "great experiment and bright dream" of the Jewish National Home policy and said it was strange "that we should turn away when [it] . . . has proved its power to succeed":

[The Jews] have made the desert bloom. They have started a score of thriving industries. . . . They have founded a great city [Tel Aviv] on the barren shore. They have harnessed the Jordan and spread its electricity throughout the land. So far from being persecuted, the Arabs have crowded into the country and multiplied till their population has increased more than even all World Jewry could lift up the Jewish population. Now we are asked to decree that all this is to stop and all this is to come to an end.

Quoted in Simon H. Rifkind et al., *The Basic Equities of the Palestine Problem* (New York: Arno Press, 1977, a reprint of the 1947 edition), 41–42. Churchill called the White Paper "plainly a breach and repudiation of the Balfour Declaration . . . a plain breach of a solemn obligation . . . the violation of the pledge . . . a breach of faith . . . a one-sided denunciation." *Ibid.*, 61. He cited previous prime ministers who had acknowledged that "the undertaking of the Mandate (embodying the pledge of the Balfour Declaration) is an undertaking to the Jewish people [as a whole] and not only to the Jewish population of Palestine." Britain had pledged a home of refuge to:

> . . . the Jews outside Palestine, to that vast, unhappy mass of scattered, perse-
> cuted, wandering Jews whose intense, unchanging, unconquerable desire has
> been for a National Home. . . . It is not with the Jews in Palestine that we have
> now or at any future time to deal, but with world Jewry, with Jews all over the
> world. That is the pledge which was given, and that is the pledge which we are
> now asked to break. . . .

*Ibid.*, 25.

20. Norman A. Rose, ed., *The Letters and Papers of Chaim Weizmann,* Letter No. 78, 87.

21. *Ibid.*, Letter No. 84, 91. Weizmann wrote that:

> . . . at some time soon I shall be going to U.S.A. As for [Arthur Hays] Sulzberger
> —he is a cowardly Jew. Now what I would like to understand however is
> whether the general attitude and feeling of the Jews is very different from Sulz-
> berger's and his paper.

Sulzberger's newspaper, *The New York Times*, had claimed that immigration was running at such a high level that it had to be restricted "to save the country from over-population and from violence at the hands of the Arabs" and urged Zionists to support the British policy in Palestine.

22. "A Survey of Palestine," prepared in December 1945 and January 1946 for the information of the Anglo-American Committee of Inquiry (Washington: The Insti-tute of Palestine Studies, 1991), 56.

23. Norman A. Rose, ed., *The Letters and Papers of Chaim Weizmann,* Letter No. 123, 145.

24. *Ibid.*, Letter No. 123, 145, n. 123.

25. *Ibid.*, Letter No. 126, 148, n. 3.

26. The unit that Weizmann had in mind was a relatively small one, composed of Jewish German refugees and other foreign Jews residing in Britain.

27. Norman A. Rose, ed., *The Letters and Papers of Chaim Weizmann,* Letter No. 143 to Malcolm J. MacDonald in London, 157–158.

28. *Ibid.*, n. 143 at 158.

29. *Ibid.*, Letter No. 153, to Lazar Braudo in Johannesburg, 171.

30. *Ibid.*, Letter No. 153, 172 ("It is too early yet for us to formulate our 'war aims' or to enter into any fundamental political discussions") and Letter 154, 173 ("It is early yet to talk of war aims in Palestine; for the time being it is our business to keep the flag flying there, and do what we can, in our small way, to help").

31. *Ibid.*, Letter No. 154, to Jan Christiaan Smuts in Pretoria, 173.

32. On November 18 Weizmann wrote to an aide to the chief of the British Impe-rial General Staff, enclosing a memorandum for Churchill that set forth ways Jews could assist in the war, confirming that the Jewish Agency could offer a Jewish divi-sion "for service wherever required."

33. Norman A. Rose, ed., *The Letters and Papers of Chaim Weizmann*, Letter No. 168 to R. MacLeod in London, 188–189.

34. *Ibid.*, Letter No. 191 to Lord Halifax in London, 214–215.

35. Lisbon's role as the escape valve was vividly portrayed in the 1942 classic film *Casablanca*, a Warner Bros. production, which opens with the narrator saying:

> With the coming of the Second World War, many eyes in imprisoned Europe turned hopefully, or desperately, toward the freedom of the Americas. Lisbon became the great embarkation point. But, not everybody could get to Lisbon directly, and so a tortuous, roundabout refugee trail sprang up—Paris to Marseilles . . . across the Mediterranean to Oran . . . then by train, or auto, or foot across the rim of Africa, to Casablanca in French Morocco.

36. The atmosphere in Lisbon in the initial years of World War II is captured in Erich Maria Remarque's novel *The Night in Lisbon* (United States: Harcourt, Brace & World, 1964), which opens with a refugee staring at a ship preparing to sail to America:

> Every ship that left Europe in those months of the year 1942 was an ark. Mount Ararat was America, and the flood waters were rising higher by the day. . . . The coast of Portugal had become the last hope of the fugitives. . . . This was the gate to America. If you couldn't reach it, you were lost, condemned to bleed away in a jungle of consulates, police stations, and government offices, where visas were refused and work and residence permits unobtainable, a jungle of internment camps, bureaucratic red tape, loneliness, homesickness, and withering universal indifference.

*Ibid.*, 3–4.

37. Chaim Weizmann, *Trial and Error*, 419.

38. See "SS 'Rex' One of the Most Famous Italian Passenger Ships," at http://vmf-cruiseshipsandliners.blogspot.com/2011/08/ss-rex-one-of-most-famous-italian.html. See also http://cruiselinehistory.com/cruise-ship-history-wonderful-youtube-video-of-the-rex-the-italian-lines-great-liner/.

39. For a description of the ship, see "Rex" at www.greatships.net/rex.html.

40. "Among Those Who Arrived from Europe on the Liner Rex last Night," *The New York Times*, January 13, 1940, http://query.nytimes.com/mem/archive/pdf?res=9F0DE1DE113EE23ABC4B52DFB766838B659EDE.

41. *The New York Times*, January 13, 1940. Weizmann issued a formal statement from the ship on his arrival, which read as follows:

> The cruel havoc wrought in the lives of hundreds of thousands of Jews in Poland constitutes one of the major human tragedies of the present conflict. . . . My mission to the United States at this time has for *its chief purpose the enlistment of American Jewry's united support for the continued development of Palestine as a haven for tens of thousands of Jews* who have been uprooted and driven from their homes by the overwhelming wave of destruction now sweeping over Central Europe. [Emphasis added.]

See "Weizmann Set for 6-week Speaking Tour; Stresses U.S. Jewry's Refugee-Aid Role," JTA, January 15, 1940.

42. "Weizmann Starts on Trip to U.S.; Assured of Status Quo on White Paper," JTA, December 22, 1939, www.jta.org/1939/12/22/archive/weizmann-starts-on-trip-to-u-s-assured-of-status-quo-on-white-paper. The same issue of the JTA included these headlines:

"Nazis Threaten to Execute 1,000 Warsaw Jews on Slightest 'Provocation'"

"Many Soviet Jews Exiled for Anti-Nazi Demonstrations, Brussels Hears"

"Polish Jewish Leaders Held by Nazis for Ransom in Foreign Currency"

"'Jewish-Polish Protectorate' Planned, Nazi Official Reveals"

43. The mosque was built on land purchased by the Shriners in 1921. See "Shriners Here Plan $2,000,000 Mosque," *The New York Times*, December 25, 1921. The Mecca Temple is today the New York City Center. See "New York City Center," http://en.wikipedia.org/wiki/NewYorkCityCenter.

44. The attendance figure of 4,000 is the one given by *The New York Times*. In Barnet Litvinoff, ed., *The Letter and Papers of Chaim Weizmann,* 384, the attendance is estimated at 6,000, with Rabbi Stephen S. Wise presiding.

The following night, Dr. Weizmann as chairman of the Hebrew University's board of governors and Salman Schocken, chairman of the Hebrew University's executive council, appeared at a dinner given by the American Friends of the Hebrew University at the Hotel Commodore. See http://www.jta.org/1940/01/10/archive/weizmann-to-be-honored-at-rally-dinner-here-next-week.

45. "Weizmann Visions Palestine Growth/Zionist Leader Outlines Aim to Achieve Jewish Ideals of Fellowship and Peace/He Speaks to 4,000 Here," *The New York Times*, January 17, 1940. The *Times* reported that:

Dr. Weizmann sketched the persecution of the last several years, declaring it had dwarfed that of the medieval period, and seemed sometimes to have been motivated by a "homicidal mania." Despite the fate of the Polish Jews, and the precarious situation of Jews in Hungary and Rumania, he forecast an era when it would be no longer be "a crime punishable by death to be a minority."

46. Louis Lipsky, *Memoirs in Profile* (Philadelphia: Jewish Publication Society of America, 1975), 205; Ezekiel Rabinowitz, *Justice Louis D. Brandeis: The Zionist Chapter of His Life* (New York: Philosophical Library, 1968), 6.

47. Brandeis was impressed that the Bible severely criticized political leaders, and he wondered "whether any government today would risk publishing a document depicting the nation's most favored ruler as the Bible does David." Solomon Goldman, ed., *The Words of Justice Brandeis* (New York: Henry Schuman, 1953), 36. He believed a Jewish homeland could conduct experiments in democracy and social justice that larger countries could not easily undertake.

48. Louis Dembitz Brandeis, *The Jewish Problem; How to Solve it* (New York: The Zionist Essays Publication Committee, 1915), 12. In the *Boston American* on July 4,

1915, Brandeis wrote that "Zionism is the Pilgrim inspiration and impulse over again." Quoted in Allon Gal, "In Search of a New Zion: New Light on Brandeis's Road to Zionism," in Jeffrey S. Gurlock, ed., *American Zionism: Mission and Politics* (New York: Routledge, 1998), 31.

49. See Rick Richman, "Zionism and Americanism: What Brandeis Saw and Why It Matters," in *What America Owes the Jews, What Jews Owe America* (New York: Mosaic Books, 2016), reprinted in *What America Owes the Jews, What Jews Owe America* (New Milford, Conn.: The Tobey Press, 2016).

50. Norman Podhoretz, born in 1930, described his reaction to his first visit to Israel the year after his 1950 graduation from both Columbia College and the College of Jewish Studies at the Jewish Theological Seminary of America:

> No doubt the Jewish people had been in exile, but not *this* Jew, not me. *My* true homeland was America, and the Jewish homeland was, so far as I was concerned, a foreign country . . . I was very happy that it had been established as a sovereign state to which persecuted Jews in need of refuge could flee, as millions of them, and at the cost of their lives, had been unable to do only a short while back. But I could not imagine any such thing ever happening to me, or to the Jews of America in general; and if, God forbid, it ever did and I was forced to settle in Israel, I would almost certainly feel that I was *now* in exile.

Norman Podhoretz, *My Love Affair with America: The Cautionary Tale of a Cheerful Conservative* (New York: The Free Press, 2000), 52 (emphasis in the original).

51. For descriptions of the history and principles of American Zionism and how it differed from European Zionism, see Naomi W. Cohen, *American Jews and the Zionist Idea* (Jersey City, N.J.: KTAV Publishing House Inc., 1975); Naomi W. Cohen, *The Americanization of Zionism, 1897–1948* (Hanover and London: Brandeis University Press, 2003); Melvin I. Urofsky, *American Zionism: From Herzl to the Holocaust* (Lincoln and London: University of Nebraska Press, 1975); Jeffrey S. Gurock, *American Jewish History, Vol. 8, American Zionism: Mission and Politics* (New York and London: Routledge, 1998). See also David Gelernter, *Americanism: The Fourth Great Western Religion* (New York: Doubleday, 2007), Chapter 3, "American Zionism: The Puritan Dream of America," 38–73.

52. See Ben Halpern, *A Clash of Heroes: Brandeis, Weizmann, and American Zionism* (New York and Oxford: Oxford University Press, 1987):

> At the close of World War I, Brandeis and Weizmann came into sharp conflict over the future direction of the Zionist work in Palestine. The differences, which seem fairly technical and rather minor in perspective, were said by both antagonists to rest upon fundamental values. It was a conflict between Washington and Pinsk, to use the imagery of the time; between the personal styles of the two leaders, each exemplifying the characteristic values of his following and his local background and each deprecating the style and values of the other. Brandeisists disparaged their opponents as undisciplined, incompetent, hysterical East Europeans; Weizmannites condemned the Brandeis coterie as American assimilationists.

53. "Weizmann Confers with Brandeis; Meeting Their First in 21 Years," JTA, February 7, 1940, www.jta.org/1940/02/07/archive/weizmann-confers-with-brandeis-meeting-their-first-in-21-years. The same issue of JTA reported that:

> Polish official circles reported today that German troops on Dec. 26 executed every tenth inhabitant of the predominantly Jewish town of Varka near Warsaw in reprisal for the shooting of a German policeman by a criminal escaping from a police raid. A total of 140 persons were executed, including 17 women and children, 4 youths under 18 years of age and 12 persons over 60 years of age. www.jta.org/1940/02/07/archive/nazis-decimated-jews-in-town-near-warsaw-poles-report.

54. Brandeis died in 1941 at age 85. In a long conversation during the last year of his life, he told Isaiah Berlin that "the money and the influence belonged to the rich and politically prominent among the [American] Jews, some of whom were, in his view, hopelessly ignorant and prejudiced, but, above all, fearful of seeming to attempt to rock the boat of American policy in some Jewish direction." In contrast, Brandeis "spoke with deep feeling of the decency of the lower-middle class and poor Jews, ill-informed, but with their hearts in the right place." Isaiah Berlin, "Zionist Politics in Wartime Washington: A Fragment of Personal Reminiscence," a lecture delivered in Jerusalem in 1972, reprinted in Henry Hardy, ed., *Flourishing: Isaiah Berlin Letters 1928–1946* (Cambridge: Cambridge University Press, 2004), 665–666.

55. "Zionist at White House/Dr. Weizmann Reports President Hopeful on Palestine Issue," *The New York Times*, February 9, 1940.

56. Weizmann recounts the meeting with FDR in a single paragraph in Chaim Weizmann, *Trial and Error,* 420. The paragraph reads in its entirety as follows:

> I had a talk with President Roosevelt early in February 1940. He showed a lively interest in the latest developments in Palestine, and I tried to sound him out on the likelihood of American interest in a new departure in Palestine, away from the White Paper, when the war was over. He showed himself friendly, but the discussion remained theoretical. Before I left he told me with great gusto the story of Felix Frankfurter's visit some time before, to a Palestinian colony where a magnificent prize bull was on show. Frankfurter asked idly what they called the bull, and received the answer "Franklin D. Roosevelt!"

*See* Allon Gal, *David Ben-Gurion and the American Alignment for a Jewish State,* 80 and fn. 29. FDR did not commit himself to any kind of action.

57. See United States Holocaust Museum, Holocaust Encyclopedia, "United States Policy and Its Impact on European Jews," http://www.ushmm.org/wlc/en/article.php?ModuleId=10007652.

> Influenced by the economic hardships of the Depression, which exacerbated popular anti-Semitism, isolationism, and xenophobia, the refugee policy of the U.S. State Department and its stringent (and questionably legal) application of the 1924 Immigration Law made it difficult for refugees to obtain entry visas, despite the ongoing persecution of Jews in Germany. . . .

Beginning in 1940, the United States further restricted immigration by ordering U.S. consuls to delay visa approvals on national security grounds. After the United States entered World War II in December 1941, the trickle of immigration virtually dried up . . . [H]owever, more than 200,000 Jews found refuge in the United States from 1933 to 1945, most of them before the end of 1941.

58. In 1938 the U.S. Department of Agriculture sent Lowdermilk, the assistant chief of the U.S. Soil Conservation Service, to survey land use in the Middle East as part of an effort to understand the Dust Bowl in the American Southwest. *See* Allis and Ronald Radosh, "Lowdermilk Makes the Case," a description of Lowdermilk's subsequent book, *Palestine, Land of Promise* (New York and London: Harper & Brothers, 1944), http://www.jbooks.com/interviews/index/IPRadosh.htm.

Lowdermilk was impressed by what the Jews "who fled to Palestine from the hatreds and persecutions of Europe" had accomplished in a short period of time. He was astonished to find 300 colonies "defying great hardships and applying the principles of co-operation and soil conservation." They have, he continued, "demonstrated the finest reclamation of old lands that I have seen in three continents." And "they have done this by the application of science, industry and devotion to the problems of reclaiming lands, draining swamps, improving agriculture and livestock and creating new industries." All this was done against "great odds and with sacrificial devotion to the ideal of redeeming the Promised Land."

*See also* Allis Radosh and Ronald Radosh, *A Safe Haven: Harry S. Truman and the Founding of Israel,* 21–23 and 55.

59. Lowdermilk, *Palestine, Land of Promise*, 78–88. Lowdermilk wrote that the decline of Palestine had begun with the Arab invasion during the seventh century, which reduced the area to "the stage of utter desolation," and continued with the Crusades of the twelfth and thirteenth centuries and the second Arab invasion, which plunged Palestine into an age of darkness. He concluded that the desolation in Palestine was not a result of the natural environment, but rather man-made devastation and neglect.

60. In a May 21, 1944, review of *Palestine: Land of Promise* in *The New York Times*, R. L. Duffus wrote that:

[Lowdermilk] is, one might say, an economic Zionist, eager to pay tribute to "the consecrated genius and vision of the Jews in Palestine development, yet seeing no real clash when Arab prosperity and population have increased in the neighborhood of all Jewish settlements and when in a space of fourteen years (1927–40) the Arab death rate dropped by one-third . . . What has been done in southern California, which in many respects is a land like Palestine, could be done along the eastern shores of the Mediterranean.

61. The story of Walter Lowdermilk is beautifully told in George Gilder, *The Israel Test* (New York and London: Encounter Books, 2012), 37–44.

62. The quoted material is from Chaim Weizmann, *Trial and Error,* 419–420. Weizmann further wrote that:

> One did not dare to say that England's cause was America's cause; one did not dare to speak of the inevitable. One did not dare to discuss even the most urgent practical problems facing England in the life and death struggle.

63. The regulations were issued on February 28, 1940, and generally prohibited transfers of land to Jews. Under the regulations, Jews could purchase land in only about 5 percent of Palestine, leaving 95 percent of Palestine off-limits to any further Jewish development.

64. Allon Gal, *David Ben-Gurion and the American Alignment for a Jewish State,* 81–82.

65. *Ibid.* The JTA reported that on February 28 the Emergency Committee on Palestine Affairs, representing all Zionist groups, held a two-hour special meeting and decided to organize nationwide rallies to protest the Palestine land restrictions, with a mass meeting in New York to be held within a week. http://www.jta.org/1940/02/29/archive/zionist-body-here-calls-protest-rallies-on-land-ordinance.

66. Chaim Weizmann, *Trial and Error,* 420.

67. Letter dated July 3, 1940, to Albert K. Epstein, Chicago, Letter No. 4 in Barnet Litvinoff, ed., *The Letters and Papers of Chaim Weizmann*, 4.

68. Back in London, in June 1940, Weizmann was concerned not only about the response of American Jews but about his own safety. As England anticipated a German invasion, Weizmann wrote to friends asking that "[i]n case I do not survive the present emergency, I would ask of my friends who do to try and collect the material regarding my forty years' work." His letter gave them directions about where the material could be found in files he had sent to Canada and Palestine. Leonard Stein, ed., *The Letters and Papers of Chaim Weizmann,* x.

After the war, a list was discovered in Berlin, prepared by the Nazis in 1940 as they planned a possible invasion of Britain, listing 2,300 names of people marked for "extermination." The list included prominent Jewish leaders in England, headed by Chaim Weizmann. "Weizmann, Other Prominent Jewish Leaders in England Marked by Gestapo for 'Extermination.'" JTA, September 16, 1945, www.jta.org/1945/09/16/archive/weizmann-other-prominent-jewish-leaders-in-england-marked-by-gestapo-for-extermination.

69. See Louis Lipsky, *Memoirs in Profile* (Philadelphia: Jewish Publication Society, 1975), 105:

> Dr. Weizmann did not qualify as an American orator. His voice was not resonant. He had few gestures. He used no groping introductions or exalted perorations. He hated the impersonation of emotion. He had no ear for the rhythmic phrase. He acquired the English gift for understatement. He did not propagandize himself as a person. He was not made for stage effects.
>
> In spite of these limitations, no Jewish speaker ever made the same deep and lasting impression. . . . He seemed to be able to capture the wisdom of Jewish

life. . . . There was a stateliness in his speech which was unique. He seemed to speak ex cathedra for the silent Jewish people.

70. Chaim Weizmann, *Trial and Error,* 418.

71. H. Sacher, ed., *Zionism and the Jewish Future* (New York: The Macmillan Company, 1916).

72. "Dr. Weizmann's Reply to His Critics," *New Palestine*, June 17, 1921.

73. Ben Halpern, *A Clash of Heroes: Brandeis, Weizmann, and American Zionism* (New York: Oxford University Press, 1987), 200, 204.

74. See George L. Berlin, "The Brandeis-Weizmann Dispute," in Jehuda Reinharz and Anita Shapira, eds., *Essential Papers on Zionism* (New York: New York University Press, 1996), 347–348.

75. Letter from Chaim Weizmann to Orde and Lorna Wingate dated June 20, 1937, http://www.shapell.org/manuscript.aspx?weizmann-wingate-partition-plan-american-jews. The Shapell Manuscript Collection, www.shapell.org. Object ID SMC #380.

## JABOTINSKY

1. In January 1940, Jabotinsky had written a letter to the American Consul General, pleading that he "reconsider your negative ruling regarding the grant of a visitor's visa to my wife, and to let her accompany me on my journey to the United States," Letter 4166, Jabotinsky Institute in Israel. She had gone to the consulate in October and had been told, erroneously, that she did not need a separate visa if her husband already had one. Jabotinsky assured the Consul General that:

> I give you my word that—if alive—we shall both of us leave the States at or before the expiry of the visa. Surely the precautions against fake visitors who overstay in order to settle in the United States are not intended to apply to visitors whose honesty cannot and should not be doubted. I am at the head of a worldwide movement. I am well known to Mr. Biddle, your ambassador in Warsaw. . . . If it were not too ludicrous I could get scores of American leaders in the world of politics, journalism etc. [to] cable you solemn guarantees that neither my wife nor I intend to live in the States permanently.

But no visa was forthcoming for Mrs. Jabotinsky.

2. Vladimir Jabotinsky, *The War and the Jew* (New York: Altalena Press, 1987), 242.

3. In *The Founding Fathers of Zionism* (Jerusalem: Gefen Publishing House Ltd. and Balfour Books, 2012), 192, Benzion Netanyahu wrote that "no phenomenon like the Legion . . . ever appeared during the long years of Jewish existence in Exile," and that "we would need to go back in history 1300 years to find it even in the Jews' own land," when Jewish legions in 614 helped Parthian armies free Palestine from Byzantium:

> However, in order to properly evaluate Jabotinsky's achievement, we need to pay attention to the differences. . . . The Jewish army that fought on the Parthian

side was established by the leadership of the Jews in Palestine, whereas the legion that Jabotinsky set up was created by him as a private person without any support from the Jewish leadership—indeed, despite its opposition.

Likewise, the soldiers of the Legion were not recruited from among a people living in its own country, that aspired to regain its freedom, but from amongst fragments of the Jewish Diaspora in Britain, whose members at first vigorously and angrily opposed their very participation in the war.

4. Leo Pinsker, *Road to Freedom: Writings and Addresses* (Westport, Conn.: Greenwood Press, 1944).

5. Thomas Paine's 47-page pamphlet, *Common Sense,* was published on January 9, 1776, and challenged the authority of the British in America in plain language. It was one of the most influential writings leading to the American Revolution. See "Thomas Paine Publishes *Common Sense*," History Channel, www.history.com/this-day-in-history/thomas-paine-publishes-common-sense.

6. *Vladimir Jabotinsky's Story of My Life*, Brian Horowitz and Leonid Katsis, eds. (Detroit: Wayne State University Press, 2016), 50. Those who have reviewed Jabotinsky's autobiographical writings differ on their factual reliability. Michael Stanislawski asserts that they are a "self-conscious and highly inventive literary creation" and that Jabotinsky's "wonderful and indeed stirring autobiography" was a "brilliant, but highly fictionalized, self-fashioning." Michael Stanislawski, Introduction to *Autobiographical Jews: Essays in Jewish Self-Fashioning* (Seattle: University of Washington Press, 2004), 3.

Brian Horowitz, the editor of the English-language edition of Jabotinsky's autobiography, takes a different position. He writes that Stanislawski "overstated the case." Horowitz states in the introduction to *The Story of My Life* that while Jabotinsky embellished details, the book "follows the basic biography of Jabotinsky's life" as reflected in his letters and documents; for example, "[i]f one wonders whether Jabotinsky was really in Istanbul . . . one can check his letters to see that he was there, and that indeed he did edit a half-dozen journals, as he claims." *Vladimir Jabotinsky's Story of My Life*, Brian Horowitz and Leonid Katsis, eds. 29. Horowitz treats *The Story of My Life* as "neither entirely nonfactual nor entirely truthful."

Jabotinsky's 2014 biographer, Hillel Halkin, concludes that "[f]or the most part, I believe, his memoirs are a sincere if artful attempt to describe times and episodes in his life as he recalled them, and I have treated them as essentially reliable accounts." Hillel Halkin, *Jabotinsky: A Life* (New Haven: Yale University Press, 2014).

7. Christopher Duggan, *The Force of Destiny: A History of Italy Since 1796* (London: Penguin Books, 2008), xvii.

8. In his 1862 book, *Rome and Jerusalem: A Study in Jewish Nationalism* (New York: Bloch Publishing Company, 1918), written at the time of Garibaldi, Hess had argued that "the [political] renaissance of Italy heralds the rise of Judah":

The orphaned children of Jerusalem will also participate in the great regeneration of nations. . . . Among the nations believed to be dead and which, when they become conscious of their historic mission, will struggle for their national rights, is also Israel—the nation which for two thousand years has defied the storms of time, and . . . has always cast yearning glances toward Jerusalem.

*Ibid.,* "Author's Preface," 36–37.

9. Leo Pinsker (1821–1891) was one of Odessa's most prominent physicians, part of the first generation of Russian Jews admitted to the country's universities. His career as a teacher and physician made him the personification of the enlightened Russian Jew, living in an optimistic stage of Russian history under the liberal Czar Alexander II.

But in 1881 Alexander II was assassinated by a group of anarchists, which allegedly included a Jewish woman, and pogroms swept through the Pale of Settlement during the course of a full year like tornadoes, beginning in 1881 and extending into 1882. The new czar was repressive, and new draconian restrictions were placed on the Russian Jews. The 60-year-old Pinsker, head of the Odessa Society for the Promotion of Culture among Russian Jews, was stunned by pogroms, which even reached Odessa, and it caused him to rethink the principles that had guided his life. In 1882, he anonymously published an extended essay entitled "Auto-Emancipation," chastising Jews for waiting expectantly "for the age of universal harmony" and urging them to embrace a different remedy, one that is "more thoroughgoing than those palliatives to which our hapless people have been turning for 2000 years." Leo Pinsker, *Road to Freedom*. He proposed a new Exodus, back to an older time and place. In his new view, the essence of the Jewish problem was that:

The Jewish people has no fatherland of its own, though many motherlands; no center of focus or gravity, no government of its own, no official representation. They are everywhere, but are nowhere at home. The nations have never to deal with a Jewish nation but always with mere Jews . . . [T]he Jews seem rather to have lost all remembrance of their former home . . . Often to please their protectors, they [renounce] their traditional individuality entirely . . .

We must prove that the misfortunes of the Jews are due, above all, to their lack of desire for national independence; and that this desire must be awakened and maintained in time if they do not wish to be subjected forever to disgraceful existence—in a word, we must prove that they must become a nation.

10. Chaim Nachman Bialik, "In the City of Slaughter," http://faculty.history.umd .edu/BCooperman/NewCity/Slaughter.html. The following is an excerpt from the opening stanzas of the poem:

Arise and go now to the city of slaughter;
Into its courtyard wind thy way;
There with thy hand, and with the eyes of thy head,
Behold on tree, on stone, on fence, on mural clay,
The spattered blood and dried brains of the dead.
. . .
Descend then, to the cellars of the town,
There where the virginal daughters of thy folk were fouled,

Where seven heathens flung a woman down,
The daughter in the presence of her mother,
The mother in the presence of her daughter,
Before slaughter, during slaughter, and after slaughter!
. . .
Note also, do not fail to note,
In that dark corner, and behind that cask
Crouched husbands, bridegrooms, brothers, peering from the cracks . . .

Crushed in their shame, they saw it all;
They did not stir nor move . . .
Perhaps, perhaps, each watcher had it in his heart to pray:
A miracle, O Lord—and spare my skin this day! . . .

Four decades later, Jabotinsky would recall the passive Jewish reaction of the Russian Jews at the time of the Kishinev pogrom in 1903. In a July 29, 1939, article in *The Jewish Herald*, in which he argued for a more aggressive response to the Arab riots in Palestine, Jabotinsky sardonically recalled an anecdote from that time:

In my native town when the news came of the Kishinev pogrom, in which 30 Jews were killed, a conversation took place between two synagogue wardens, one from the Shalashne Synagogue and the other from the Goldsmiths' Synagogue:

"Have you done anything?"

"Nothing—what can we do?"

"What do you mean—nothing? You're good-for-nothings in your Shalashne Street. We in the Goldsmith, as soon as we heard of the tragedy, we stayed at the Synagogue all night and cried and read psalms and lamentations. . . . Do you think we'll just allow things to happen?"

11. See Lewis Glinert, *The Story of Hebrew* (Princeton and Oxford: Princeton University Press, 2017), 207: "*the* historic moment in modern Hebrew poetry, for the literary historian Dan Miron, was the appearance in 1924 of the translations from Dante and Poe by the charismatic Russian-Zionist politician-litterateur [Vladimir] Jabotinsky—in an Israeli rhythm and graphic modernistic style. . . ." [Emphasis in original]. For a discussion of Jabotinsky's plays, see Michael Stanislawski, *Zionism and the Fin de Siècle: Cosmopolitanism and Nationalism from Nordau to Jabotinsky* (Berkeley and Los Angeles: University of California Press, 2001). For a review of Jabotinsky's great Russian novel, *The Five*, translated by Michael R. Katz (Ithaca: Cornell University Press, 2005), see Hillel Halkin, "Sacrifices," *The New Republic*, December 18, 2005, www.newrepublic.com/article/62680/sacrifices.

12. Jabotinsky wrote two novels of lasting significance: *Samson* in 1928 and *The Five* in 1935. *Samson* was purchased by Cecil B. De Mille and was made into the movie *Samson and Delilah*. *The Five* was translated into English in 2005 and was treated as a major Russian novel by numerous reviewers. See Hillel Halkin, "Sacrifices"; Michael Stanislawski, *Zionism and the Fin de Siècle*, 227–28. Jabotinsky's most famous essay is

"The Iron Wall," written in 1923: http://en.jabotinsky.org/media/9747/the-iron-wall.pdf. See Rick Richman, "Why Jabotinsky Still Matters," *The Tower Magazine* (June 2014), http://www.thetower.org/article/why-jabotinsky-still-matters/.

13. Vladimir Jabotinsky, *The Story of the Jewish Legion* (New York: Bernard Ackerman, Incorporated 1945), 29.

14. Vladimir Jabotinsky's *Story of My Life*, Brian Horowitz and Leonid Katsis, eds., *ibid.*

15. For an extensive treatment of the Jewish experience with the morality of power and powerlessness, see Ruth R. Wisse, *Jews and Power* (New York: Nextbook Schocken, 2007).

16. Col. John Henry Patterson, Forward to Vladimir Jabotinsky, *The Story of the Jewish Legion* (New York: Bernard Ackerman Inc., 1945), 14–15.

17. Vladimir Jabotinsky, *The Story of the Jewish Legion*, 59. Vera Weizmann, in *The Impossible Takes Longer: The Memoirs of Vera Weizmann*, 58–59, recalled her friendship with Jabotinsky, beginning in early 1916, when "I had moved from Manchester to London, joining Chaim and 'Jabo' in their bachelor establishment at 3 Justice Walk, a few days before our removal to our first Kensington address":

> On Jabo's arrival in England, he lived with us in Manchester for some time. He then . . . began his historic, if contentious, struggle to form the Jewish Legion, in which endeavor both Chaim and I were his fervent supporters. . . . For a time, while he was promoting the Legion, he lived with us in Kensington.

> A furious storm of controversy broke over Jabo's and our heads over the whole issue of the Jewish Legion. Even pro-Zionists thought such a force was unnecessary and positively harmful to the Jewish cause since many Jews were already enrolled in Allied armies: Ahad Ha'am, Chaim's closest friend, went so far as to castigate the scheme as an "empty demonstration"; but Jabo, with my husband's support, continued to press the idea, and both Chaim and I followed his recruiting campaign with the deepest interest. . . . [Jabotinsky] in the widest sense of the word . . . was the founder of the Jewish Legion."

18. Jehuda Reinharz, *Chaim Weizmann: The Making of a Statesman* (New York: Oxford University Press, 1993), 183–184.

19. John Patterson, *With the Judaeans in the Palestine Campaign* (London: Hatchenson & Co., 1922), 19–20.

20. Vladimir Jabotinsky, *The Story of the Jewish Legion*, 104.

21. Jabotinsky's claim is supported in Bernard Wasserstein, *Britain and the Jews of Europe: 1939–1945*, 272 ("That 'Jewish Legion' had helped secure the favorable atmosphere towards Zionism in which the Balfour Declaration had been issued in 1917").

22. Vladimir Jabotinsky, *The Story of the Jewish Legion*, 181–182.

23. Joseph B. Schechtman, *Fighter and Prophet: The Vladimir Jabotinsky Story: The Last Years* (New York: Thomas Yoseloff, 1961), 370–371.

24. Letter to Louis I. Newman, October 22, 1939, Letter No. 6721, Jabotinsky Institute in Israel. In that letter, Jabotinsky explained why neither a Jewish legion nor Jewish units within other nations' armies would be sufficient:

I do not know whether the Allies will eventually agree to forming Jewish units, but even if they do it will be of no political significance. The situation has tremendously changed since 1917 when the formation of a Judean Regiment was such a revolutionary symbol: today a step of this kind will be unable to put us "on the map".

In short: if (I underline the "if" as heavily as I can) there is a force that still can place the Jewish problem in the forefront and compel the Allies to treat us at least as they do [others], that force can only come from within American Jewry.

25. Rafael Medoff, *Militant Zionism in America: The Rise and Impact of the Jabotinsky Movement in the United States, 1926–1948* (Tuscaloosa: The University of Alabama Press, 2002), 47–49; 84; Naomi W. Cohen, *The Americanization of Zionism, 1897–1948* (Hanover and London: Brandeis University Press, 2003), 154. Akzin was the editor of the *American Jewish Chronicle* and taught at the City College of New York. Two senior aides traveled to the United States on the *SS Samaria* with Jabotinsky: 34-year-old Aaron Kopelowicz and 38-year-old Eliahu Ben-Horin. In July, the 25-year-old Hillel Kook (later known as Peter Bergson) joined them. Medoff, *Militant Zionism in America*, 49.

26. Jabotinsky gave his speech extemporaneously, but a detailed outline of his remarks with lengthy quotations can be found in "Address by Vladimir Jabotinsky at Manhattan Center, March 19, 1940, 'The Fate of Jewry.'" Reference Code A-1 8/59, Jabotinsky Institute In Israel.

27. Max Nordau was a leading journalist and a prominent public intellectual at the turn of the nineteenth century. He became Theodor Herzl's closest associate and co-founded the Zionist Organization, serving as vice president of the first six Zionist Congresses and president of the seventh through tenth. His addresses and writings became classics of Zionist literature. See "Address at the First Zionist Congress" (1897); "Zionism and Anti-Semitism Zionism by Nordau; and Anti-Semitism by Gottheil" (Amazon Digital Services LLC); "Address by Max Nordau at the Sixth Zionist Congress" (1903). In 1919, when a new wave of pogroms swept through Russia, he advocated transferring 600,000 Jews to Palestine within a matter of months. See "Nordau, Max," Jewish Virtual Library, www.jewishvirtuallibrary.org/jsource/judaica/ejud0002_0015_0_14907.html.

28. The portrayal of Jabotinsky as a "militarist" was always pejorative and an oversimplification of his views. See Vladimir Jabotinsky, "The Aims of Zionism," *The Zionist*, May 14, 1926, 6–7:

I know that many Jews scoff at "moral pressure," pretending to believe that "Goyim" can only be convinced by physical coercion. But we Revisionists reject this non-Jewish pessimism. Against robbers and pogrom-makers, we are "militarists": but the really essential problems of humanity and history can only be decided on those "battlefields" where the weapons are spiritual weapons, and on those "battlefields" the Jewish People is second to none in power. The mightiest force on earth is a *justa causa*—if you have the courage to fight for it.

29. Melvin Urofsky, *A Voice that Spoke for Justice: The Life and Times of Stephen S. Wise* (Albany: State University of New York Press, 1981).

30. Surveying the American Jewish scene in 1940 in New York, Samuel Merlin found that:

> The established Zionist leaders . . . largely kept Jewish concerns within the fold, that is, within the Jewish community, instead of actively bringing Jewish problems to wider attention and trying to influence general public opinion.

Samuel Merlin, *Millions of Jews to Rescue* (Washington, D.C.: The David S. Wyman Institute for Holocaust Studies, 2011), 34.

31. Melvin I. Urofsky, *A Voice that Spoke for Justice: The Life and Times of Stephen S. Wise*, 312.

32. Rafael Medoff, *Militant Zionism in America*, 51. One indication of the electrifying effect that Jabotinsky's oratory had is that a young student who heard him on the evening of March 19 still recalled the feeling nearly half a century later, telling Jabotinsky's biographer that:

> My father had tickets for the meeting [at the Manhattan Center] and invited me to go with him. I had better things to do than to listen to a lecturer; but I gave in and went along. *It was the experience of my life.* I sat on the edge of my chair, afraid to move lest I should miss a word. [Emphasis added.]

Shmuel Katz, *Lone Wolf: A Biography of Vladimir (Ze'ev) Jabotinsky*, Vol. 2 (New York: Barricade Books, 1996), 1755.

33. *"Revisionism—A Destructive Force,"* a twenty-six-page printed booklet, issued under the sponsorship of the entire American Zionist leadership. See Yitzhak Ben-Ami, *Years of Wrath, Days of Glory*, 331–332.

34. Regarding Max Nordau, *see* fn. 27.

35. Jabotinsky also contacted James G. McDonald, the High Commissioner for Refugees (Jewish and Other) of the League of Nations. In a 1938 cable, Jabotinsky thanked him for his interest in salvaging German Jewry and argued that the "most just way to solve the tragic problem that engages your and the whole decent world's attention at the moment would be to allow us to repatriate into Palestine within the next two years the whole of German Jewry and some 500,000 more from other countries of Jewish distress," and he told McDonald:

> This can be done. Stop. . . . May I remind you that over a million Greeks were transferred from Asia Minor in less than a year. Stop. Of these, 800,000 were settled in Macedonia which is smaller than Palestine. Stop. They were helped by a League of Nations loan of ten million pounds. Stop. We Jewish people can raise the necessary funds. We can make the supreme effort. We can with your help solve the problem. . . . I beseech you to use your influence with British Government to secure its consent to this radical way of solving the problem confronting us all.

Letter No. 3911, Reference Code A-1 2/28, Jabotinsky Institute In Israel.

36. The full text of Jabotinsky's testimony before the Peel Commission on February 11, 1937, can be found at https://www.scribd.com/document/287215998/Jabotinsky-Testimony-to-Peel-Commission.

37. See also Vladimir Jabotinsky, "Justice of the Jewish Claim," *Canadian Jewish Chronicle* (Montreal), May 12, 1922, 7:

> The principle of self-determination can only be applied to peoples as entities, not to every square mile of the world's populated surface. It takes account of every nation to live, not only the present racial composition of every province. . . . And if your statistics show you one people possessing five times more land than it is able to cultivate, while another has no land at all, then it is only just that the former should be requested to concede a fraction of its surplus so that the latter may have a homestead. This is exactly the case of the Jews and the Arabs.

Quoted in Louis Gordon, "The Unknown Essays of Vladimir Jabotinsky," *Jewish Political Studies Review* 9:1–2 (Spring 1997), 99.

38. Quoted by Benzion Netanyahu in Benzion Netanyahu, *The Founding Fathers of Zionism* (Jerusalem: Balfour Books, co-published with Gefen Publishing House Ltd., 2012), 229–230.

39. Vladimir Jabotinsky, "A White Paper Against Diaspora Jewry," *The Jewish Herald*, June 23, 1939. In May 1939, Jabotinsky delivered twenty-one lectures in Poland, Latvia, Lithuania, and Finland, and then held a series of meetings in Rumania, Yugoslavia, and Bulgaria, including a long meeting with the president and prime minister of Lithuania. He had previously met twice with the president of the Free Irish State, Eamon De Valera. Schechtman, *Fighter and Prophet: The Vladimir Jabotinsky Story,* 363.

40. Letter from Vladimir Jabotinsky, as president of the New Zionist Organization, to Prime Minister Neville Chamberlain, September 4, 1939. The Jabotinsky Institute in Israel, Letter No. 4115, Reference Code A-1 2/29/2.

41. Letter from Vladimir Jabotinsky to Lt. Col. John Patterson, April 14, 1940. The Jabotinsky Institute in Israel, Letter No. 4232, Reference Code A-1 2/30/1.

42. See Samuel Merlin, *Millions of Jews to Rescue*, 42–43:

> The Zionist leadership appears to have been motivated by three factors. First, a determination to combat Jabotinsky, regardless of the merits of his project, because he was a rival who posed competition for the hearts and minds of Jewry. Second, a fear that since the United States was still neutral, a campaign for a Jewish army might cast a shadow over their patriotism as Americans. Third, some kind of breakdown in communication between the American Zionist establishment and the London and Jerusalem offices of the Zionist movement, since the latter favored the creation of a Jewish military force within the British army, an idea not so distant from Jabotinsky's.

See also Henry L. Feingold, *The Politics of Rescue: The Roosevelt Administration and the Holocaust, 1938–1945* (New York, 1980), 174–175, referring to "bickering major organizations . . . [and] the large number of unaffiliated Jews who were growing impatient with the inability of the regular organizations to take effective action").

Arye Bruce Saposnik argues in "Advertisement or Achievement? American Jewry and the Campaign for a Jewish Army, 1939–1944: A Reassessment," *The Journal of Israeli History* 17, no. 2 (1996), that America's established Jewish leadership was actually sympathetic to the creation of a Jewish army. Rafael Medoff rebuts that view in "Who Fought for the 'Right to Fight'? A response to Arye Bruce Saposnik's Article on the Campaign for a Jewish Army, 1939–1944," *The Journal of Israeli History* 18, no. 1 (Spring 1997).

43. Rafael Medoff, *Militant Zionism in America*, 50. The address was given on March 31, 1940, at the Capitol Hotel. A copy is in the archives at the Jabotinsky Institute. Reference Code A-1 8/58.

44. See the entry for "Betar" in the *YIVO Encyclopedia of Jews in Eastern Europe*, which explains that the acronym stood for "Berit Yosef Trumpeldor (Joseph Trumpeldor Alliance)," and that Betar's goals and principles, as adopted in a 1929 conference of representatives from 24 countries, were:

> (1) a stress on Zionist monism, which meant devotion to the idea of a purified Zionism [unaffected by other "isms" such as socialism]; (2) an aspiration to create a Jewish state on both sides of the Jordan River; (3) compulsory army training and immigration to Palestine; (4) nurturing of the concept of *hadar* (dignity), in the broadest meaning of that word; (5) a commitment to learn Hebrew; and (6) total obedience to the institutions of the Betar movement.

The entry states that by the end of 1938, there was a worldwide membership of 90,000 in twenty-six countries, with the majority in Poland. Melzer, Emanuel. 2017. Betar. YIVO Encyclopedia of Jews in Eastern Europe. http://www.yivoencyclopedia.org/article.aspx/Betar.

45. Joseph B. Schechtman, *Fighter and Prophet: The Vladimir Jabotinsky Story*, 418.

46. The "new Jewish mentality" that Jabotinsky sought was not ideological, but rather one in which Jews could stand up for themselves. See footnotes 47 and 49 below.

47. Midge Decter has noted a key difference between Jabotinsky's goal of *hadar* and the aim of socialist equality and fraternity that motivated the Labor Zionists:

> Jabotinsky's insistence that behind the Jews of his time stood "some 70 generations of people who were literate, who learned and spoke of God and history, of peoples and kingdoms, of ideas, justice and righteousness . . ." is a startling reminder of something that now tends to get lost: namely, that the goal of Zionism on the part of its true founding fathers was to be the creation not of a "new Middle East" but of a sturdy, dignified, and self-respecting Jewish people.

Midge Decter, "Return and Exile," a review of Shmuel Katz's biography of Jabotinsky, *Commentary Magazine*, July 1996, 66.

48. In an essay published in the March 17, 1935, issue of the *Jewish Daily Bulletin*, Jabotinsky responded to an assertion by Rabbi Stephen S. Wise, published in the *Bulletin* the week before, that the Revisionist movement was "fascism" (because it allegedly held the view that "the state is everything and the individual nothing"). Jabotinsky challenged Wise to cite any Revisionist resolution, declaration, or authoritative article that had expressed that view, and he wrote:

Personally, I hate the very idea of a "totalitarian State," whether Communist or Fascist . . . and prefer old-fashioned parliamentarism, however clumsy or inefficient; and ninety-nine percent of my comrades share this attitude. What Dr. Wise obviously mistook for his bogey is the fact that we maintain and will go on maintaining—that striving for the creation of a Jewish State should be . . . miles above any class or individual interest. But so did Garibaldi hold the creation of the Italian State paramount, so did Lincoln the unity of America; which does not mean that they wanted an Italy or an America where the State would be everything and the individual nothing.

Hillel Halkin described Jabotinsky in a 2005 article in *The New Republic* as "a European liberal who despised fascism . . . one of the most intelligent, talented, honest, and likeable of all twentieth-century politicians." Hillel Halkin, "Sacrifices," *The New Republic*, December 18, 2005, https://newrepublic.com/article/62680/sacrifices.

49. In a May 7, 1940, interview in New York, Oscar Kraines, a member of the radical-left Hashomer Hatzair youth movement (an ideological rival of Jabotinsky's movement), asked Jabotinsky why he believed socialism was not good for Zionism. He responded as follows:

When the Arabs massacred Jewish settlers in 1936, 1938 and 1939, socialist Zionists were shocked that gentile socialists and the communists, including Jewish communists, described those massacres as nationalist uprisings against imperialism. Also, socialist Zionists are too pacifistic. The world has yet to accept Jews as fighters, trained and disciplined soldiers who know how to use weapons.

In an article I wrote in 1936, entitled "On the Hearth" (Yiddish) I pointed out that each generation of Jews has its own alef-bet to learn, and the lessons are different for each generation. I wrote: "For this generation now growing before our own eyes, and on whose shoulders will fall the responsibility for the greatest turning point in our history, the alef-bet is very plain and simple: 'Young men, learn to shoot!' Being educated is not enough. Being educated and also skilled workers and farmers is still not enough. But knowing how to shoot will give us hope. This is not militarism or fascism. This is historical reality. It is necessary for our survival in Palestine and elsewhere.

We Jews have too long been a people of contemplation only. Now we need generations of young founders and builders who can ride horses, climb trees, and use weapons and their fists. It is not morality and contemplation that move nations. It is power and military force—just what we Jews have lacked everywhere for centuries and even now in Palestine.

Oscar Kraines and Rafael Medoff, "Jabotinsky's Campaign in America: A Previously Unpublished Interview," *The Journal of Israeli History* 15, no. 2 (1994).

See also Ayre Naor, "Jabotinsky's New Jew: Concept and Models," *The Journal of Israeli History* 30, no. 2 (September 2011), 141–159, quoting from a Jabotinsky essay written in Hebrew, "Al ha-ad (ha-alef-bet he-hadash)" (At the Fireside—The New Alphabet):

Recognition of historical reality commands us: . . . if all of you speak Hebrew and are knowledgeable in all of our national literature . . . but do not know how to shoot, there will be no hope for you. . . . Of all the conditions for our political renaissance, knowing how to shoot is, regrettably, the most important.

In *The Founding Fathers of Zionism*, Benzion Netanyahu summarized Jabotinsky's view as:

You can cultivate a dream of perpetual peace and even work to advance and attain it. But if you want to reach the day when this dream is realized, you must in the meanwhile wage a war with predators. Therefore, you must use your teeth and nails; and if you do not have these, you must grow them.

50. Jabotinsky, Ze'ev, "Speech to Betar Formation," March 31, 1940. Reference Code A-1 8/58, Jabotinsky Institute in Israel. The 1930s were a time of great growth for the Communist Party USA and for Jewish involvement in it. See Priscilla Murolo, "Communism in the United States," in *Jewish Women: A Comprehensive Historical Encyclopedia,* March 1, 2009, Jewish Women's Archive, http://jwa.org/encyclopedia/article/communism-in-united-states:

The party swelled from just under ten thousand members in 1929 to about forty thousand in 1936 and to eighty-three thousand in 1943. Female membership expanded from about 15 percent in the early 1930s to 30 or 40 percent at the end of the decade and to about 46 percent in 1943. CP historians estimate, moreover, that almost half of the party's membership was Jewish in the 1930s and 1940s, and that approximately 100,000 Jews passed through the party in those decades of high member turnover.

See also Howard Sachar, "Jews in Radical Politics," http://www.myjewishlearning.com/article/jews-in-radical-politics/#, describing Jewish involvement in communist-front organizations during the late 1930s:

Altogether, tens of thousands of Jews throughout the country were drawn to Communist-front organizations, particularly to the various "anti-Fascist" groups. One of the most popular of these, founded in 1937, was the American League against War and Fascism, later to be renamed the American League for Peace and Democracy. The Jewish People's Committee against Fascism and Anti-Semitism was formed in 1939, when the American Jewish Congress rejected applicants from the leftist International Workers Organization.

Impressionable and idealistic, students were uniquely susceptible to these leagues and alliances. In 1936, the American Student Union—later the American Youth Congress—listed 200,000 members, of whom possibly a fourth were Jews. For these young people, witnessing the rise of anti-Semitism in Europe and experiencing raw discrimination at home, almost any "progressive" movement would have claimed their loyalty. But with their own strong Jewish cultural traditions, they were particularly impressed by the intellectualism of the

Left, by a movement that included so many admired thinkers, writers, and other individuals of cultivated tastes.

51. Cahan's article was reprinted by *Forward* on May 26, 2000, in a story entitled *"'An Old Jewish Journalist to Another': The Private Correspondence of Ze'ev Jabotinsky and Ab. Cahan."* The *Forward* also published on that date an essay on the Cahan-Jabotinsky correspondence by Louis Gordon, a longtime Jabotinsky researcher who had discovered the correspondence in the archives of the Jabotinsky Institute in Israel and the YIVO Institute for Jewish Research in New York.

52. Weizmann's profession of ignorance about the likely fate of the Jews in Europe was less than candid. James G. McDonald, the first U.S. ambassador to Israel, in his memoir entitled *My Mission in Israel, 1948–1951* (New York: Simon and Schuster, 1951), 249, 251, wrote of Weizmann as follows:

> I had known Weizmann for fifteen years before we began to work together in Israel [in 1948]. Ever since the fall of 1933, when he first came to see me in my office as League of Nations High Commissioner for German Refugees, our paths had frequently crossed and we had become good friends. . . .

> Dr. Weizmann's prescience was impressed upon me during the first interview nearly two decades earlier in Geneva. Then it was that he unfolded to me his basic philosophy about his people and his hopes for their future. I was appalled but not surprised at his ruthless analysis of the fate of the Jewish communities in Germany and Eastern Europe. *He foresaw the extermination of millions of his fellow Jews and the persecution and displacement of other millions.* Only in Palestine did he foresee a secure haven. *"If before I die," he said, "there are half a million Jews in Palestine, I shall be content because I shall know that this 'saving remnant' will survive.* They, not the millions in the Diaspora, are what really matter. . . ." [Emphasis added.]

53. Jabotinsky would doubtless have been far more critical of Weizmann had he known about the testimony Weizmann gave in 1936 to the Peel Commission in a session held *in camera*, where Weizmann was more candid than in his public testimony. Weizmann told the Commission that:

> I have always thought it is a mistake to say that Palestine is a quantitative solution of the Jewish problem. . . . [W]e could not bring six million Jews to Palestine in a reasonable time. . . . *We can only try to salvage from this destruction the young, the vigorous, the adaptable, those who have their life before them.* . . . Therefore, I divide the number of six million by three. The problem thus reduces itself to two million . . . half must be brought into Palestine, or be destroyed. . . . [O]ne has to face realities and limit oneself to that element which has its life before it, and *what will happen to the other Jews, I do not know.* [Emphasis added.]

Barnet Litvinoff, editor, *The Letters and Papers of Chaim Weizmann*, 175, 179 (Paper 24, December 18, 1936 testimony). On the other hand, Jabotinsky was probably aware of the speech Weizmann gave to the following Zionist Congress, in which Weizmann told the delegates:

The old ones will pass; they will bear their fate or they will not. They are dust, economic and moral dust in a cruel world. . . . Two million, and perhaps less: "She'erith Hapleta"—only a remnant shall survive. We have to accept it.

Quoted in Oskar K. Rabinowicz, *Fifty Years of Zionism: A Historical Analysis of Dr. Weizmann's "Trial and Error"* (London: Robert Anscombe & Co. Ltd., 1950), 85.

54. Letter from Jabotinsky to Cahan, Letter No. 4228, Reference Code: A-1 2/30/1, Jabotinsky Institute in Israel.

55. Cahan's letter dated April 17, 1940, stated that he had heard a great deal about Jabotinsky's place in Russian journalism, and had read his novel of Odessa (*The Five*). He told Jabotinsky:

To be sure, you and I look at things from two different points of view, but as I tried to make it clear in my article about you, I sincerely admire your talent. So much so that that part you play in the Zionist movement is of secondary importance from my point of view. . . . Frankly speaking, I regret that you have not devoted your great gifts to journalism and literature.

Quoted by Louis Gordon in *Forward, supra*, May 26, 2000.

56. Jabotinsky published *Samson the Nazirite* in 1926 and *The Five* in 1936. *Samson* was based on the Biblical story of a powerful individual enticed by the sophisticated non-Jewish culture of the Philistines, which Jabotinsky portrayed as a world in which power was understood and respected. Cecil B. De Mille bought the movie rights to Jabotinsky's novel and eventually produced the film *Samson and Delilah,* starring Hedy Lamarr and Victor Mature.

Ruth R. Wisse, in her 2000 book, *The Modern Jewish Canon: A Journey Through Language and Culture* (New York: The Free Press, 2000), lists both Jabotinsky's *Samson* and Cahan's *The Rise of David Levinsky* as part of the Modern Jewish Canon.

Jabotinsky's novel *The Five* was not translated into English until 2005. It was written by Jabotinsky in Russian, as *Samson* had been, and Cahan probably read it in Russian (which Cahan knew from the first twenty-one years of his life that he lived in Russia). If anything, the book is more accomplished than *Samson*, praised by Hillel Halkin in *The New Republic* in 2005 for its literary merit, noting how good it was not only as a novel by a political figure, but indeed for any writer. Hillel Halkin, "Sacrifices." It is a remarkably moving novel about Zionism, in which none of the characters are zionists (except perhaps the narrator, who survives, or perhaps the character who sacrifices herself to save her children).

57. See Abraham Cahan, *The Education of Abraham Cahan* (Philadelphia: The Jewish Publication Society, 1969), 185, in which Cahan describes two groups of Russian Jews in the years after the 1881 assassination of Czar Alexander II led to a wave of pogroms throughout the Pale of Settlement:

One [group] believed that a new home for the Jews should be started in America, the land of rich resources and opportunity. The other urged a return to Palestine, the historical home of the Jewish people. . . . I could not subscribe to the Palestine idea [because] I was first of all a socialist . . .

58. Quoted in Seth Lipsky, *The Rise of Abraham Cahan* (New York: Schocken Books, 2013), 125 and 126.

59. *Ibid.*, 127.

60. Letter dated April 17, 1940, from Abraham Cahan to Mr. V. Jabotinsky. Archives of the Jabotinsky Institute in Israel.

61. On April 3, 1940—just after Cahan published his indictment of Jabotinsky but before Jabotinsky wrote to him—Jabotinsky spoke at the Brooklyn Academy of Music on "Lublin or Palestine, Which?" under the auspices of the Brooklyn-Queens Council and the American Friends of a Jewish Palestine. He used the occasion to plead for funds to help Jews escape expulsion to Lublin by facilitating their movement to Palestine. See JTA, "*Share in U.P.A. funds for Palestine Revisionists Urged by Jabotinsky,*" April 4, 1940, www.jta.org/1940/04/04/archive/share-in-u-p-a-funds-for-palestine-revisionists-urged-by-jabotinsky.

A month after Jabotinsky's speech—several weeks after the Jabotinsky-Cahan correspondence—the JTA reported that Polish authorities were interested in reducing the "surplus" Jewish population but that "responsible representatives of the Jewish community [said they] could not consider any proposals derogating from full equality for Jewish citizens." The Revisionists, on the other hand, were reportedly "willing to support a policy of Jewish emigration." JTA, "Polish Leaders Seek Views of Jewish Groups on Future Status in Poland," May 12, 1940, www.jta.org/1940/05/12/archive/polish-leaders-seek-views-of-jewish-groups-on-future-status-in-poland. Faced with the opposition of mainstream Jewish leaders, nothing further happened.

See also Seth Lipsky, "Abraham Cahan Speaks," *Tablet Magazine*, July 7, 2012, an imaginary interview with Cahan on the occasion of his 150th birthday, in which Lipsky imagines Cahan telling the fictional interviewer:

I met my match in Jabotinsky. It was an important error in my life, my denunciation of him after his speech at the Manhattan Opera House. That was 1940. He called then for the urgent evacuation of the Jews from Europe to Eretz Israel, and I turned around and belittled him in the pages of the Forward. I gave a whole page to it, and that's when I wrote, "Six million is a pretty small state." I was derisive, and I was wrong.

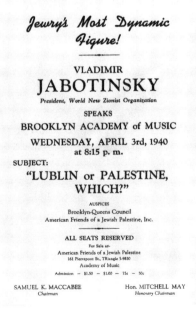

*http://collection.mjhnyc.org/index*
*.php?g=detail&objectid=1886*

62. Sent just two days after Churchill became prime minister, Jabotinsky's cable read as follows:

> Wishing success in your formidable mission. I as spokesman of movement principally identified with Jewry's revived military tradition offer you plan of cooperation. I am cabling upon assumption that you realize necessity to reverse all those features of previous policy which nearly killed magnetism of Allied cause abroad. One feature was absurd shrinking from Jewish aspects of present crisis, forgetful that when in anti-Nazi war even Jews are forced into indifference gentile isolationism feels doubly justified.

> I offer to raise Jewish army for all Allied fronts provided status similar to Polish Army and provided MacDonald policy stopped, leaving Palestine's destiny officially unprejudiced till peace conference. Discounting at present further possibilities foresee 130,000 recruits in Eastern hemisphere alone plus worldwide network of centers radiating new attitude to Allied cause among all creeds. Details in Memorandum submitted to War Office by New Zionist Presidency last March.

63. In his letter to Sinclair, Jabotinsky wrote that:

> This big blind America has suddenly awakened, but is still unable to realize that what she really longs for is to fight at once. Some of the magnetic centres dominating this peculiar public mentality are still asleep. Perhaps you remember the offer I outlined to you last autumn: to try and set in motion here a trail of electricity which, starting from Jews, will reach the Gentile bulk. I cabled to Mr. Churchill repeating it the other day. The focal idea is to form a nucleus called "the Jewish Army". Now more than ever I am sure of success. Please help; please fight the suicidal tendency of neglect of "small" things which may look small but are pivotal.

Letter No. 4264, Reference Code A-1 2/30/1, the Jabotinsky Institute in Israel.

64. Letter No. 4263, Reference Code A-1 2/30/1, Jabotinsky Institute in Israel. Jabotinsky wrote that with the new developments in the war, things might change quickly:

> The development of the Jewish mentality will now flow in the direction we have always desired. Jews are still shy of saying any decisive word lest they be charged with war-mongering (I have never seen American Jewry so scared of local antisemitism as now—the danger seems really tangible and widespread). But soon it will become safe to speak more openly. If anything by way of a nucleus of attraction is born, for instance in Canada, wonders could be accomplished within a few months.

65. Letter No. 4265, Reference Code A-1 2/30/1, Jabotinsky Institute in Israel.

66. See Letter dated May 19, 1940, to Abraham Cahan, Letter No. 4377, Reference Code A-1 2/30/1 in the Archives of the Jabotinsky Institute in Israel. The letter has Jabotinsky's handwritten list of all recipients of his individually addressed letters and

his handwritten description of the response from Finkelstein. The letters to the other individuals are Letters Nos. 4269 (Baerwald), 4270 (Monaky), 4271 (Wise), 4272 (Goldman), 4273 (Brandeis), *et seq.* in Reference Code A-1 2/30/1.

67. In a letter dated May 29, 1940, to Francis Gunther (the daughter of Russian Jews, a graduate of Barnard College, a foreign correspondent for the *London News Chronicle,* and the wife of writer and journalist John Gunther), Jabotinsky wrote that his aim in sending the letter to the American Jewish leaders "was not so much to get those men to make a move as, on the contrary, to fix their inability or unwillingness to move, in case we'll have to move alone." He continued:

> You remember how I tortured you trying to explain about the impending earthquake, etc. and how our plans ought to be awfully big to fit in the picture? Now the earthquake is yawning bigger than I expected and threatens to swallow all the plans of the mighty ones, not only mine.

68. Louis Finkelstein was the head of the Jewish Theological Seminary of America in New York. His letter dated May 20, 1940, informed Jabotinsky that he "deeply appreciate[d]" Jabotinsky's letter to "establish a World Jewish Committee to concentrate the care and defense of the interests of Jews in the Eastern Hemisphere," but that "commitments I have already made prevent my associating myself with your committee."

By letter dated May 23, 1940, Henry Monaky, president of the B'nai B'Brith, writing from Omaha, Nebraska, said he would give Jabotinsky's suggestion "my earnest consideration" and that he hoped "the opportunity may present itself on some occasion when I am in New York, to discuss the matter with you."

Rabbi David de Sola Pool, the preeminent Sephardic rabbi in America and longtime spiritual leader of Congregation Shearith Israel in New York, wrote that he had "no doubt that every one of those whom you have approached, even as myself, is giving constant thought to [your suggestion on our peace efforts] even in these desperately dark days," but promised nothing further.

Solomon Goldman, president of the Zionist Organization of America, thanked Jabotinsky for his "very kind letter," noted that several American Jewish leaders had agreed to meet in Washington "to consider the grave situation confronting our people the world over," and suggested that perhaps after that it might be deemed wise to follow Jabotinsky's suggestion.

Paul Baerwald, chairman of the American Jewish Joint Distribution Committee, wrote that "[a]s a philanthropic organization, we refrain from participating in any world Jewish committees as you suggest, and this is one of the reasons why it is not possible for me to be instrumental in the proposal you have made."

All of these letters are in the Archives of the Jabotinsky Institute in Israel, under a file entitled "Letters addressed to V. Jabotinsky . . . 1940." Reference Code A-1 3/28/1. There are no responses in that file from the other recipients of Jabotinsky's May 19 letter.

69. Rafael Medoff, *Militant Zionism in America,* 53–54.

70. The full text of the telegram (Letter 4200 and Letter 4385, Reference Code A-1 2/30/1, Jabotinsky Institute in Israel), signed simply "Jabotinsky," read as follows:

Akzin leaving tonight for Washington carrying information of essential importance. Would appreciate your receiving him urgently.

71. Rafael Medoff, *Militant Zionism in America,* 56.

72. *Ibid.,* 57, fn. 42.

73. Unknown to Jabotinsky and his associates, but perhaps not to Lord Lothian, on May 23, 1940—two weeks after becoming prime minister—Churchill had written to his secretary of state for the colonies, encouraging him to arm the Jews in Palestine to relieve the British forces from their obligation to protect them there, freeing up more forces for use in Europe. "For this purpose," he wrote, "the Jews should be armed in their own defense, and properly organized as soon as possible." Winston S. Churchill, *The Gathering Storm,* Appendix A, 559. Two days later, Churchill wrote to the secretary of state again, in a memorandum reading:

> The cruel penalties imposed by your predecessor upon the Jews in Palestine for arming have made it necessary to tie up needless forces for their protection. Pray let me know exactly what weapons and organization the Jews have for self-defense.

*Ibid.,* 564. The next day, Lord Lothian met with Jabotinsky's representative in Washington and heard a presentation on Jabotinsky's plans to form a Jewish army.

74. A handwritten letter to Jabotinsky dated June 7, 1940, written from Washington and signed with a signature that is indecipherable, reported that the writer:

> Had a long chat with Lothian, got him to send a cable to London asking permission to raise a Jewish Army. If answer is favorable he will be glad to meet you at the World's Fair on the 12th either before or after he opens the pavillon. . . .

Archives of the Jabotinsky Institute in Israel, file entitled "Letters addressed to V. Jabotinsky . . . 1940."

75. Joseph B. Schechtman, *Fighter and Prophet: The Vladimir Jabotinsky Story,* 389; Rafael Medoff, *Militant Zionism in America.*

76. Rafael Medoff, *Militant Zionism in America,* 60–61; Joseph B. Schechtman, *Fighter and Prophet: The Vladimir Jabotinsky Story,* 389.

77. "Zionist Leaders Here Frown on Jabotinsky's Army Plan," JTA, June 19, 1940, 3.

78. Dunkirk was "the greatest crisis in nine centuries of English history." Peter Stansky, "80 Days that Saved the World: The Duel 10 May–31 July 1940," March 3, 1991.

79. Drew Middleton, *"At 'Their Finest Hour,'" The New York Times,* January 24, 1965, 70. Middleton, one of the greatest war correspondents in the modern era, had been an eyewitness.

80. See Drew Middleton, *"At 'Their Finest Hour/Churchill's Confidence in Dark Days of 1940 Inspired the British People," The New York Times,* January 24, 1965. In December 1942, Churchill disclosed to the House of Commons that on June 11, 1940, Britain had only 100 tanks. See Associated Press, December 16, 1942, "Only 100 Tanks in Britain at First, Churchill Reveals":

Britain had only 100 tanks and they were of the thin-skinned kind which had proved ineffective against German anti-tank fire in France when the German threat of invasion seemed greatest on June 11, 1940, Prime Minister Churchill disclosed to the House of Commons today. . . . He made the disclosure in discussing the emergency measures taken to provide Britain with armor and the new tanks which bear his name.

81. The full text is at http://www
.guardian.co.uk/theguardian/2007/apr/29/
greatspeeches1. Here is an excerpt:

*Winston Churchill in 1941, U.S. Library of Congress Prints and Photographs Division*

True, we have suffered a major defeat. We lost the battle of France through a faulty military system, mistakes in the conduct of operations, and the defeatist spirit shown by the government during recent battles. But we still have a vast empire, our fleet is intact, and we possess large sums in gold. We still have the gigantic potentialities of American industry. The same war conditions which caused us to be beaten by 5,000 planes and 6,000 tanks can tomorrow bring victory by means of 20,000 tanks and 20,000 planes.

. . . [T]his is not a Franco-German war to be decided by a single battle. This is a world war. No one can foresee whether the neutral countries of today will not be at war tomorrow, or whether Germany's allies will always remain her allies. . . . I call upon all French servicemen of the land, sea, and air forces; I call upon French engineers and skilled armaments workers who are on British soil, or have the means of getting here, to come and join me. . . . I call upon all Frenchmen who want to remain free to listen to my voice and follow me.

82. Max Colchester, "French Remember De Gaulle on Day of Historic Address," *Wall Street Journal*, June 18, 2010. In 2006 French President Jacques Chirac declared June 18 a national commemorative day. In 2010 President Sarkozy traveled to London for the commemoration. In 2012 French President Francois Hollande, in the course of an address about the Holocaust, said that "France's honor was embodied by General de Gaulle, who stood up on June 18, 1940."

See "A Certain June 18," http://www.historytoday.com/anne-corbett/certain-june-18th:

Every French child learns that [June 18] was the day that General de Gaulle broadcast on the BBC from London his appeal to French officers, soldiers, engineers and munition workers to resist the Pétain government's surrender. . . . The

June 18th speech is seen as a turning point in French national history. . . . By the same token June 18th, 1940, is also an event in British history . . . This was the moment of Churchill's broadcast on 'their finest hour.' . . . In France . . . 'le 18 juin' is so engraved in French memory that there is no need to affix it to the year 1940 . . .

83. Martin Gilbert, *The Second World War: A Complete History* (Revised Edition) (New York: Henry Holt and Company, 1989), 101.

84. "Estimate of Losses Made by De Gaulle," *The New York Times,* June 30, 1940.

85. "British and Nazi Armies," *The New York Times*, June 28, 1940.

86. "Mr. V. Jabotinsky's Address, Manhattan Centre, 19.6.1940," entitled "The Second World War and a Jewish Army," Reference Code A-1 8/60 in the archives of the Jabotinsky Institute in Israel.

*Gen. Charles de Gaulle, circa 1942.*
*Photo credit: Office of War Information,*
*Overseas Picture Division*

87. Col. Patterson attended the press conference as well, telling the press:

I saw Jewish youth fighting in the Zion Mule Corps in Gallipoli, and in the Jewish battalions in Palestine. They came from every corner of God's earth, from America, Canada, Britain, Russia, Eastern Europe, Palestine, all animated by the great ideal of their national redemption. I saw them facing death courageously for they believed that their sacrifices would not be in vain. I have no words to praise their bravery and valor.

88. Jabotinsky's reference was to Czech Consul Hudec, who was a speaker at the rally. See "Jabotinsky, at Rally Here, Predicts Jewish Army Fighting at Britain's Side," JTA, June 20, 1940.

89. Rafael Medoff, *Militant Zionism in America*, 62–63. See Shmuel Katz, *Lone Wolf: A Biography of Vladimir (Ze'ev) Jabotinsky*, Vol. 2 (New York: Barricade Books, 1996), 1773, 1774:

The meeting of June 19 at the Manhattan Center . . . exceeded all expectations. Messages of support had come from a number of public figures—senators and academics. . . . Ben-Horin reported [that]:

"The most interesting results are to be found in the hundreds of letters, telegrams, telephone and personal calls which were received at our office every day on behalf of people who wished to enlist or to give their support and assistance."

See also Robert Silverberg, *If I Forget Thee O Jerusalem: American Jews and The State of Israel* (New York: William Morrow and Co., 1979), 182:

[Jabotinsky's] zeal and personal magnetism struck a sympathetic response in the United States, as it had in World War I. Newspapers all over the country commented favorably, and many Americans, Jewish and Gentile, offered to join Jabotinsky's army; they included many experienced soldiers, including aviators and radio operators.

90. Rafael Medoff, *Militant Zionism in America,* 63. Finances for Jabotinsky's movement were in fact in poor shape. In a letter dated June 24, 1940 to Abraham Abrahams, in charge of the NZO office in London while Jabotinsky was in America, Jabotinsky wrote that the movement was "facing days of extreme poverty . . . but we will still not surrender." Letter No. 4304, Jabotinsky Institute in Israel Archives.

91. Vladimir Jabotinsky, Letter to Lord Lothian, June 21, 1940, Letter No. 4302, Reference Code A-1 2/30/2, Jabotinsky Institute in Israel.

92. Jabotinsky Institute in Israel, Document 202/1940. The *Jewish Standard* was formed in 1931 as a newspaper for New Jersey. See http://jewishstandard.timesofisrael .com/about-us/?/content/item/aboutus.

93. Jabotinsky had determined that if his wife were not permitted to join him in America, he would have to return home.

94. On July 9, 1940, Jabotinsky had written to Henry G. Koppell of Alliance Book Corporation, proposing that he rewrite his book *The Jewish War Front*, which had been published in Britain earlier in the year, into a U.S. edition in which Jabotinsky proposed to "give a piece of my mind to American Jews." He told Koppell he could finish the book by the middle of August, in exchange for a $250 honorarium. Letter No. 4325, Jabotinsky Institute in Israel, Reference Code A-1 2/30/3. On August 29, 1940, *The New York Times* reported that Jabotinsky had been putting the final touches to the book in the first week of August.

95. Lindbergh had begun speaking and writing against any involvement in the European war in 1939. In March, 1940, *The Atlantic Monthly* published an article by him asserting that the "history of Europe has always been interwoven with conflict . . . the Ethiopian war, the World War, the Boer War, the Franco-Prussian War, the war between Germany and Austria, the war between Prussia and Denmark, the Franco-Sardinian war against Austria, the Crimean War, the British opium war; revolutions and uprisings in Spain, Germany, Italy, France, Ireland, and the Balkans; British actions in Africa, India, China, Afghanistan, Palestine, and elsewhere; French action in Africa, Indo-China, and Mexico"—all taking place within the last hundred years. He wrote that the new continental war was simply an intra-European conflict:

> This present war is a continuation of the old struggle among western nations for the material benefits of the world. It is a struggle by the German people to gain territory and power. It is a struggle by the English and French to prevent another European nation from becoming strong enough to demand a share in influence and empire.

See Scott Berg, *Lindbergh* (New York: G. P. Putnam's Sons, 1998), 395. The August 3, 1940, rally was organized by Chicago builder (and head of the American Olympic

Association) Avery Brundage, and was supported by the publisher of the *Chicago Tribune*, Col. Robert R. McCormick, who offered extensive publicity in the newspaper for the rally. *Ibid.*, 438.

96. The editorial is quoted in Seth Lipsky, "Abraham Cahan Speaks," *Tablet Magazine*, July 7, 2012. A longer quotation appears in Lipsky's article, "Abraham Cahan," in *Commentary*, June 1997:

> "The death of Vladimir Jabotinsky at this grim time for the Jewish people is, in the true sense of the word, a national catastrophe," the editorial began. It proceeded to laud him as a person, a writer, and an orator; when he spoke, the paper asserted, "even the deaf could hear." But the sentence that struck me with particular force was the one predicting that Jabotinsky would be missed "not only now, in the middle of the storm, but also later, when the storm is over and the time comes to heal the wounds and rebuild Jewish life on new foundations in a new time."

97. The honorary pallbearers included: Col. John H. Patterson; James G. McDonald, former League of Nations High Commissioner for Refugees; James Freeman, President of the Canadian Zionist Organization; Col. A. Ralph Steinberg, Past Master of B'nai B'rith; the author John Gunther, the editor Jacob Landau, and the publisher William B. Ziff; William G. Stanton, Chairman of the American Friends of Jewish Palestine; K.B. Friedman, Assistant U.S. District Attorney; and Col. Maurice Mendelsohn, past National Commander of the Jewish War Veterans.

The Jewish Telegraphic Agency reported, "Revisionist leaders present included Prof. Benjamin Akzin, Eliahu Ben-Horin and Captain Jeremiah Halpern. Others who attended were Edmund I. Kaufmann, president of the Zionist Organization of America; Dr. Hirsch J. Gordon, commander of the American Palestine Jewish Legion; Sol Masch, State Commander of the Jewish War Veterans; Maurice Schwartz, the actor; John Gunther, the author; Willard G. Stanton, secretary of the American Friends of a Jewish Palestine, and Col. J. H. Patterson, commander of the 1918 Palestine Jewish Legion."

98. "Weizmann Pays Tribute at London Meeting," JTA, August 8, 1940, http://www.jta.org/1940/08/08/archive/weizmann-pays-tribute-at-london-meeting.

99. *Ibid.*

100. *Ibid.* The August 16, 1940, issue of the *Palestine Post* included an article entitled "Jabotinsky: Tribute to an Adversary." Zweig wrote that Jabotinsky "never lacked imagination and enthusiasm; the impatience of his heart and mind probably surpassed that of all his contemporaries."

101. See Yitshaq Ben-Ami, *Years of Wrath, Days of Glory*, 244:

> Standing with thousands of others outside the funeral parlor on the Lower East Side in New York, I felt orphaned, and a bitter anger welled up in me. Fate had taken Jabotinsky from our people at the most crucial time in our history. The Nazis had starved and dislocated entire communities in Poland and central Europe and hundreds of thousands of Jews were already dead. . . . Jabotinsky was

the one leader who could have injected pride and courage in the Jews around the world. . . . He could have rallied thousands of people to halls . . . sounding the alarm and awakening America's conscience. . . . The one leader who may have moderated the catastrophe, was gone.

102. Moshe Arens, interviewed for the author in May 2012 in Tel Aviv by Ms. Cincinnati Lieberman.

103. After the completion of his public service for the State of Israel, Arens wrote *Flags Over the Warsaw Ghetto: The Untold Story of the Warsaw Ghetto Uprising* (Jerusalem: Gefen Publishing House, 2011), which recounted the story of the Betar fighters under the command of Pawel Frenkel in the uprising, and the internecine fighting among the Jews themselves.

104. Menachem Begin, *White Nights: The Story of a Prisoner in Russia* (Harper & Row: New York, 1957), 15, 28.

105. Koestler had met Jabotinsky in Tel Aviv in Palestine in October 1926 and was present at an open-air meeting where Jabotinsky spoke for three or four hours before 40,000 people, which Koestler described as follows:

> There was a recurrent refrain in that speech, a quotation from Cicero's In Catilinam ["Oration Against Catiline"], probably *quo usque tandem* ["how much longer?"], which had a chilling and terrifying effect. It was not a speech—it was an earthquake sustained for several hours.

Quoted in Michael Scammell, *Koestler: The Literary and Political Odyssey of a Twentieth-Century Skeptic* (New York: Random House, 2009).

106. Arthur Koestler, *Scum of the Earth* (New York: The Macmillan Co., 1941), quoted in Louis A. Gordon, "Arthur Koestler and His Ties to Zionism and Jabotinsky," *Studies in Zionism* 12, no. 2 (1991).

107. "Palestine Mourns Jabotinsky; Work Stoppage Called; Son Freed from Jail," JTA, August 6, 1940.

108. *Ibid.*

109. *Ibid.*

110. "5,000 Attend Memorial in Montevideo," JTA, August 11, 1940.

111. "Tributes in London," JTA, August 11, 1940.

112. Stephen S. Wise, "Vladimir Jabotinsky," 1940, reprinted in Stephen S. Wise, *As I See It* (New York: Marstin Press, 1944), 228–229.

113. See Yitshaq Ben-Ami, *Years of Wrath, Days of Glory*, 244:

> The last time I saw Jabotinsky he looked tired and gray. I attributed his appearance to the troubles with the split of the Irgun, to the slow progress here [in America], to the bad news from Europe, and to his separation from his beloved wife, whom he had to leave behind in the London blitz.

One of Jabotinsky's closest colleagues later wrote, "In New York, he often looked worn out and complained of utter weariness." Joseph B. Schechtman, *Fighter and Prophet: The Vladimir Jabotinsky Story: The Last Years* (New York: Thomas Yoseloff, 1961), 396. "Those who met him in the summer of 1940, are unanimous in stressing the gloominess of his general outlook." *Ibid.*, 394. He told colleagues, "The Europe I knew is lost," and he felt guilty for leaving his wife alone in London—a violation, he thought, of *hadar*, even though he had repeatedly written personal letters to Lord Lothian seeking to get a visa for her to come to America. *Ibid.*, 394.

Jabotinsky's June 27, 1940, letter to Lord Lothian—with whom he had had a relationship since the formation of the Jewish Legion in 1917—is heartbreaking:

> Dear Lord Lothian,
>
> You would oblige me more than I can say if you would intercede with the American authorities so that my wife, now in London, could join me here . . . I solemnly promise that we shall depart as soon as the crisis is over.
>
> I need not explain how painful it is for me, at a time like this and in the middle of a mission . . . [that] is a replica of the one you helped years ago, to have to write . . . about my wife. Will you at least believe me if I say that I would never have done it had I not seen in all that needless and irritating handicaps in a work which—forgive my bitterness—a wiser and more farsighted Whitehall would have encouraged nine months ago when the plan was first submitted. . . .
>
> I thank you in advance for anything you may do. [Letter 4310, Jabotinsky Institute Archives]

Lord Lothian responded with a letter promising to help, but with no further reply from the passport authorities, Jabotinsky cabled Lord Lothian again:

> I fear that it soon may become impossible in London for an elderly woman in poor health to continue active demarches at American Consulate and Cunard Line office and so on. I therefore beg you now to intervene with Secretary of State for telegraphic instructions to London consulate. . . . Be assured of my profound gratitude.

Jabotinsky wrote to the American secretary of state as well:

> Sir,
>
> I apologize for addressing you on a matter that sounds personal. It is not entirely so. I understand it has already been brought to your attention, but recent events have lent it, for me, a painful urgency.
>
> In view of the menace to England—where I left my wife—I must either be allowed to bring her over, or return to London myself. . . . If my work here is useful it would be logical to make my stay here morally possible. Apart from its value to me as a Zionist, and trying to gauge it from the viewpoint of general interest, I submit that in agitating the Jewish Army issue I seek to consolidate, at least among one section of the public, a more decisive attitude to war problems. If such is not your opinion, I have nothing to add. If, however, my effort is of use, please help me without delay. . . .
>
> I can only offer my word of honor that we do not intend to settle in this country and will leave when required to do so. . . .

Believe me,

Sir,

Yours faithfully

Vladimir Jabotinsky

Schechtman writes, "During the last weeks of his life, [Jabotinsky] looked worn out; his face was thin, ash-grey, and pinched; his eyes were sunken and seemed to have lost their lustre; he had visibly aged." Joseph B. Schechtman, *Fighter and Prophet*, 395. Jabotinsky knew he had a heart condition—he sought a doctor's permission to go to the Betar camp in the Catskills—but he kept it secret from everyone but his doctors. *Ibid.*

114. See "All Revisionists but Eri Jabotinsky Reported Released in Palestine," JTA, June 24, 1940, www.jta.org/1940/06/24/archive/all-revisionists-but-eri-jabotinsky-reported-released-in-palestine. For background on Eri Jabotinsky's arrest, see Rafael Medoff, "Eri Jabotinsky's Race Against Death," *Haaretz*, June 12, 2009, www.haaretz.com/eri-jabotinsky-s-race-against-death-1.277829:

> The case of the SS Sakarya was particularly agonizing. It took on more than 2,000 passengers—including Eri—at the Romanian port of Sulina in late 1939, but could not proceed because its Turkish owners demanded a huge extra payment as insurance against British seizure. Irgun fundraising efforts in the U.S. were rebuffed by mainstream Jewish leaders, who were reluctant to anger America's ally Great Britain. Eventually the money was secured, and on February 13, the Sakarya reached Haifa. The passengers were detained by the British, but then released, and allowed to stay in the country (many subsequent arrivals were less fortunate—they were deported to Mauritius). Eri, as the mastermind, was sent to Acre Prison.

115. During the mid-1930s, Jabotinsky had been advised by his doctors about the condition of his heart, and urged to rest lest his habitual overworking lead to serious complications. But Jabotinsky responded that he could not change his way of life. Joseph B. Schechtman, *Fighter and Prophet,* 396–398. Shmuel Katz, *Lone Wolf: A Biography of Vladimir (Ze'ev) Jabotinsky, Vol. Two* (New York: Barricade Books Inc., 1996), 1776, describes Jabotinsky's last hours, based on Schechtman's account:

> Before reaching the [Betar] camp, he showed signs of exhaustion. He alighted from the car with great difficulty and made only a peremptory review of the Betar guard of honor which awaited him. He then immediately went to the building where he was housed. He slowly mounted the stairs to his room on the upper floor, obviously in great pain. . . . As [Aaron] Kopelowicz helped him to undress, he heard him say, "I am so tired, I am so tired." These were Jabotinsky's last words.

> Another physician was called from neighboring Hunter; oxygen equipment was also brought. But he did not recover consciousness, and two hours later he died.

DAVID BEN-GURION

1. Letter from David Ben-Gurion to Charles L. Pilzer dated January 7, 1941. Ben-Gurion Archives and Library, Ben-Gurion University of the Negev (original in English). Pilzer wrote in part as follows:

> I am taking the liberty of writing to you, as one of our foremost Jewish Leaders, of an item which has come to my attention. The papers for the past few days have carried the story of one of England's greatest needs—Ships. They have also published an offer by the British Purchasing Commission to Our Government of three million dollars for approximately twenty-six merchant ships now owned by our Maritime Commission.
>
> Here is a great opportunity for us to actively and concretely demonstrate that we are siding as a People in the prosecution of this War. I am earnestly suggesting to you, and I hope through your voice to all Jewry, that the Jewish people purchase these ships and loan them to England for the duration of the War. Let us purchase these ships through a popular subscription, and let it be known that the Jewish Nation, that Palestine, is the owner of these ships, and that we lend them to our Ally for the duration of the War.
>
> I feel certain that we could quickly and easily raise the necessary funds. It would also be a sound investment for the Jewish People.

2. Letter from David Ben-Gurion to Charles L. Pilzer. Ben-Gurion preceded the quoted sentences with this analysis:

> As you rightly said, we must fight for the right to live as a nation, and by that I understand not philanthropic help to England, but simply that we should fight—just as England is fighting. . . . I see no reason why the Jewish people, as a people, should not actually fight as you say "side by side with the allies." It is for this reason that, in my view, the task of the Jews is to form a Jewish army with Jews in Palestine and Jews in any other country where they are free to do so: to fight as an ally and not merely give money . . .
>
> [I]t does not follow that a British victory by itself will safeguard our future as a free, independent people in its own free, independent homeland. In order to enjoy the benefit of the victory at the end of the war, as a free people, we must try to achieve the status of a free people and an allied people during the war. This can be achieved only through the formation of a Jewish army.

3. Shabtai Teveth, *Ben-Gurion: The Burning Ground 1886–1948* (Boston: Houghton Mifflin Company, 1987), 767.

4. The portions of Ben-Gurion's diaries in the following pages were obtained for the author from the Ben-Gurion Archives in Israel by the Israeli biographer Avi Shilom, PhD, and were translated for the author by Alisa Klaiman and Ophir Klaiman, edited slightly for clarity by the author.

5. Shabtai Teveth, *Ben-Gurion*, 5.

6. David Ben-Gurion, *Letters to Paula* (London: Vallentine, Mitchell & Co., 1971), 241.

7. Quoted in Shimon Peres, *The Imaginary Voyage: With Theodor Herzl in Israel* (New York: Arcade Publishing, 1998), 22.

8. Ben-Gurion briefly left Palestine to attend law school in Turkey, at a time when he thought learning Turkish law would be the key to dealing with the Ottoman rulers in Palestine.

9. Ben-Gurion Diary, October 15, 1940. Ben-Gurion listed sixty-five books he bought in New York, most of them by ancient Greek authors. In his diary entry for November 17, Ben-Gurion listed another thirty books, mostly in Greek. He also purchased a volume of *Masterpiece Books*, a history of Rome, and a book entitled *The Founders of the Church*. In his entry for November 26, he listed another fifty books, including *History of the Language* (Greek and Roman), a volume on Roman literature, Demosthenes' *Speeches*, Sherman's *Life of the Prophets*, and Plato's *The State*.

10. Amos Oz, "David Ben-Gurion," *Time Magazine*, April 13, 1998, http://content. time.com/time/magazine/article/0,9171,988160,00.html.

11. Ben-Gurion was captivated by Lenin and admired him as a leader. Anita Shapira, *Israel: A History* (Waltham, Mass.: Brandeis University Press, 2012), 108, 118. He idolized him, describing him in his diary as "the prophet of the Russian Revolution." Michael Bar-Zohar, *Ben-Gurion: A Biography* (New York: Delacorte Press, 1978), 51. Ben-Gurion thought the ideal leader was a composite of Herzl and Lenin. Shabtai Teveth, *Ben-Gurion,* 233.

12. The Agency had been established by the Zionist Organization in 1929 pursuant to the League of Nations' Mandate for Palestine, which called for an "appropriate Jewish agency" to be established and recognized as a public body to advise and cooperate with Britain on the "establishment of the Jewish National Home and the interests of the Jewish population in Palestine." See *Modern History Sourcebook*, "League of Nations: The Mandate for Palestine," July 24, 1922, http://www.fordham.edu/ halsall/mod/1922mandate.html.

13. Allon Gal, *David Ben-Gurion and the American Alignment for a Jewish State,* 12. See also Louis Lipsky, *Memoirs in Profile*, 316, where Lipsky described Ben-Gurion as having "organized, led and tyrannized over [the labor movement] in Palestine." Lipsky wrote further that Ben-Gurion "[f]rom his first days on . . . had his own dogmatic views on problems of Jewish life and of Zionism. . . . In fact, he was by nature dictatorial."

14. Shabtai Teveth, *Ben-Gurion*, 664. Louis Lipsky in his memoir was more direct: "Ben-Gurion's hot blood, his uncontrollable indignations, his egotistical drive, his impatience, could not long endure the moderation of Dr. Weizmann." Louis Lipsky, *Memoirs in Profile,* 318.

15. Shabtai Teveth, *Ben-Gurion,* 747.

16. *Ibid.*, 736.

17. *Ibid.*

18. "Palestine Curbs Jews' Land Buying—Britain Bans Purchases in Big Area, Limits Them in Another—Jewish Agency Defiant," *The New York Times*, Febru-

ary 29, 1940. The regulations divided Palestine into three areas: (1) Zone A, where the transfer of land to anyone other than a Palestinian Arab was prohibited, "including the Hill Country as a whole, together with certain areas of the Gaza and Beersheba sub-districts"; (2) Zone B, where Jewish purchases were prohibited except by special permission; and (3) Zone C, where Jewish purchases were permitted.

19. Shabtai Teveth, *Ben-Gurion*, 736–737.

20. *Ibid.*, 738.

21. *Ibid.*, 738–739.

22. *Ibid.*, 743–744.

23. *Ibid.*, 745–746.

24. *Ibid.*, 746.

25. *Ibid.*, 747.

26. "Zionists Make Plea For Broad Support," *The New York Times*, July 3, 1940.

27. Shabtai Teveth, *Ben-Gurion*, 761.

28. *Ibid.*, 762.

29. *Ibid.*, 760. On September 9 Ben-Gurion wrote a letter to Weizmann, telling him, "I hope to be able to leave London very soon, and in case I should not see you again here, I would like to take this opportunity of wishing you a heart-felt God-speed. . . . I shall always be ready to give whatever help I can, whenever my assistance should be required, and wherever I may happen to be." Ben-Gurion regarded this as a polite farewell letter, from which Weizmann "should have understood that I have no intention of seeing him ever again." *Ibid.*

30. Michael J. Cohen, ed., *The Letters and Papers of Chaim Weizmann, Vol. XX, Series A, July 1940–January 1943*, (Jerusalem: Transaction Books, Rutgers University, Israel Universities Press, 1979), No. 45, dated September 23, 1940, 45. Credit Yad Chaim Weizmann, Rehovot, Israel.

31. Brigit Wells, one of the children on board, has described the voyage at The Wartimes Memory Project:

> We sailed on 24th September from Liverpool, a week after the "City of Benares" was torpedoed carrying 90 children, only 13 of whom were saved. . . .
>
> We were escorted by a couple of small Naval vessels for a couple of days and then split up to go as fast as we could. Both we and the "Samaria" got to New York on 3rd October. It was astonishing to see the tops of the skyscrapers pointing out of the mist in the very early morning.
>
> We were not allowed to take our clothes off at any time, so we slept in all-in-one ski-suits, then quite fashionable as "siren suits". There was boat drill every day, and we carried Mae West lifejackets around at all times.

John Bedwell, another one of the children on board, contributed his memory of the trip at www.royalnavyresearcharchive.org.uk/MEMScythia.htm.

32. Martin Gilbert, *The Second World War: A Complete History* (Revised Edition) (New York: Henry Holt and Company, 1989), 126. On October 5, 1940, the Germans began air raids that came only at night. According to Gilbert:

Hundreds of thousands of Londoners took to sleeping, for safety, in the deep stations and tunnels of the Underground; one tunnel, a mile long, between Bethnal Green and Liverpool Street station, provided shelter for 4,000 people. Hundreds of thousands of children again left London, to live in the countryside; by mid-October, the number of child evacuees had reached 489,000.

*Ibid.*, 130.

33. "London Views Pact as Warning to U.S.—Intimidate on Meddling in Europe or Asia Is Read Into Axis Alliance With Japan," *The New York Times*, September 28, 1940.

34. Diary of David Ben-Gurion, entry dated October 3, 1940, Ben-Gurion Archives and Library, Ben-Gurion University of the Negev (original in Hebrew; English translation commissioned by the author): "No one was seen near the ship, even though we sent two telegrams to the Zionist Federation and the Workers of Zion this morning. . . . I found out that the two telegrams were received only at 2:30 in the afternoon and that everyone was at the synagogue that morning."

Was it really possible that Ben-Gurion had not known that October 3 was Rosh Hashanah? An answer can be derived from an incident that Rabbi Arthur Hertzberg, who eventually served as president of the American Jewish Congress, records in his autobiography, *A Jew in America*. Hertzberg had a chance encounter with Ben-Gurion in Tiberias in 1949, on the evening of Tisha B'Av at the hotel where they both happened to be staying:

He recognized me, so his aides let me approach him. Ben-Gurion offered me tea, and he was visibly surprised when I told him that I was fasting that night, in accordance with tradition. Ben-Gurion chided me for observing this fast; our ancestors fasted and prayed when they should have acted.

Ben-Gurion told him that history had begun again with Zionism and the Diaspora was irrelevant: Jews in the Land were putting their lives on the line to remake Jewish history; American Jews merely gave money. Arthur Hertzberg, *A Jew in America: My Life and a People's Struggle for Identity* (New York: HarperCollins, 2002), 203–204. In *The Paradox of Liberation: Secular Revolutions and Religious Counterrevolutions* (New Haven and London: Yale University Press, 2015), Michael Walzer writes that:

Zionist negation was first of all a denial that there was a Jewish politics in the exile—or even a collective history. "Since our last national tragedy"—the suppression of the Bar Kochba rebellion in 135 CE—"we have had 'histories' of persecution, of legal discrimination, of the Inquisition, and pogroms of . . . martyrdom," but, wrote Ben-Gurion, "we did not have a Jewish history anymore, because [the] history of a people is only what the people create as a whole," and, he insisted, the Jews created nothing in the centuries of exile.

Walzer disagreed with that analysis: "In fact, the internal politics of the Jewish Diaspora, through which the people as a whole sustained itself, in scattered communities, without coercive power, for many centuries, is one of the more remarkable stories in the history of humankind." Walzer, 128.

35. Memorandum dated October 4, 1940, entitled "David Ben-Gurion's Arrival in the United States," by Bernard Kornblith, director of Port Reception Services, in YIVO Institute of Jewish Research in New York City.

36. Letter dated November 8, 1940, from David Ben-Gurion to Justice Louis D. Brandeis.

37. Memorandum dated October 4, 1940, entitled "David Ben-Gurion's Arrival in the United States," by Bernard Kornblith.

38. Shabtai Teveth, *Ben-Gurion,* 768. Ben-Gurion wrote in his diary for that day that he was impressed that everyone at the pier knew Rabbi Wise—"the immigration clerks, the doctors, the policemen, the drivers, and the porters." Diary of David Ben-Gurion, entry dated October 3, 1940, Ben-Gurion Archives and Library, Ben-Gurion University of the Negev (original in Hebrew; English translation commissioned by the author). A week later, Ben-Gurion appeared before the authorities at Ellis Island and was interrogated for more than an hour by officials who he thought suspected that he might be planning to stay in America beyond a visa period. Diary of David Ben-Gurion, entry dated October 9, 1940, Ben-Gurion Archives and Library, Ben-Gurion University of the Negev (original in Hebrew; English translation commissioned by the author).

39. A portion of the banner headline in *The New York Times* on October 3, 1940, read: "Nazi Led Drive in Egypt Foreseen . . . German Officers Said to Be in 'De Facto' Charge of Africa Campaign, Suez is Held Objective."

40. The Jacob Rader Marcus Center of the American Jewish Archives, Stephen S. Wise Collection, Manuscript Collection 49, Cincinnati, Ohio, http://collections.americanjewisharchives.org/ms/ms0049/ms0049.html.

41. In his memoirs, Wise's discussion of 1940 is devoted entirely to recounting his support for FDR in the presidential election that year.

42. Harold I. Saperstein, *Witness from the Pulpit: Topical Sermons 1933–1980,* edited by Marc Saperstein (Lanham, Md: Lexington Books, 2000).

43. The source of the picture is Harold I. Saperstein, *Witness from the Pulpit.*

44. *Ibid.,* 77–78. Saperstein's words were a reference to Job XIII:24–25:

Wherefore hidest thou thy face,
And holdest me for thine enemy?
Wilt thou harass a driven leaf

45. *Ibid.,* 75.

46. Abba Hillel Silver, *Therefore Choose Life: Selected Sermons, Addresses, and Writing of Abba Hillel Silver, Volume One,* ed. Herbert Weiner (Cleveland: The World Publishing Company, 1967), 60–66.

47. Israel H. Levinthal, *A New World is Born: Sermons and Addresses* (New York: Funk & Wagnalls, 1943), 141–147. The Brooklyn Jewish Center, known affectionately as the "shul with the pool" for its dedication to the concept that a synagogue should also be a cultural and even a sports center for its members, who were excluded from gentile clubs, described itself as "a beacon of American Jewish life." Its membership was in the thousands, making it the largest Conservative or Orthodox congregation in the country:

Thousands would stream to hear Rabbi Levinthal's popular sermons on Friday evenings. Walking from surrounding Jewish neighborhoods, they often arrived to find standing-room-only crowds filling the great sanctuary.

From an early membership of several hundred, the center grew to a peak of about 3,500. At its height, recalls a long-time member, there was no prominent Jew in Brooklyn who did not have some association with the Center. The first Jewish mayor of New York City, Abraham Beame, was a member, as were the judges, doctors, lawyers and politicians who made up the elite of Jewish society. Magnificent weddings and celebrations were held in the grand ballroom of the Center, which is famous to this day for its old-world style with its impressive chandeliers and luxurious décor.

Among the notable figures associated with the Brooklyn Jewish Center were: Chaim Weizmann, Albert Einstein and Menachem Ussishkin, who came in 1921 as a delegation on behalf of the Zionist movement; Moss Hart, who served as a social director in 1927; Heinz Liepmann, Einstein, Stephen Wise and Will Durant, who were involved with the establishment of a Library of Nazi Banned Books; Rollo G. Reynolds (Provost of Teachers College), who was the founding Educational Adviser of the Center Academy in 1928; Mark Rothko, the world famous artist, was the arts teacher in the School Academy, Samuel Lemberg (philanthropist), who initiated plans for the mortgage redemption; and Abraham D. Beame (later mayor of New York City), was an active member. Richard Tucker served the congregation as its cantor for many years.

"Brooklyn Jewish Center—Origins," www.brooklynjewishcenter.org/history.html.

48. For other sermons in 1939–1941, see Marc Eli Saperstein, *Jewish Preaching in Times of War, 1800–2001* (Oxford: Littman Library of Jewish Civilization, 2008); Rabbi Sidney D. Tedesche, *A Set of Holiday Sermons, 5701–1940* (Cincinnati: The Tract Commission, 1940); Israel Goldstein, *Toward a Solution* (New York: G. P. Putnam's Sons, 1940).

Israel Goldstein was the rabbi of Congregation B'nai Jeshurun in Manhattan. On May 14, 1939, he delivered an address before a conference on "The Jew and the World Crisis," held under the auspices of the Jewish Theological Seminary of America. In that address, given months before World War II broke out, he described "the isolationist in the Jewish camp":

> For religion in general or for Judaism in particular, he had no use, considering himself too enlightened for religious commitments and too cosmopolitan for synagogue affiliation. His favorite rationalization was his doctrine of Americanism, that America is a melting pot and that Jewish loyalty is a narrowing, stultifying influence inconsistent with the spirit of true Americanism. Zionism, his pet aversion, he condemned with charges of dual allegiance. . . . He both hated and feared it.

Rabbi Goldstein asserted that "[o]n all counts, isolationism has been discredited," and that "[u]pon American Jews there devolves a special responsibility":

In the desperate plight of the Jewish people today, American Jewry, strong, free and relatively comfortable, represent the one strong staff of support. . . . As one after another of the great Jewish communities in Europe are laid low, the finger of destiny points to us. It is as if the voice of Mordecai were challenging us, "Who knows but that for just such a time as this hast thou attained thy royal estate?" . . . An organized, integrated American Jewry of four and a half millions can become a tremendous force. A disorganized, disintegrated American Jewry is impotent.

*Ibid.*, 99–108.

49. In Ben-Gurion's diary for October 4, he wrote that "the main action, in my opinion, is the establishment of the Jewish Army. The time will not come until the end of the American elections [the following month] and I do not know if I will stay here until then, or if I will return home early—we'll see." Diary of David Ben-Gurion, entry dated October 4, 1940, Ben-Gurion Archives and Library, Ben-Gurion University of the Negev (original in Hebrew; English translation commissioned by the author). In his diary entry for October 6, Ben-Gurion wrote, "Only one thing occupies my mind right now: the effort to build a Jewish Army," and that if a favorable decision about establishing a Jewish army could be obtained from the British government, it "will be the main focus of the Zionist Movement at this time, especially in America." Diary of David Ben-Gurion, entry dated October 6, 1940, Ben-Gurion Archives and Library, Ben-Gurion University of the Negev (original in Hebrew; English translation commissioned by the author).

50. "Ben-Gurion Here en Route to Palestine," JTA, October 7, 1940 (published originally as "Palestine's Future Depends on Jewish Army—Says David Ben-Gurion"), http://www.jta.org/1940/10/07/archive/ben-gurion-here-en-route-to-palestine.

51. In reply to Ben-Gurion, Jabotinsky described himself as the "type of Zionist who doesn't care what kind of society our state will have":

If I were to know that the only way to a state was via socialism, or even that this would hasten it by a generation, I'd welcome it. More than that: give me a religiously Orthodox state in which I would be forced to eat gefillte fish all day long (but only if there were no other way) and I'll take it. More even than that: make it a Yiddish-speaking state, which for me would mean the loss of all the magic in the thing—if there's no other way, I'll take that too. In the will I leave my son I'll tell him to start a revolution, but on the envelope I'll write: "To be opened only five years after a Jewish state is established."

Hillel Halkin, *Jabotinsky: A Life* (2014), 196.

52. Diary of David Ben-Gurion, entry dated October 4, 1940, Ben-Gurion Archives and Library, Ben-Gurion University of the Negev (original in Hebrew; English translation commissioned by the author).

53. *Ibid.*

54. "Jews Fight for Britain—Palestine Recruiting Already Above Quota and Closed," *The New York Times*, October 3, 1940.

55. Diary of David Ben-Gurion, entry dated October 5, 1940, Ben-Gurion Archives and Library, Ben-Gurion University of the Negev (original in Hebrew; English translation commissioned by the author).

56. Diary of David Ben-Gurion, entry dated October 6, 1940.

57. Shlomo Bardin (1898–1976) was a Jewish activist born in Lithuania who moved to Palestine and came to America at the beginning of World War II. After the war, he became one of the most influential Jewish educators in America. See "Shlomo Bardin," www.jewishvirtuallibrary.org/jsource/judaica/ejud0002003002031.html.

58. Diary of David Ben-Gurion, entry dated October 6, 1940.

59. Diary of David Ben-Gurion, entry dated October 10, 1940, Ben-Gurion Archives and Library, Ben-Gurion University of the Negev (original in Hebrew; English translation commissioned by the author).

60. *Ibid.*

61. Shabtai Teveth, *Ben-Gurion,* 771.

62. *Ibid.*, 772–773.

63. Diary of David Ben-Gurion, entry dated October 16, 1940, Ben-Gurion Archives and Library, Ben-Gurion University of the Negev (original in Hebrew; English translation commissioned by the author).

64. *Ibid.*

65. Diary of David Ben-Gurion, entry dated October 18, 1940, Ben-Gurion Archives and Library, Ben-Gurion University of the Negev (original in Hebrew; English translation commissioned by the author).

66. Ben-Gurion's descriptions of Akzin and Ben-Horin seem to have been intemperate. In America, Benjamin Akzin later joined the legal department of the Library of Congress, and then served on the staff of the War Refugee Board after it was established in 1944. He prepared a memorandum in 1944 in which he proposed the bombing of Auschwitz. See the Encyclopedia of America's Response to the Holocaust, http://enc.wymaninstitute.org/?p=40.

Eliahu Ben-Horin (1902–1966) began his Zionist activities as chairman of the Zionist Students' Union at the University of Odessa before immigrating to Palestine in 1921, where he joined the Labor Zionist movement but left in 1928 to join Jabotinsky's Revisionist movement. In America during the 1940s, he wrote for *The Atlantic, Harper's*, and *Foreign Affairs*. See the Encyclopedia Britannica, http://www.encyclopedia.com/article-1G2-2587502474/ben-horin-zelig-bidner.html.

67. "Mr. Ben-Gurion Suggests 'Living Exhibit' of American Jewry," JTA, October 27, 1940.

68. Diary of David Ben-Gurion, entry dated November 9, 1940, Ben-Gurion Archives and Library, Ben-Gurion University of the Negev (original in Hebrew; English translation commissioned by the author).

69. *Ibid.*

70. Letter dated November 9, 1940, from David Ben-Gurion to Paula Ben-Gurion.

71. *Ibid.*

72. *Ibid.*

73. The article is republished in Louis Lipsky, *Memoirs in Profile,* 557–558.

74. Brandeis and Frankfurter opposed any public announcement that might put stress on U.S. relations with Britain, and Wise thought that secret diplomacy with Britain would be spoiled by public statements. Wise took a position similar to that of Weizmann: the Jews had an obligation to help Britain win the war against Hitler and to ignore the White Paper for the time being, because if Britain fell, the whole issue would be moot.

75. His diary records his pride in being able to deliver a speech in English, but he just as often spoke Yiddish to his American audiences.

76. David Ben-Gurion, *Israel: A Personal History* (New York and Tel Aviv: Funk & Wagnalls and Sabra Books, 1971), 54. The sentence read as follows: "In my capacity as chairman of the Executive in Jerusalem, I traveled to the United States in 1940 and 1942 to enlist the support of American Jewry in the struggle to cancel out the White Paper and establish a Jewish State after the war." In David Ben-Gurion, *Memoirs* (New York and Cleveland: World Publishing Co., 1970), a 216-page volume, Ben-Gurion does not mention the trip at all.

77. A full discussion of the contributions of American Jews in 1947–1948 is beyond the scope of this book and cannot be summarized even in a long footnote. Two contributions in particular, however, are worth noting here:

A. As the United Nations approached the momentous decision in 1947 to endorse a Jewish and an Arab state in a partitioned Palestine, some of the most prominent Jewish lawyers in America prepared and printed a remarkably comprehensive 107-page lawyer's brief, "based upon fair argument and unchallengeable fact," to support the case for a Jewish state in all of Western Palestine. Simon H. Rifkind et al., *The Basic Equities of the Palestine Problem* (New York: Arno Press, 1977). The brief was prepared by Rifkind, Jerome N. Frank, Stanley H. Fuld, Abraham Tulin, Milton Handler, Murray I. Gurfein, Abe Fortas, and Lawrence R. Eno—a combination of Zionists and non-Zionists who saw "no other just or equitable solution of the Palestine problem."

B. Rabbi Abba Hillel Silver—who in 1943 founded the American Zionist Emergency Council (AZEC) and in 1945 became the president of the Zionist Organization of America (ZOA)—addressed the United Nations on May 7, 1947, and said in part:

> A generation ago, the international community of the world, of which the United Nations today is the political and spiritual heir, decreed that the Jewish people should be given the right, long denied, and the opportunity to reconstitute its national home in Palestine. . . .
>
> The Jewish people belongs in this society of nations. Surely the Jewish people is no less deserving than other peoples whose national freedom and independence have been established and whose representatives are now seated here. . . . We hope that the representatives of the people which gave to mankind spiritual and ethical values, inspiring human personalities and sacred texts which are your treasured possessions, and which is now rebuilding its national life in its ancient homeland, will be welcomed before long by you to this noble fellowship of the United Nations.

The full text of the Silver address can be accessed at https://israeled.org/rabbi-abba-silver-addresses-the-un-general-assembly/. The video of the address is at https://www.youtube.com/watch?v=kWWN2PaEzzM.

78. Letter from David Ben-Gurion to Mrs. David de Sola Pool dated January 16, 1941. Ben-Gurion Archives and Library, Ben-Gurion University of the Negev (original in English).

79. Allon Gal, *David Ben-Gurion and the American Alignment for a Jewish State*, 158–159.

## EPILOGUE

1. In a handwritten letter to Lorna Wingate dated September 30, 1944, after her husband, Orde, had died, Weizmann wrote mournfully: "Now, at last that some sort of a Jewish Brigade has been belatedly sanctioned I'm thinking all the time of Orde. At present, it's a small thing[.] If he were with us it might have become a powerful force." The letter can be seen at the website of the Shapell Manuscript Foundation: http://www.shapell.org/manuscript/british-palestinian-jewish-brigade-fights-nazi-germany-1944. Churchill considered Orde Wingate "a man of genius." See letter from Winston Churchill to Lorna Wingate dated September 10, 1994, http://www.shapell.org/manuscript/winston-churchill-zionism-orde-wingate.

Had Jabotinsky lived, would he have been successful in forming a new Jewish Legion? There were obviously huge obstacles, not only with respect to the British government but also from the inadequate support of Jewish leaders in America, such as Stephen S. Wise and Abraham Cahan. But one of Jabotinsky's closest associates in America thought he would have succeeded. See Yitshaq Ben-Ami, *Years of Wrath, Days of Glory*, 244:

> Jabotinsky was the one leader who could have injected pride and courage in the Jews around the world; despite the opposition and indifference he encountered, he could have rallied thousands of people to halls in New York, Philadelphia, Chicago and Los Angeles. . . . He could have reached the White House and represented the Jewish people as not just another pleader but as an acclaimed national leader.

2. Yad Vashem, "The Jewish Brigade," http://www.yadvashem.org/odotpdf/Microsoft%20Word%20-%206365.pdf. See also Shabtai Teveth, *Ben-Gurion*, 764; Mahross, "The Jewish Brigade," January 1, 2004, www.ww2f.com/topic/8959-the-jewish-brigade/; "Brigadier Benjamin, Commander of Jewish Brigade, Comes from Family Active in Jewish Life," JTA, October 25, 1944. World War II ended in Europe on May 8, 1945, when Germany surrendered unconditionally. "World War II—1945—Victory in Europe," www.history.com/this-day-in-history/victory-in-europe.

3. Morris Beckman, *The Jewish Brigade: An Army with Two Masters 1944–1945* (New York: The History Press, 2008); see also Monty Noam Penkower, *The Jews Were Expendable: Free World Diplomacy and the Holocaust* (Champaign: University of Illinois Press, 1983).

4. Vera Weizmann, *The Impossible Takes Longer: The Memoirs of Vera Weizmann*, 232. Michael Bar-Zohar, *Ben-Gurion*, 145. "Lt. Gen. Yaacov Dori (1947–49)," https://www.idfblog.com/about-the-idf/past-chiefs-of-staff/lt-gen-yaacov-dori-1947–49/.

5. The vote by both the United States and the Soviet Union in favor of the resolution, and the support within America of both the left and right in favor of a Jewish State, were part of a historic moment of unity. See Ronald Radosh, "When the Radical American Left Loved Israel," *Commentary Magazine*, September 2012.

6. The thirty-three nations that voted in favor of the resolution were: Australia, Belgium, Bolivia, Brazil, Byelorussian S.S.R., Canada, Costa Rica, Czechoslovakia, Denmark, Dominican Republic, Ecuador, France, Guatemala, Haiti, Iceland, Liberia, Luxemburg, Netherlands, New Zealand, Nicaragua, Norway, Panama, Paraguay, Peru, Philippines, Poland, Sweden, Ukrainian S.S.R., Union of South Africa, U.S.A., U.S.S.R., Uruguay, Venezuela.

The ten abstentions came from: Argentina, Chile, China, Colombia, El Salvador, Ethiopia, Honduras, Mexico, United Kingdom, Yugoslavia.

"How They Voted, UN General Assembly Resolution 181," www.theicenter.org/sites/default/files/resources/icenter-nov29ungeneralassemblyresolution181.pdf.

7. In his 700-page volume, *Israel: A History* (United States: Harper Perennial, 2008), Martin Gilbert describes what happened in Palestine immediately after the United Nations adopted its resolution:

> From the moment of the United Nations vote, Arab terrorists and armed bands attacked Jewish men, women and children all over the country, killing eighty Jews in the twelve days following the vote, looting Jewish shops, and attacking Jewish civilian buses on all the highways.

> For the Arabs outside Palestine, a similar wave of anti-Jewish hatred led to violence against Jews in almost every Arab city. . . . There followed, in Palestine, five and a half months of terrorism and violence.

8. Shabtai Teveth, *Ben-Gurion*, 875. Louis Lipsky in his memoir wrote that Ben-Gurion forced Weizmann's retirement "with an intensity and ruthlessness difficult to understand, and against the will of over half his party." Louis Lipsky, *Memoirs in Profile,* 318–319.

9. In January 1948, both the State Department and the Defense Department warned Truman that a partition of Palestine would require more than 150,000 American troops to enforce.

10. Quoted in Allis Radosh and Ronald Radosh, *A Safe Haven,* 298.

11. Harry S. Truman, *Years of Trial and Hope*, 188, quoted in Allis Radosh and Ronald Radosh, *Ibid.*, 296.

12. Vera Weizmann, *The Impossible Takes Longer: The Memoirs of Vera Weizmann,* 221–222.

13. Chaim Weizmann, *Trial and Error*, 471.

14. Quoted by Abba Eban in his chapter entitled "Tragedy and Triumph" in Meyer W. Weisgal and Joel Carmichael, editors, *Chaim Weizmann: A Biography by*

*Several Hands* (New York: Atheneum, 1963), 304; see also Allis Radosh and Ronald Radosh, *A Safe Haven*, 297, 221.

15. *Weisgal and Carmichael, Chaim Weizmann: A Biography by Several Hands, 304.*

16. Vera Weizmann, *The Impossible Takes Longer,* 223.

17. *Ibid.*, 223–224.

18. See Barnet Litvinoff, ed., *The Letters and Papers of Chaim Weizmann, 690,* Paper No. 95 ("W. had arrived ill, and was confined to his hotel room . . . for over a week"). In her memoir, Vera Weizmann, in the course of recounting the final days before the announcement of Israel's independence, writes that "in all these exciting events, with all that was happening around us, poor Chaim was in bed, solemn and sad, issuing directions, using the telephone at his bedside, drafting letters and memoranda, holding conferences." Vera Weizmann, *The Impossible Takes Longer,* 233.

19. *Ibid., Letter 121.*

20. *Ibid.*, Letter 125.

21. For a video history of Eddie Jacobson and his relationship with Harry S. Truman, see "Remarks of Bob Cohen and Truman-Jacobson Video," shown at the 2016 AIPAC Policy Conference, in Washington, D.C., March 20, 2016, www.aipac.hubs .vidyard.com/watch/oDme2r4xIqA6Gpe-Gdeugg?vyemail=ortor.

22. Quoted in Norman Rose, *Chaim Weizmann: A Biography,* 436–437, and Allis Radosh and Ronald Radosh, *A Safe Haven,* 300.

23. Harry S. Truman, *Years of Trial and Hope,* 171–172; cited in Vera Weizmann, *The Impossible Takes Longer,* 228–229.

24. Harry S. Truman, *Years of Trial and Hope,* 171–172.

25. See Barnet Litvinoff, ed., *The Letters and Papers of Chaim Weizmann,* Paper No. 96 ("American Trusteeship Scheme Condemned," Weizmann Statement of Press, New York, March 25, 1948), 694. According to Weizmann's statement to the press, the "gravity of the present moment" compelled him to speak:

> There are three established principles in the Palestine question. The first is that to prolong tutelage and delay a final solution based on independence is to increase confusion and bloodshed. The second is that to make Arab consent a condition of a settlement is to rule out all chance of a settlement. The third is that to abandon a judgment under pressure of Arab violence is to give an incentive to further violence. . . .
>
> The [partition] plan worked about by the [General] Assembly was the result of a long and careful process of deliberation in which the conflicting claims of the various parties were judged in the light of international equity. In order to achieve a compromise between Jewish and Arab national claims, the Jews were asked to be content with one-eighth of the original area of the Palestine Mandate. Their consent was sought for the recognition of a second Arab State in seven-eighths of the area originally designated—as I can personally testify—for the creation of the Jewish homeland. . . . We accepted these limitations. . . .
>
> To pursue Arab consent by further concessions at our expense as a necessary basis for a settlement is thus pure appeasement of aggression—it is not concilia-

tion. Indeed the worst feature of any change in policy now is the undeniable fact that it arises purely as an act of submission to Arab violence.

26. Allis Radosh and Ronald Radosh, *A Safe Haven*, 302.

27. The description of Weizmann's feelings was set forth by Vera Weizmann in her diary. See Vera Weizmann, *The Impossible Takes Longer*, 229. She called it the "Black Friday" of Jewish diplomatic history, and wrote that Weizmann believed that Truman had deceived him.

28. Allis Radosh and Ronald Radosh, *A Safe Haven*, 303, citing "Clifford Sets the Record Straight: Talk Delivered before the American Jewish Historical Society and the American Historical Association," *New East Report*, December 29, 1972, *inter alia*. Truman noted that there were lower-level people in the State Department who had "always wanted to cut my throat" and that they had just "succeeded in doing it." Quoted in Allis Radosh and Ronald Radosh, *A Safe Haven*, 303, citing an entry on Truman's calendar for March 19, 1948, in Margaret Truman, *Harry S. Truman* (Avon Books, 1993), 424–425.

On March 25, 1948, Truman issued a statement that it had "become clear that the partition plan cannot be carried out at this time by peaceful means" and that partition could not be imposed "by the use of American troops." He stated that a trusteeship was "not proposed as a substitute for the partition plan but as an effort to fill the vacuum soon to be created by the termination of the [British] mandate on May 15," and he called for a truce between Arabs and Jews to avoid bloodshed and reach a peaceful settlement. "Truman's Palestine Views," *The New York Times*, March 26, 1948.

29. Chaim Weizmann, *Trial and Error*, 474. In full at *The Letters and Papers of Chaim Weizmann, Series A, August 1947–1952*, 99–101, Letter 138.

30. Vera Weizmann, *The Impossible Takes Longer*, 232–233.

31. Barnet Litvinoff, ed., *The Letters and Papers of Chaim Weizmann*, 116, Letter 154.

32. Abba Eban, "Tragedy and Triumph," in Meyer W. Weisgal and Joel Carmichael, eds., *Chaim Weizmann: A Biography by Several Hands*, 311–312.

33. Vera Weizmann, *The Impossible Takes Longer*, 235; Howard M. Sachar, *A History of Israel: From the Rise of Zionism to Our Time* (New York: Alfred A. Knopf, 1976), 311.

34. Barnet Litvinoff, ed., *The Letters and Papers of Chaim Weizmann*, Letter 154, fn. 2.

35. The Torah was originally prepared in honor of a Bar Mitzvah in 1940, and belonged to the Synagogue at the Jewish Theological Seminary of America in New York. During World War II, it was loaned to a chaplain for use in religious services in the armed services. After the war, it was returned to the Jewish Theological Seminary until it was presented to President Truman. Harry S. Truman Library, "Creation of the State of Israel, 1948, Torah Scroll," www.trumanlibrary.org/israel/torah.htm.

36. Michael Bar-Zohar, *Ben-Gurion: A Biography*, 156–157.

37. *Ibid.*

38. See Chaim Herzog, *The Arab-Israeli Wars: War and Peace in the Middle East from the War of Independence through Lebanon* (New York: Vintage Books, 1984), 42–44, describing the siege of the Jewish Etzion settlements between Bethlehem and Hebron, overrun by the Arab League and other irregular Arab forces on May 12, who

killed the defenders and massacred prisoners, and then plundered, looted, and destroyed the villages.

39. Declaration of Independence of the State of Israel, May 14, 1948, www.mfa .gov.il/MFA/ForeignPolicy/Peace/Guide/Pages/Declaration%20of%20Establishment %20of%20State%20of%20Israel.aspx.

40. David Ben-Gurion, *The Eternity of Israel* (Jerusalem: The Government Yearbook, 1954), 14–23, excerpted in Michael Walzer, Menachem Lorberbaum, Noam J. Zohar, eds., *The Jewish Political Tradition: Volume One: Authority* (New Haven and London: Yale University Press, 2000), 491. The compromise is also described by Shimon Peres, in conversation with David Landau, *Ben-Gurion: A Political Life* (New York: Nextbook Schocken, 2011), 117.

41. Robert Wexler, president of American Jewish University, in conversation with the author, March 2016; see Anita Shapira, *Israel: A History*, 242–243 ("It is doubtful if among the leadership of the Yishuv or of the Jewish people as a whole there was anyone else capable of making such a decision"); Shimon Peres, *Ben-Gurion: A Political Life* ("at the Yishuv's moment of decision, in May 1948" Ben-Gurion applied "inner strength and determination" like no other; "I truly believe that without Ben-Gurion the State of Israel would not have come into being").

42. Michael Bar-Zohar, *Ben-Gurion: A Biography*, 156–157. It should be noted, however, that Ben-Gurion's efforts also got a timely assist from Chaim Weizmann, who at a key moment sent a cable from Washington to his colleagues, stating: "Either the state is established now or, God forbid, it will never be established."

43. Ben-Gurion became not only the first head of the new state of Israel but also commander-in-chief of a unified armed force (the IDF) that was then still under formation. It came into existence on May 26, 1948, formed by combining the Haganah, Palmach, Irgun, and Lehi into a single force. See Eliot A. Cohen, *Supreme Command: Soldiers, Statesmen, and Leadership in Wartime* (New York: Anchor Books, 2003), 164. Ben-Gurion became one of the great democratic war statesmen in history. *Ibid.*, 132–172.

44. The quote is from Begin's interview in the video "Flames of Revolt: The Story of the Irgun," http://www.ergomedia .com/IS503.HTM.

45. For much of the time, Begin was disguised as "Rabbi Sassover" and his family.

46. For the history of the Irgun's revolt against the British, see Menachem Begin, *The Revolt: The Story of the Irgun* (New York: Henry Schuman, 1951); Samuel Katz, *Days of Fire* (Jerusalem, Tel Aviv, and Haifa: Steimatzky's Agency Ltd., 1966); Yitshaq Ben-Ami, *Years of Wrath, Days of Glory*; Bruce Hoffman, *Anonymous Soldiers: The*

"Rabbi Sassover," Menachem, and Aliza Begin, with their son, Ze'ev Binyamin Begin, 1943. Courtesy Jabotinsky Institute in Israel

*Struggle for Israel, 1917–1947* (New York: Alfred A. Knopf, 2015). "Anonymous Soldiers" was the name of the Irgun's anthem.

In his 1949 autobiography, Chaim Weizmann noted both the influence of the Irgun and his opposition to its tactics:

> There is a tendency to say that it was the activities of the Irgun which largely succeeded in drawing the attention of the world to the Palestine problem and in bringing it before the international forum of the United Nations. How the world was affected by the terror in Palestine it is difficult to gauge. We received more publicity than Herostrafus, and I do not think that it is desirable to attract attention in that form.

Chaim Weizmann, *Trial and Error*, 454.

47. Menachem Begin, *The Revolt*, 376–377.

48. *Ibid.*, 373, 376–377.

49. Louis Lipsky, *Memoirs in Profile*, 154–155. Joseph Schechtman—a close associate of Jabotinsky for thirty years—observed in 1961 that:

> For Churchill's eightieth birthday, England's Poet Laureate John Masefield wrote a quatrain, the first three lines of which succinctly formulate the service both Churchill and Jabotinsky had rendered to their respective nations:
>
> > This Man, in darkness, saw; in doubting, led;
> > In danger, did; in uttermost despair,
> > Shone, with Hope that made the midnight fair.

Joseph B. Schechtman, *Fighter and Prophet: The Vladimir Jabotinsky Story*, 548.

50. Jabotinsky's last will, executed in 1935, had directed that he should be buried "wherever death finds me, and my remains (should I be buried outside of Palestine) may not be transferred to Palestine unless by order of that country's eventual Jewish Government." Joseph B. Schechtman, *Fighter and Prophet: The Vladimir Jabotinsky Story*, 400.

51. *Ibid.*, 401.

52. The Prime Minister's Office—Levi Eshkol, http://www.pmo.gov.il/English/Memorials/PrimeMinisters/Pages/LeviEshkol.aspx.

53. "Huge Crowds Participate in Jabotinsky Funeral Procession in New York," JTA, July 7, 1964.

54. See "Kol Brama Nishma—Rachel's Voice," http://finkorswim.com/2009/12/31a-lesson-from-our-matriarch-rachel-about-unity-a-guest-post/. Jer. 31:15 reads, in the New International Version (NIV) Study Bible (Grand Rapids, Mich., 1985): This is what the Lord says:

> "A voice is heard in Ramah,
> mourning and great weeping,
> Rachel weeping for her children
> and refusing to be comforted,
> because they are no more."

55. *Ibid.* "Mourners Pay Homage to Jabotinsky; Funeral Procession Set for Today," JTA, July 6, 1964; "Eshkol Pays Respects to Remains of Jabotinsky at Paris Airport," JTA, July 8, 1964; "Israel to Bury Jabotinsky, American Zionist Leader," *The New York Times*, June 14, 1964. Rick Richman, "70 Years Ago Today," *Commentary Magazine*, August 3, 2010, https://www.commentarymagazine.com/culture-civilization/history/70-years-ago-today/.

56. "Thousands in Tel Aviv View Jabotinsky Coffin," *The New York Times*, July 8, 1964.

57. Jabotinsky's remains lay in state in Tel Aviv and then were moved in a procession through the city to Jerusalem. An estimated 250,000 people took part in the funeral activities in Israel. Shmuel Katz, *Lone Wolf: A Biography of Vladimir (Ze'ev) Jabotinsky, Vol. 2* (New York: Barricade Books, 1996), 1792.

58. "Address by PM Benjamin Netanyahu Knesset Session in Memory of Ze'ev Jabotinsky," July 22, 2009, http://www.pmo.gov.il/English/MediaCenter/Speeches/Pages/speechjabo220709.aspx.

59. "Benzion Netanyahu to be laid to rest in Jerusalem," *The Jerusalem Post*, May 1, 2012, www.jpost.com/National-News/Benzion-Netanyahu-to-be-laid-to-rest-in-Jerusalem.

60. See Yehuda Avner, *The Prime Ministers: An Intimate Narrative of Israeli Leadership* (New Milford: The Toby Press, 2010), 84:

> The election of 1949 was to be the first of many that Menachem Begin would lose. David Ben-Gurion demonstratively excluded him from every coalition government he headed, and he headed many. . . . Only in 1967 did Ben-Gurion's successor, Prime Minister Levi Eshkol, end the boycott, when he invited Menachem Begin to join his national unity government on the eve of the Six-Day War.

In the days leading up to the Six-Day War, Israel watched as Arab forces mobilized to invade it, complete with chilling, genocidal rhetoric. See Anne Lieberman, "Six Days Remembered," *The Jewish Press*, June 1, 2005, www.jewish press.com/indepth/front-page/six-days-remembered/2005/06/01/. The U.S. government repeatedly made it clear to Israel that it could expect no support if it acted preemptively, as did France. See Michael B. Oren, *Six Days of War: June 1967 and the Making of the Modern Middle East* (Oxford: Oxford University Press, 2002), 100, 115, 139, 157. As Israel was faced with the necessity to act even if it had to act

*Benjamin Netanyahu in his office in January 2009, in front of photographs of Vladimir Jabotinsky and Menachem Begin. Photo credit: © Michal Fattal Photography http://www.michalfattal.com*

alone, its internal unity was essential to the decision to proceed—and the ultimate outcome.

Menachem Begin went on to lose eight successive elections before finally succeeding in 1977 with his Likud Party. In 1996 Benjamin Netanyahu headed the Likud Party and served as prime minister from 1996 to 1999, and then again from 2009 to the present.

61. George Eliot, "The Modern Hep! Hep! Hep!" http://www.online-literature.com/georgeeliot/theophrastus-such/18/. See Gertrude Himmelfarb, *The Jewish Odyssey of George Eliot* (New York: Encounter Books, 2009), 105, 120 ("a remarkable essay . . . Eliot's final testament, her bequest to the Jews"); William Kristol, "The Jewish State at 60," *The New York Times*, May 12, 2008, www.nytimes.com/2008/05/12/opinion/12kristol.html?r=0 ("the amazing essay by the novelist George Eliot who made a case for Zionism in 1879—17 years before the publication of Theodor Herzl's 'The Jewish State'").

62. George Eliot's last book was *Impressions of Theophrastus Such*, published in May 1879—a year and a half before her death on December 22, 1880. Gertrude Himmelfarb, *The Jewish Odyssey of George Eliot* (New York: Encounter Books, 2009), 105. Eliot studied Latin, Greek, Hebrew, Italian, German, and French in order to read sources in the original. Her notebooks included thousands of excerpts from the Bible, the Mishnah and Talmud, Maimonides, medieval rabbis and Kabbalistic works, and scores of others. *Ibid.*, 68. The list of books Eliot consulted covers twenty-three pages. *Ibid.*, 8.

"Hep! Hep! Hep!" was the acronym for "*Hierosolyma est perdita*" ("Jerusalem is destroyed")—the eleventh-century chant of the Crusaders as they annihilated Jewish communities on their way to the Holy Land, and the rallying cry of German anti-Jewish rioters in the early nineteenth century. Cynthia Ozick, "The Modern Hep! Hep! Hep!," in the Afterword to Ron Rosenbaum, ed., *Those Who Forget the Past: The Question of Anti-Semitism* (New York: Random House, 2004), 596.

Ruth R. Wisse describes Eliot's final novel, *Daniel Deronda*—the story of a man who discovers his Jewish identity and undertakes a Zionist mission—as "the imaginative equivalent of the Balfour Declaration." Ruth R. Wisse, *The Modern Jewish Canon* (Chicago: University of Chicago Press, 2003), 238. See Ruth R. Wisse, "Daniel Deronda, George Eliot's Novel of Jewish Nationalism," https://tikvahfund.org/course/daniel-deronda/. See also Edward Alexander, "Daniel Deronda: 'The Zionist Fate in English Hands' and 'The Liberal Betrayal of the Jews,'" in Cammy, Horn, Quint, Rubinstein, eds., *Arguing the Modern Jewish Canon: Essays on Literature and Culture in Honor of Ruth R. Wisse* (Cambridge, Mass.: Harvard University Press, 2008), 189.

63. Menachem Begin's party lost eight consecutive elections before ultimately achieving victory in 1977. The story of his fidelity to democracy as part of the loyal opposition is expertly recounted by Louis Gordon in a presentation before Children of Jewish Holocaust Survivors, "The Evolution of the Israeli Right: From Jabotinsky to Begin to Netanyahu," August 12, 2012, https://www.youtube.com/watch?v=u4tM27r3cbg.

# PHOTOGRAPH AND IMAGE CREDITS

## PREFACE

p. xv   Chaim Weizmann. *Bettmann/Bettmann Collection/Getty Images*
Vladimir Jabotinsky. *Public Domain/Wikimedia Commons*
David Ben-Gurion. *Bettmann/Bettmann Collection/Getty Images*

## INTRODUCTION

p. 1   German Invasion of Poland, September 1, 1939. *U.S. Holocaust Memorial Museum*

p. 2   Eastern Europe After the German-Soviet Pact. *U.S. Holocaust Memorial Museum*

p. 8   AJC Annual Report of the Executive Committee, 1940. *Photograph by Rick Richman*

p. 10   Jews Face Crisis in Eastern Europe. *From* The New York Times, *February 7, 1937. © 1937 The New York Times. All rights reserved. Used by permission and protected by the Copyright Laws of the United States. The printing, copying, redistribution, or retransmission of this Content without express written permission is prohibited.*

p. 12   Rabbi Isaac Mayer Wise. *Public Domain/Wikimedia Commons*

p. 17   Cyrus Adler. *JHU Sheridan Libraries/Gado/Archive Photos/Getty Images*
Rabbi Stephen S. Wise. *Edward Steichen/Conde Nast Collection/Getty Images*

p. 18   Rabbi David Philipson. *My Life As An American Jew by David Philipson. Published by John Kidd & Son, Inc.*

p. 20   Irvin Berlin. *Public Domain/Wikimedia Commons*

## CHAIM WEIZMANN

p. 30   Map of Palestine. *Public Domain/Wikimedia Commons*

p. 32   Hitler Seizes Memel, March 23, 1939. *Corbis Historical/Getty Images*

p. 41   Weizmann pictured in *The New York Times. From* The New York Times, *January 13, 1940. © 1940 The New York Times. All rights reserved. Used by permission and protected by the Copyright Laws of the United States. The printing, copying, redistribution, or retransmission of this Content without express written permission is prohibited.*

p. 52    Weizmann handwritten letter. *The Shapell Manuscript Collection of The Shapell Manuscript Foundation*

## VLADIMIR JABOTINSKY

p. 58    Leader Says Jews Will Fight as Unit. *From The New York Times, March 14, 1940. © 1940 The New York Times. All rights reserved. Used by permission and protected by the Copyright Laws of the United States. The printing, copying, redistribution, or retransmission of this Content without express written permission is prohibited.*

p. 65    38th Battalion, Royal Fusiliers marching in London. *Jabotinsky Institute in Israel*

p. 67    Jabotinsky with soldiers of the Jewish Legion, 1918. *Jabotinsky Institute in Israel*
         38th Battalion, Royal Fusiliers, First Judeans, January 1918. *Jabotinsky Institute in Israel*

p. 70    New Zionist Leader Heard by 5,000 Here. *From The New York Times, March 20, 1940. © 1940 The New York Times. All rights reserved. Used by permission and protected by the Copyright Laws of the United States. The printing, copying, redistribution, or retransmission of this Content without express written permission is prohibited.*

p. 73    Jabotinsky testifying before the Peel Commission. *Jabotinsky Institute in Israel*

p. 81    Abraham Cahan, 1937. *Library of Congress Prints & Photographs Division [LC-USZ62-119095]*

p. 90    Jabotinsky Asks Jews for Army of 100,000. *From The New York Times, June 20, 1940. © 1940 The New York Times. All rights reserved. Used by permission and protected by the Copyright Laws of the United States. The printing, copying, redistribution, or retransmission of this Content without express written permission is prohibited.*

p. 91    Jabotinsky at the Manhattan Center, June 1940. *Jabotinsky Institute in Israel*

p. 93    Jabotinsky meeting Betar campers on August 3, 1940. *Jabotinsky Institute in Israel*

p. 94    Text of Col. Lindbergh's Speech. *From The New York Times, August 5, 1940. © 1940 The New York Times. All rights reserved. Used by permission and protected by the Copyright Laws of the United States. The printing, copying, redistribution, or retransmission of this Content without express written permission is prohibited.*

p. 95    Jabotinsky Dead; Led New Zionists. *From The New York Times, August 5, 1940 © 1940 The New York Times. All rights reserved. Used by permission and protected by the Copyright Laws of the United States. The printing, copying, redistribution, or retransmission of this Content without express written permission is prohibited.*

p. 96    Jabotinsky Rites Today. *From The New York Times, August 6, 1940. © 1940 The New York Times. All rights reserved. Used by permission and protected by the Copyright Laws of the United States. The printing, copying, redistribution, or retransmission of this Content without express written permission is prohibited.*

Tribute by 12,000 Paid Jabotinsky. *From The New York Times, August 7, 1940. © 1940 The New York Times. All rights reserved. Used by permission and protected by the Copyright Laws of the United States. The printing, copying, redistribution, or retransmission of this Content without express written permission is prohibited.*

p. 97   The crowd in front of the Second Avenue Chapel for Jabotinsky's funeral. *Jabotinsky Institute in Israel*

p. 98   Crowds on both sides of Second Avenue for Jabotinsky funeral cortege. *Jabotinsky Institute in Israel*
New Yorkers standing ten-deep at other locations along the cortege route. *Jabotinsky Institute in Israel*

p. 100  Menachem Begin with Jabotinsky in Poland in 1939. *Jabotinsky Institute in Israel*

p. 102  Kupat Holim nurses marching in Tel Aviv memorial procession. *Jabotinsky Institute in Israel*

p. 103  Vladimir, Joanna, and Eri Jabotinsky, 1921. *Jabotinsky Institute in Israel*

## DAVID BEN-GURION

p. 109  Private David Ben-Gurion in his Jewish Legion uniform. *Public Domain/ Martin Gilbert/Wikimedia Commons*

p. 119  Rabbi Harold I. Saperstein. *Harold I. Saperstein, Witness from the Pulpit: Topical Sermons 1933–1980, edited by Marc Saperstein (Lexington Books, 2000), all rights reserved*

p. 121  Rabbi Abba Hillel Silver. *Time Life Pictures/The LIFE Picture Collection/ Getty Images.*

p. 123  Rabbi Israel H. Levinthal. *© Brooklyn Jewish Center*

p. 134  Tamar de Sola Pool. *Collection of American Jewish Historical Society*

## EPILOGUE

p. 138  Map of Palestine. *Public Domain/UN Partition Plan for Palestine 1947/ Wikimedia Commons*

p. 143  President Truman and President Weizmann at the White House, May 25, 1948. *Bettmann/Getty Images*

p. 145  Ben-Gurion reading the Declaration of Independence, May 14, 1948. *Public Domain/Israel Ministry of Foreign Affairs/Wikimedia Commons*

p. 148  Jabotinsky Casket in New York Funeral Procession, 1964. *Jabotinsky Institute in Israel*

p. 149  Procession Transferring Jabotinsky Caskets to Jerusalem in 1964. *Jabotinsky Institute in Israel*

p. 150  Jabotinsky's grave. *Deror avi/Wikimedia Commons/CC-BY-SA-3.0 GNU Free Documentation License.*

p. 151  Benzion Netanyahu and his son, Benjamin Netanyahu, February 9, 2009. *Photograph © Michal Fattal 2009*

## ENDNOTES

p. 187 Balfour Declaration. *Published in The Times of London, November 9, 1917*

p. 210 Flyer for Jabotinsky Speech, April 3, 1940. © *Museum of Jewish Heritage*

p. 214 Winston Churchill, 1941. *Library of Congress Prints & Photographs Division [LC-USZ62-64419]*

p. 215 Gen. Charles de Gaulle, circa 1942. Office of War Information, Overseas Picture Division. *Public Domain/Wikimedia Commons*
Benjamin Netanyahu at his desk, with photographs of Jabotinsky and Menachem Begin. *Photograph © Michal Fattal 2009*

p. 234 Menachem Begin disguised as a rabbi, with his wife, Aliza and their son, Ze'ev Binyamin, 1943. *Jabotinsky Institute in Israel*

p. 236 Benjamin Netanyahu at his desk, with photographs of Jabotinsky and Menachem Begin. *Photograph © Michal Fattal 2009*

# INDEX